Christ's Sudden and Certain Appearance to Judgment

by
Thomas Vincent
Sometime Minister of Magdalen,
Milk Street, London

"For yet a little while, and he that shall come,
will come, and will not tarry." Hebrews 10:37

Soli Deo Gloria Publications
. . . for instruction in righteousness . . .

Soli Deo Gloria Publications
P.O. Box 451, Morgan, PA 15064
(412) 221-1901/FAX 221-1902

*

*

ISBN 1-57358-023-6

Contents

To The Citizens of London

You have heard God's terrible voice in the city expressing itself in the late dreadful, desolating judgments of plague and fire; the sound of which has gone forth not only unto every corner of the land, but, I believe, also by this time unto the farthest end of the world. Give me leave to sound another trumpet in your ears, and to forewarn you of a judgment ten thousand times more dreadful. I mean the last and general judgment of the whole world at the second appearance of the Lord Jesus Christ, who will most certainly, and very quickly, be revealed from heaven in flaming fire to take vengeance upon all them which shall be found ungodly on that day.

Could I have certainly foretold the many thousands that fell by the plague in the year 1665, of their so near approaching death, surely they would have endeavored to prepare that the sting and fear of death might have been removed. Could I have foretold the citizens of London of the many thousand houses which should fall by the fire in the year 1666, surely they would have endeavored to prevent the fire or, at least, have removed all their goods beforehand; but these things could not be foreseen and, therefore, as the judgments were unexpected, so they took them most unprovided. But I can certainly foretell you from God, who cannot lie, of the future last judgment by the Lord Jesus Christ at the last day, which is the subject of this ensuing treatise. And when you are warned hereof out of the Word of truth, and given awakening motives to prepare by dreadful temporal judgments, if you should neglect to do it, and after all be found unprovided at the appearance of Christ, as your sins shall be the greater and more inexcusable, so your dread will be the greater at the sight of your Judge, whom these very eyes which read these lines will behold ere long coming in the clouds, and your punishment will be more intolerable. But if the Lord inclines your hearts to follow the directions and counsels of His Word, to prepare for this great and notable day, you will lift up your heads with joy when the greatest part of the world shall be filled with terror and confusion and, when the Lord Jesus appears, you shall also appear with Him in glory. The design of these sheets is to set forth the glorious appearance of Christ with the certainty and suddenness thereof, that sinners might be awakened to repent, and believers might be comforted with hopes of it, and all might be in readiness for the day which is so sure and near: which that you may be, and that my endeavors may be blessed for your help herein, is the prayer of an earnest well-wisher to your souls:

Thomas Vincent

Chapter 1

The Doctrines Stated

"Surely I come quickly, Amen.
Even so, come Lord Jesus."

The last words of a dear friend are usually most remarked and best remembered, especially when he speaks with great affection. These are the last words of Jesus Christ, the best Friend that the children of men ever had, when He sent angels from heaven after He had been some years in glory with the Father, to speak His name unto His churches upon the earth. Revelation 22:16: "I, Jesus have sent Mine angel to testify these things in the churches." Of all these things which He testifies by His angels, this is the last and sweetest in the text: "Surely I come quickly"; which word of promise coming down from heaven, and expressing so much love to the church, is charged with an echo and resound of the church's earnest desire: "Amen. Even so, come, Lord Jesus."

Hence observe:

DOCTRINE 1. The Lord Jesus Christ will certainly and quickly appear.

DOCTRINE 2. There is an earnest desire and longing in the church for Christ's appearance.

DOCTRINE 1. The Lord Jesus Christ will certainly and quickly appear.

In this book I shall:

1. Speak concerning Christ's appearance.
2. Show that He will certainly appear.
3. Show that He will quickly appear.
4. Lastly, apply it.

1. Concerning Christ's appearance. There is a twofold appearance of Christ which the Scriptures make mention of:

In the flesh;

In glory.

The first appearance of Christ was in the flesh about seventeen hundred years ago in the land of Judah, unto the people of the Jews, the only then-visible Church upon the earth. There it was that the Word was made flesh; and among that people He dwelt for awhile, some of whom beheld His glory. "The glory of the only begotten of the Father, full of grace and truth." There it was that the eternal Son of God was made man, being conceived miraculously by the power of the Holy Ghost in the womb of the virgin Mary, without the contamination of original sin, which all ordinary conceptions introduce. His real mother and supposed father were both of the tribe of Judah and of the lineage of David. And He was born in the town of Bethlehem according to the Scriptures' prediction.

After He had lived thirty years in obscurity, he was baptized by John the Baptist, his forerunner and harbinger, in whose baptism, when John saw the heavens opened and the Spirit of God descending

like a dove, lighting upon Him, and heard the voice
of the excellent glory saying, "This is My beloved
Son in whom I am well pleased," he gave his
testimony concerning Him that He was the Son of
God, and the Lamb of God who takes away the sins
of the world. After His own baptism and temptation,
and John's imprisonment, he made His appearance
more openly unto Israel, showing forth His glory
not in outward pomp and splendor, but in a more
high, eminent and wonderful manner, altogether
divine, exceeding the imitation of any earthly
monarch in the world. He spewed forth the glory of
His power in the miracles which He worked;
namely, in opening the eyes of the blind and the
ears of the deaf, in loosing the tongues of the dumb
and the bonds of other infirmities, in cleansing the
lepers and healing other diseases with a word, in
casting out devils after long possessions, in calming
the sea and wind when boisterous and stormy, in
raising up the dead before and after burial for some
days, and the like.

He showed forth the glory of His knowledge in
looking into the hearts of those who came unto
Him, being able to perceive their most secret
thoughts and imaginations, and needed not that
any should testify of man, for He knew what was in
man.

He showed forth the glory of His wisdom in His
most wise answers to the ensnaring questions of the
Pharisees and others, in the most excellent and
heavenly doctrine which He preached, wherein He
did not teach His disciples subtle and empty specu-
lations, which the greatest wits in the world have

busied themselves about, but great soul-saving truths. Indeed, He revealed such great and deep mysteries above the reach of the highest wit of the greatest scholar without the teaching of His Spirit, which were momentous and needful in order unto practice, but the greatest part of His doctrine was plain and easy.

He showed forth the glory of His holiness in His exact walking and perfect obedience unto the law of God, without the least deviation of sin.

He showed forth the glory of His goodness and tenderness towards the children of men in going about to do them good and give succor to those who were in misery, casting out none which came unto Him.

Especially, He showed forth the glory of His mercy and infinite love to His own people in submitting to so low a condition as He lived in for their sakes; in humbling Himself and becoming obedient unto death, even the cursed, disgraceful, painful death of the cross, besides the soul miseries which He endured through a sense of God's wrath due for their sins, that He might satisfy God's justice and deliver them from eternal death and wrath to come, and purchase life and glory from Him.

Thus Christ lived, and thus Christ died for our sins, according to the Scriptures; and, though He was dead, the bonds of death could not hold Him; neither did the Holy One see corruption, but the third day rose again from the dead, according to the Scriptures and, after His resurrection, was seen of Mary Magdalene, of Peter, of James, all the apostles, of five hundred brethren at once, according to the

Scriptures. After forty days, He was taken up into heaven and is there in His human nature at the right hand of the throne of the Majesty in the heavens making intercession for His people, where He will abide until the second appearance. Thus concerning Christ's appearance in the flesh.

I will speak of His appearance in glory in the next chapter.

Chapter 2

The Second Appearance of Christ

The second appearance of Christ will be in glory at the last day, when the world shall come to an end; this is the appearance we are treating of and, therefore, I will speak of it more largely and show:

The manner of this appearance.

The end and transactions of this appearance.

Concerning the nature of Christ's second appearance. What tongue of men or angels is able to set forth, what heart can conceive the splendor thereof? The Scripture reveals something; and, taking the Scripture for my guide, I shall endeavor to speak something of it. See Luke 21:27: "Then shall they see the Son of man coming in a cloud, with power and great glory. "

Christ at His second appearance will come with power, with great power. He has all power put into His hands in heaven and in earth now, and exercises it more secretly; then He will exercise it more visibly and apparently in the sight of the whole world. To give instance:

He will come with power over death. Death has had great power since the fall, and is the greatest conqueror in the world; death has made universal conquest over all the sons and daughters of Adam (Enoch and Elijah only excepted) which lived in former generations, and has led them captive, binding their faces in secret, chaining their hands and their feet, and clapping them up close prisoners in the grave, and none have been able to make resistance. Yea, death assailed the Lord of life Himself and got the victory for a while and shut Him up in prison; but He got loose before three days were at an end, broke open the doors, and gave death a deep wound, as it were, and an abolishing stroke in His resurrection, 2 Timothy 1:10, pursuing the complete victory which afterwards He would obtain over this enemy of mankind.

Now, when Christ makes His second appearance in the world at the last day, He will exercise His power over death. He will lead captivity captive. He will lay first His hands on death and tread this conqueror under His feet and strip him of his force and spoil which he has been treasuring up for so many years. He will snatch the keys of the grave out of the hand of death and open the prison doors and let forth all his captives. He will loosen all the bonds of death, and knock off his chains and bring out all his prisoners into freedom and enlargement, as it is said, Hosea 13:14, "I will ransom them from the power of the grave; I will redeem them from death. O death! I will be thy plague: O grave! I will be thy destruction." And it is said in 1 Corinthians 15:25–26 that all enemies shall be put under the feet of Jesus Christ, and the last enemy which He shall destroy is death. And verse 25 says that when this mortal shall put on immortality, then death shall be swallowed up in victory. And surely Christ must come with great power to get victory over such a potent enemy.

He will come with power over men and devils. He will have power over all His enemies which have rebelled against Him, over all the principalities and powers on the earth that exercise lordship and dominion in the world. He will bring the kings of the earth down from their seats and pluck off the robes of princes, He will take the staff and the sword out of their hand and divest them of all their royalty and greatness, and they who have employed their borrowed power against Him, how will they quake and tremble before Him! See Revelation 11:15–18: "When the seventh angel sounded, there were great voices in heaven, saying, 'The kingdoms of the world are become the kingdom of our Lord, and of His Christ, and He shall reign for ever and ever.' And the four and twenty elders fell on their faces, saying, 'We give Thee thanks, O Lord God Almighty, which art, and wast, and art to come, because Thou hast taken to Thee Thy great power, and hast reigned. And the nations were angry, and Thy wrath is come, and the time of the dead, that they should be judged, and that Thou shouldst give rewards unto Thy servants the prophets, and to Thy saints, and them that fear Thy name, small and great, and shouldst destroy them, which destroy the earth.' "

The kings of the earth, and great potentates, will be angry when they will be dethroned; and the wicked of the earth will be troubled when the Lord Jesus shall come down from heaven to call them to judgment. If all the powers of wicked men and devils too (who are greater in power than men) could, they would make head and resist the Lord Jesus Christ and pull Him from His throne and put Him to death as the Jews did at His first appearance. If they had any hopes of making their party good against Him, how would they call their forces and gather their armies and wage war with this great King, especially when all the wicked shall be raised up and the ancient rebels, the giants of the old world, shall come forth of their dust and the prison of hell, where some of them have been tormented by Him many years! O how would they combine their strength, and so many millions of them together would rush upon Him with rage and violence and endeavor to avenge themselves upon Him, at least defend themselves against Him when He comes to torment them. But Christ will come with such great power that He will be able to deal with the whole world of wicked men together when they are raised and united in one body and have obtained more strength of body, and are filled with more rage and spite of mind than here they had, and are out of all hopes of making peace with Him, and have the whole stock of all the devils in hell to join in their company. I say, Christ will come with sufficiency of strength to bind them all in chains and so to hold them all down that they shall not be able to make the least resistance. He that has power to raise the wicked from the dead will have power to keep all His enemies from rebellion. He will come with power.

Christ will come at His second appearance with great glory. At His first appearance, He came like a servant; yea, like a servant of servants. At His second appearance, He will come like a Lord; yea, like a Lord of lords, like the great Lord of glory. At His first appearance, He was clothed with great dishonor, and a chain of contempt was put about Him; but, at His second appearance, He will be clothed with glory and honor, and most excellent majesty will be put upon Him. At His first appearance, His deity was veiled; His beauty was masked with infirmed flesh; His brightness was under a cloud, though sometimes some beams broke forth with such a dazzling luster as made Peter to fall at His feet, saying, "Depart from me, for I am a sinful man, O Lord," Luke 5:8, and others in the ship to worship Him, acknowledging, "Of a truth Thou art the Son of God," Matthew 14:33. He often filled His disciples with fear and astonishment; but He was so disguised in flesh that few knew Him at all. None knew much of Him when He was so disrobed and so meanly attired and attended. It is said, the princes of the world knew Him not, else surely they would have laid down their scepters at His feet. Had they known Him, they would not have dared so disgracefully to have crucified the Lord of glory, 1 Corinthians 2:8.

But, at the second appearance, the veil will be so drawn aside that the deity of Christ will shine forth with amazing splendor to the view of the whole world; His human nature will be glorious beyond any other creature. But, oh! How glorious will His Divine nature be when the eyes of the whole world shall be opened to see God in such a way as now we are not able to conceive! He will appear in the brightness of His Father's glory so that they who see Him will see the Father; the majesty, authority, dominion, power, holiness, justice, and love of the Father will be like so many sparkling gems to deck the crown of Christ at His appearance. But who can conceive the reality and surpassing excellency of Jesus Christ when He comes down out of His Father's palace into the world! He will come in great glory; God will come down in Him and with Him. The throne of God will be removed; the palace will be below; the heaven will be upon the earth. Where Christ is, there is heaven; there is God in His greatest glory to be seen. He will come in glory. Never was there such glory seen upon the face of the earth; never did the eye of man behold such a sight as then it will behold. We read of great and pompous shows which some princes have made in their triumphs, but never was there such pomp in the world as will be at this appearance of Jesus Christ when He comes with the spoils of principalities and powers, making a show of them openly, and decked with such excellent glory.

A little further to set this forth:

He will come attended with a glorious retinue of angels. We read in Matthew 26:53 of more than twelve legions of angels, and in Daniel 7:10 of thousand thousands, yea, ten thousand times ten thousands, which minister about the throne of God. Yea, further, Revelation 5:11, of a number of ten thousand times ten thousands, thousands of thousands of angels. All these angels will attend upon Jesus Christ at His second appearance. It is said in Matthew 25:31 that all the holy angels shall come with Him. Now the angels are dispersed in several places; some of them are upright on the earth, ministering unto the saints, which shall be heirs of salvation, Hebrews 1:14. Others are in heaven beholding the face of the Father, ready to execute His will.

Some are ascending, some descending, but when they will be all gathered together into one company, and like so many courtiers wait upon this great King in this His glorious appearance to the world, all will descend with Christ. Heaven will be emptied of angels; they will all come forth and come down from their old habitation. And, oh, how glorious will the train be!

He will come with all the holy angels, angels that are holy and glorious; not like those rotten courtiers which attend upon these earthly kings who have no other glory upon them but what lies in their rich and splendid apparel, the bodies of some of which, if they were uncased, would appear to be full of loathsome diseases, but whose souls are monstrously ugly and deformed, full of loathsome and noisome lusts, besmeared with dung and filthiness, who, could their insides be turned outward, and the deformity of their sin be seen with bodily eyes, would appear to be hideously black and swarthy, and more misshapen than those that are born with the greatest blemishes of nature, who carry hell in their bosoms and, like so many bears and ugly hounds, are led about by the devil in chains. Such follow many kings on earth, when they appear abroad with hearts full of lust, with eyes full of adultery, with mouths full of oaths and filthy ribaldry; who are like so many spots in the faces of their princes, like a cloud about their brow which darkens their glory in the eyes of the serious and sober-minded. But Christ will come attended with millions of holy angels, arrayed in such pure and white garments as will not have the least spot or tincture of sin upon them. He will come with His holy angels who will be like so many flames of fire, full of sweet burning love, covered with such light and glorious excellency as will not darken, but illustrate the glory of the Lord and Prince they attend upon.

Christ will come with a glorious brightness and great noise; such a light will shine in Him and about Him as will a thousandfold surpass the light of the sun when it shines in its full strength. We read in Matthew 13:43 that the righteous shall shine like the sun in the kingdom of their Father. How, then, will the Son of righteousness shine, from whom they will receive all their brightness by reflection as the moon and some other stars do from the sun in the firmament! It is said in Matthew 24:29–30 that at the coming of Christ "the sun will be darkened, and the moon shall not give her light, and the stars of heaven shall fall." And Revelation 6:12–14: "The sun shall be black as sackcloth of hair, the moon shall be like blood, and the stars of the heavens shall fall to the earth, even as a fig-tree casteth her untimely figs, when she is shaken of a mighty wind, and the heavens shall depart away as a scroll when it is rolled together, and every island and mountain shall be removed out of their places."

At the coming of Christ, there shall be such brightness as will darken the sun and other luminaries in the heavens, even as the sun darkens the lesser stars who, though shining all night with a twinkling light, and like so many candles in the firmament, yet upon the sun first lifting up its head in the morning, and casting about its beams, they presently sink in their sockets and disappear. So the sun itself, and other luminaries of heaven, will disappear, when this more glorious Son arises in the morning of the last day; they will then lose their light, and what further need of them? In heaven it will be all day. Revelation 21:23 says that in the city of the new Jerusalem, "there will be no need of the sun, neither of the moon to shine in it, for the glory of God will lighten it, and the Lamb will be the light of it." Chapter 22:5: "There shall be no night there, and they shall need no candle nor the light of the sun, but the Lord God giveth them light, and they shall reign for ever and ever."

In hell it will be all night and no day; there will be blackness and darkness for ever, and not the least beam of light shall shine into the place. And if the sun and other stars are given for the measure and distinction of time and seasons, when the last day is come, time will be no longer and all must launch forth from the confines of time into the vast ocean of eternity, which cannot be bounded nor measured. It is said in Revelation 20:11 that when the great white throne shall be set, and Christ is placed thereon, the heavens and the earth shall flee away from before His face, and no more place be found for them. 2 Peter 3:10: "When the day of the Lord cometh, that the heavens shall pass away with a great noise, the elements shall melt with fervent heat, and the earth with all its work shall be burnt up." Christ will come with a glorious light and a roaring dreadful noise, which will further set forth the glory of His appearance.

See this expressed in 1 Thessalonians 4:16: "The Lord Himself shall descend from heaven with a shout, with the voice of archangels, and with the trump of God." And Matthew 24:31: "He shall send forth His angels with a great sound of a trumpet, who shall gather His elect from the four winds." Never was there such a noise heard in the world as will be then heard. When Christ shall appear, the heavens will roar; the earth will be in flames of fire; there will be a great shout, and the sound of the last trumpet in the air. This shout will be given by Jesus Christ Himself, as is likely, for it is said, John 5:28–29, "The hour is coming, in the which all that are in their graves shall hear His voice, and shall come forth."

We read in John 11:43 that when Christ came to raise Lazarus He cried with a loud voice, "Lazarus, come forth." Surely when He comes to raise the world, He will cry and shout with a much louder voice. Such a voice likely will come down from Him in a roaring shout, "Awake ye dead, and come to judgment"; or, "Arise, ye children of men, and come forth out of your graves." Never was there such a shout given as then will be given, which shall be accompanied with the sound of the last trumpet. The angels shall sound the trumpet. We read in Exodus 19:16 that, when the Lord gave the Law from Mount Sinai, there were thunderings and lightnings and the voice of a trumpet, exceedingly loud, which made the people which were in the camp to tremble. O what thunderings will there be in the air at Christ's second appearance! And how exceedingly loud will the sound of this last trumpet be when Christ comes to judge them which have broken His Law! That trumpet was heard only by the nation of the Jews, which were together about the mount; this trumpet will be heard by all nations throughout the world. That trumpet was heard only by those that were alive at that time; this trumpet will be heard not only by them that shall remain alive upon the earth at the last day, but also by those which have died throughout all generations, from the beginning of the creation. Such a noise there will be as will awaken all that shall be asleep in their graves. Such a noise as will make all the corners of the earth to ring and the pillars of the world to tremble. But, oh! How will it startle the wicked when they hear it, and fill them with terror and amazement!

Thus you have something in the manner of Christ's second appearance set forth unto you. He shall come with power and great glory.

Chapter 3

The End of Christ's Second Appearance

2. The next thing is to speak of the end of Christ's second appearance and the transactions of that day. The end of Christ's second appearance will be to judge the world. The end of His first coming was not to judge, but to redeem and save, as He told His disciples when they desired Him to execute some judgment from heaven upon those Samaritans who would not receive Him. Luke 9:55–56: "Ye know not what spirit ye are of; the Son of man came not to destroy men's lives, but to save them." John 12:47: "If any man hear my words and believe not, I judge him not, for I came not to judge, but to save." But when Christ will appear the second time, He will come to judge the world. Jude 14: "Behold the Lord cometh with ten thousand of His saints to execute judgment upon all." Matthew 25:31–32: "When the Son of man shall come in His glory, and all His holy angels with Him, then shall He sit upon the throne of His glory, and before Him shall be gathered all nations." And so He goes on in description of the last judgment.

In speaking of Christ's judging the world and the transactions of that day, I will show that:

Christ will raise up all the dead out of their graves.

He will gather all nations before His judgment seat.

He will separate the righteous from the wicked.

He will open the books out of which all must be judged.

I shall then, in chapter 4, speak more particularly of the judgment of the righteous and of the wicked.

Christ, at His second appearance, will raise up all the dead out of their graves. There shall be a general resurrection. John 5:28–29: "The hour cometh, in the which all that are in their graves shall hear His voice and come forth; they that have done good unto the resurrection of life; and they that have done evil unto the resurrection of damnation." Something has been spoken already concerning Christ's victory over death and loosing all his prisoners, but give me leave to illustrate the resurrection a little further: and here I shall endeavor to set it forth with an allusion to Ezekiel 37:1–11:

> The hand of the Lord was upon me and carried me out in the Spirit of the Lord, and set me down in the midst of the valley, which was full of bones, and caused me to pass by them round about; there were very many in the open valley; and lo they were very dry. And He said unto me, son of man, can these bones live? And I answered, O Lord God, thou knowest. And He said unto Me, prophesy upon these bones, and say unto them, O ye dry bones, hear the word of the Lord: thus saith the Lord God unto these bones, behold I will cause breath to enter into you, and ye shall live. And I will lay sinews upon you, and bring up flesh upon you, and cover you with skin, and put breath in you: and ye shall live, and know that I am the Lord.

> So I prophesied as I was commanded, and as I prophesied there was a noise, and behold a shaking, and the bones came together, bone to his bone. And when I beheld, lo, the sinews and the flesh, came upon them, and the skin covered them about, but there was no breath in them. Then said He unto me, prophesy unto the wind, prophesy, son of man, and say to the wind, Thus saith the Lord God, come from the four winds, O breath, and breathe upon these slain, that they may live. So I prophesied as He commanded me, and the breath came into them, and they lived, and stood upon their feet, an exceeding great army.

Something like this will the resurrection be at the last day. Now the bones and bodies of all former generations are scattered up and down in the shadow of the valley of death; some are sunk into the depth, others are buried in the earth; the flesh is consumed and dissolved into its first elements, and the bones of some remain, of others are moldered into earth. Now, when the Lord Jesus Christ, the Son of God, shall come down from Mount Zion which is above, into the valley of this inferior world, He will prophesy over all the bodies and bones of the children of men that are dead, and speak unto them to live. He will say unto them while they lie rotting in their graves, "Live." He will say, "Awake, ye that sleep in the dust"; and oh, what a noise and shaking will there be then in the ground! What a clattering of bones together in the coming of bone to his bone! If the body has been quartered and buried, part in one place and part in another, as the Levite's concubine who was divided into twelve parts and sent to the twelve tribes of Israel, and it is likely buried in twelve distinct places, the bones will fly through the air out of all these places, and meet in one body. Oh, what a great part of the air, water, and earth will there run into conjunction by the command of Christ and be turned into those very bodies which were dissolved into them by death and the corruption of the pit; but, with the addition of such new qualities as shall sublimate, spiritualize, and refine them from all that dreggishness and ill humor that shall be the foundation of any sickness or death forever. Then bones will come together and be made like the stones for strength. Then the sinews will be, as it were, iron sinews and the flesh brass; such strength will be put into them as I conceive is not found in the strongest creatures hitherto God has made; that they might be fitted, the bodies of the righteous for an eternal life of happiness, and bearing the glory of heaven; the bodies of the wicked for an eternal life of misery, and bearing the torments of hell; either of which the body, now as it is, would sink under. Then the sea will give up her dead and the earth will give up her dead, Revelation 20:13. As the whale cast Jonah upon the shore after he had lain three days in his belly, so the sea will give up all the dead that for so many years have been buried into its bowels.

But what a stirring will there be in the earth! Those which are alive will wonder to see such a strange metamorphosis of the ground, to feel men and women stirring and moving under their feet, arising and crowding for room among them. Then will the Lord bring down all the souls of the righteous, which have been in paradise with Him many years. And they shall find out their own bodies, and He will open the prison of hell and let out the souls of the wicked for a while that they also may find out their own bodies which shall be prepared for both, that they might be both prepared for the last judgment; of which more when I come to the particular judgment of the righteous and wicked. Thus Christ will raise up all the dead out of their graves.

Christ, at His second appearance, will gather all nations before His judgment seat. Revelation 20:11–12: "I saw a great white throne, and Him that sat on it. And I saw the dead, small and great, stand before God." 2 Corinthians 5:10: "We must all appear before the judgment seat of Christ." Matthew 25:31–32: "When the Son of man shall sit on His throne, all nations shall be gathered before Him." Oh, what a vast number will there be when so many hundred generations of people shall be alive together and gathered together into one place! If so be, the multitude of the righteous will be so great when they are gotten together into one body that no man can number them. Revelation 7:9: "After I beheld, and lo, a great multitude which no man could number, of all nations and kindreds, and people and tongues stood before the throne, and before the Lamb, clothed with white robes, and palms in their hands." What, then, will the multitude of the wicked be when they are gathered together in comparison with whom the righteous are but few? All nations shall be gathered before Christ's judgment seat.

Christ, at His second appearance, will separate the righteous from the wicked; the chaff will be purged from the wheat, Matthew 3:12. The tares shall be gathered from the corn, Matthew 13:30. The bad shall be divided from the good, verse 38. The goats shall be separated from the sheep, Matthew 25:32. By the chaff, tares, bad fish, and goats we are to understand the wicked; by the good corn, good fish, and sheep we are to understand the righteous, who will be separated one from another, however they are now, in some places, mingled and linked together. The elect will be gathered together into one company from the four winds, Matthew 24:31. And they shall stand on the right hand of Christ, and the reprobate wicked shall stand on the left, Matthew 25:33. In which gathering and separation there shall be no mistake, as there may be now.

Many close hypocrites may in this world pass for the true children of God; they may live together, and hear together, and pray together, and receive the sacrament together, and make the same profession of religion; yea, some hypocrites may, as to outward appearance, seem to outdo some of God's own children in zeal and forwardness. The lamps of the foolish virgins may seem to shine with a greater blaze than some of the lamps of the wise, when they have not the least dram of the oil of true grace in the vessel of their hearts, Matthew 251–13. Yea, some of God's own children may here be mistaken for hypocrites, their chiefest life being secret and out of view, by them that are uncharitable; and they may also mistake themselves, through the temptations of the devil, and the doubtings of their misgiving, unbelieving hearts. But at the last day there will be no mistake; not only the more openly profane, and notorious vile generations of the wicked, who are even professed enemies of God's people, and shun their company, and separate themselves now, shall be separated themselves by Jesus Christ at the last day; but also all those that were more sober, and had some kind of love for them, but none for Jesus Christ; yea, all hypocrites who seemed to be of their company shall be parted from them.

Christ will look upon them all with a piercing, distinguishing eye, He will easily discern and discover all the hypocrites, however they may plead that they have eaten and drunk in His presence, and some of them cast out devils in His name; He will not judge according to the outward appearance, but according to the truth which has been in the heart, and they which have so much deceived men shall not be able to deceive Him. None of them shall twine themselves imperceivably and crowd into heaven among the righteous. Then the lamps of the foolish virgins will be gone out. Then the veil and mask of an outward show will be rent and torn to pieces. Then the sheepskin will be plucked off, and they will appear unto the whole world to have been but goats, and among the goats they must go. Christ will not leave one of the goats among the sheep, and He will not leave one of the sheep among the goats. All who belong to His fold shall be gathered into one society. Of their meeting, I will say more in their particular judgment.

At the second appearance of Jesus Christ the books must be opened out of which all must be judged. Revelation 20:12: "I saw the dead small and great stand before God, and the books were opened, and another book was opened, which is the book of life, and the dead were judged out of those things which were written in these books according to their works."

The Five Books To Be Opened at the Final Judgment

There are five books which will then be opened: the book of God's remembrance; the book of men's own consciences; the book of the Law; the book of the gospel; and the book of life.

The book of God's remembrance will be opened. This we are to understand in a spiritual sense; not as if there were a real book which God made use of for His remembrance of things, like men do who have frail and weak memories which would let slip many things of note without such a help. But hereby we are to understand that God takes an exact notice of things, and remembers them as if He had them written in a book by Him. The book of God's remembrance will be opened wherein will be found recorded:

First, the names of all the sons and daughters of Adam, whatever age and generation they have lived in, from the beginning of the creation unto the consummation of all things, as also the relations they stood in and the charge committed to them. Such and such were magistrates, and had such and such subjects under them; such had the sword of justice put into their hands, and their charge was to rule under Christ, to encourage and reward them that ruled well and to punish evildoers. Such and such were ministers, and they were entrusted with the care of souls; they were set by the Lord as watchmen to forewarn the people of judgments, stewards to dispense the food of the Word and to give everyone their portion. Such and such were governors of families whose work was to set up religion and the worship of God in their houses, and labor in their places after the salvation of their souls, as well as to set those under them about their civil work and to provide for their bodies. Such and such were children and servants whose charge was to yield obedience to parents and governors in the Lord with meekness and fear, readiness and diligence.

Second, there will be found recorded the place where such persons lived; such indeed lived in the dark places of heathenism and idolatry; but such and such lived in Israel, in a Goshen, in a land of light. Such and such lived in England, in London, in such a religious family. There will be recorded the means of grace which they have enjoyed in those places. Such lived under such a powerful ministry, heard such heart-awakening and heart-warning sermons, and had such sweet showers of the Word dropping upon them. They were planted in a fertile soil and they had fat pastures to feed in.

Third, there will be found recorded the various dispensations of God's providence towards them for their good. Such and such had not only God's Word, but also God's rod to teach them; they lived under the sound of awakening judgments; they lived in London when the plague raged so sorely, and when the fire broke forth and consumed the city. And such were preserved when thousands fell into the pit; they were brought down to the doors of the grave and eternity, and they were brought up again; they were preserved and provided for, and every day tasted the cup of God's goodness; they were loaded with His mercies.

Fourth, especially there will be found recorded all the actions of the children of men and their carriage towards God and one another in those places, in those relations, under those ordinances and providences.

There will be found recorded all the good that has been found in, or done by, any from the day of their childhood to their dying hour. Such and such were obedient to parents when they were young. They were diligent in learning their catechism, and ready to receive instructions in the principles of religion; such were acquainted with the Scriptures when they were but children; such had tender hearts in their tender years. Such loved God and followed God when they were but youths; such and such had their hearts opened in hearing the Word, and enlarged hearts in prayer; such were awakened by such sermons and convinced and humbled for sin, and persuaded to repent and turn to the Lord. Such opened the door to Jesus Christ when He knocked, and set up His throne in their hearts; they put their necks under His yoke. Such and such were frequenters and lovers of the ordinances and ministers of Jesus Christ. Such made it their business to be religious; such walked with God in their families and were upright in their dealings in the world. Such used to deny themselves and took up His cross and labored to follow Jesus Christ wherever He led them; such mourned for the sins they could not reform; they were thankful for the mercies they received, were thankful in the relations they were placed in, were faithful under the means they enjoyed, were merciful to their brethren in misery, were patient and cheerful under the rod which was laid upon them, and all the good actions of men will be had in remembrance.

There will be found recorded all the evil actions, all the sins of the children of men. Such and such were disobedient and froward children; slighted the commands of God and their parents, were idle and careless of instruction and would not open their ears to discipline. Such were old in sin when young in years, were strong and skillful in wicked and sinful practices when their bodies were but weak and minds sottishly ignorant in the things of God. Such had good examples before them, but they would not follow them; they saw dreadful judgments, but were hardened under them; they received many mercies, but abused them; they had seasons of grace, but they misspent them; they had calls, but they shut their ears against them; they had convictions of conscience, but they stifled them; they had motions of the Spirit, but they quenched them; they had proffers of Christ, pardon, and salvation, but they refused them and turned God's glory into shame and His grace into wantonness. Such and such were sabbath-breakers; such were swearers; such were drunk-

ards; such were unclean persons and adulterers;
such were thieves; such were covetous persons and
idolaters; such were unjust and unrighteous in their
dealings; such were bitter and reproachful in their
speeches; such were injurious in their action.

All the sins of men and women will be found in
the book of God's remembrance. Deuteronomy
32:34: "Is not this laid up with me and sealed
amongst my treasures?" God stores and treasures up
the sins of the wicked and ungodly against the day
of His wrath, and their perdition. It is said in Job
14:16–17: "Thou numberest my steps; dost Thou not
watch over my sin? My transgressions are sealed up
in a bag, and Thou sewest up mine iniquities." God
numbered the steps of sinners one by one, sin by
sin, as a man would number every step; and He
watches that He may number aright. He takes exact
notice of the footsteps of the body when a man
walks in soft clay. He puts the transgression in a
bag, sews the bag, and seals the bag; all which expressions denote God's exactness in recording and
laying up the sins of men. It is said in Jeremiah 17:1
that "the sin of Judah is written with a pen of iron,
and with the point of a diamond." All secret sins will
be found there recorded, for nothing is secret to
God whose eyes are like a flame of fire which gives
light to every dark corner; darkness hides not from
Him, but the night shines as the day. He looks into
every corner of the earth and into every corner of
the heart, and has set the secret sins in the light of
His countenance; and all open sins will be found
there recorded. No man has taken so much notice
of others' sins as God has done. He does, as it were,

write all down in His remembrance; and, when Christ comes at the last day, the book of God's remembrance will be opened.

The second book which will be opened at Christ's coming will be the book of men's consciences. And this will be the counterpart to every man's particular of what is written in the book of God's remembrance. They will find the same thing there registered; indeed, conscience may now seem to be asleep and say nothing while men are eating, drinking, and sinning; yet conscience is secretly awake and busy in writing and taking notice of every man's actions every day. Conscience has its daybook which has not an empty page. The mouth of conscience may be shut and, with much ado for the present, restrained from speaking and biting; but the eye of conscience cannot be shut from seeing, nor the hand of conscience restrained from registering what it takes notice of. Everyone in the world has, as it were, whole volumes of his own actions in his bosom written down by conscience; and, though the letters of some things done long ago may seem to be razed and worn out so that a man cannot read them now, yet when this book shall be opened at the last day, they will appear in very legible characters.

When a man writes with the juice of a lemon upon fair paper, the juice is white and the paper is white, and he cannot read a word when it is written, or while he is writing; but, let him keep the paper many years by him, and later bring the paper close to the fire, the white letters will turn black and become very legible. So the consciences of wicked persons are writing while they are sinning, and they do not perceive it after it is written. They forget many of their old sins; yea, they do not take notice of them as sins while they are committing them, but when the last day is come, and Christ is come, who will be revealed from heaven in flaming fire to take vengeance upon them, and the book of their conscience shall be opened before them, and all the notes of conscience will be plain and easy to be read, and a ready confirmation, conscience will give all that is written in the book of God's remembrance. And oh, how sweet will the testimony of conscience be of good actions! How bitter will its records be of sin!

The third book which will be opened will be the book of the Law, which requires perfect and perpetual obedience. It will condemn all, both righteous and wicked, because all have sinned and, by the Law, are cursed. Galatians 3:10: "Cursed is every one that continueth not in all things which are written in the book of the law to do them." But then an appeal will be made.

The fourth book which will be opened is the book of the gospel. And there the righteous will find the merits of Christ, though they have had none of their own. They will find exceedingly great and precious promises of pardon and salvation and eternal happiness, which have been made to all them that repented and believed in Christ, and testify the same by their sincere love to God, making choice of Him for their chief good and happiness, and laying up their treasure in heaven by their sincere obedience to His commands and walking in heaven's way. And then conscience will give an evidence, and God's remembrance will confirm it, and the Spirit will witness, and Christ Himself will acknowledge that all His true disciples have had the qualifications which have shown their interest in the promises.

Yea, the weakest of believers, whatever doubts and fears they have now, will then certainly know and confidently plead these qualifications which they have had. They will be able to say that they had true faith, though it was but weak; that they truly laid hold on Christ, though it was but with a trembling hand; that they had the faith of reliance and recumbence, though they had not the faith of assurance and strong confidence; that they heartily repented and grieved for sin, though they had not that measure of godly sorrow which they desired; that sin did not reign in them, though sometime it raged and domineered; that they had chosen God for their chief good above the whole world, and the bias of their wills was towards Him; and that they had a sincere love to Him, though they fell short in the fervency which they desired to have; that they walked and kept on in God's way; and, if sometimes they wandered, that they found their way again; if, sometimes they stumbled, that they got up again. And this book of the gospel will give all true believers such acquittal that they shall not come into condemnation. John 3:16: "Whosoever believeth in the Son shall not perish, but have everlasting life." And Romans 8:1: "There is no condemnation to them that are in Christ Jesus, who walk not after the flesh, but after the Spirit."

But unbelievers will get no benefit by this book. They may find great and sweet promises, but not one promise in the whole book of the gospel belonging to them because they do not belong to Christ. They lived and died in impenitence, unbelief, and neglect of Christ and salvation, and now they cannot find one favorable word for themselves. Therefore, they will be sent back to be tried by the book of the Law; only the gospel will double the condemnation of such as have not yielded up themselves unto its obedience.

A fifth book which will be opened will be the book of life. This is where all the names of the elect are enrolled which, when they read, how will they adore the riches of the free grace of God in choosing them before the foundation of the world was laid! And all those whose names are not enrolled in this book shall be condemned and cast into the lake of fire, Revelation 20:12, 15.

Chapter 4

Christ's Judging the Righteous

3. The third thing proposed, and the chief, is to speak more particularly of Christ's judging both the righteous and the wicked at His second appearance.

And here I shall speak of their particular judgment, concerning the judgment of the righteous and the wicked. The judgment of the righteous will be first, and therefore I shall first treat the immediate antecedents to their judgment, and then of the judgment itself.

Concerning the immediate antecedents of the judgment of the righteous.

The first antecedent to the righteous judgment will be the resurrection from the dead. 1 Thessalonians 4:16: "The dead in Christ shall rise first." When Christ descends from heaven, the souls of the righteous shall descend with Him. 1 Thessalonians 4:14: "Them that sleep in Jesus will God bring with Him." The spirits of all the just men and women made perfect shall then come down and find out their own bodies which have been sleeping in the bed of their graves; they shall enter again into their old habitations. They went out of them, it may be, with fear and trembling, with grief and sorrow, being unwilling to leave them behind, though they were so rotten and ruinous; but oh, with what joy will they return and enter again when the building shall be repaired, when their bodies shall be raised by the power of the Lord Jesus Christ and healed of all infirmities, when they shall be made incorruptible and immortal! 1 Corinthians 15:52: "In a moment, in the twinkling of an eye, at the last trump, for the trumpet shall sound and the dead shall be raised incorruptible, and we shall be changed." And verse 54: "So when this corruptible shall have put on incorruption, and this mortal shall have put on immortality, then shall be brought to pass the saying that was written, Death is swallowed up in victory." Then shall they triumph over death and the grave, saying, "O death, where is thy victory?" The Lord Jesus will then make them victorious over this conqueror. Verse 57: "Thanks be to God who hath given us the victory through our Lord Jesus Christ."

The parting of soul and body was never so sad unto any of the saints at their death as the meeting will be sweet at the resurrection. Oh, how will the soul wonder at the sudden and strange metamorphosis of the body when the soul left the body vile, to putrefy and corrupt in the grave, and shall find it come forth more bright and glorious than gold after it had been refined like unto Christ's more glorious body! Philippians 3:21. Oh, how will the soul delight in the beauty, strength, and immortality which then shall be put upon the body, whereby it will be more suited to its nature and fitted for its operations and participation in its glory! And oh, how will the body delight in the wonderful glories and shining excellencies which the soul has attained since its separation! If the love between the soul and the body were so great when the body was so vile and the soul so sinful, what will it be when both are glorified? If the conjunction between the soul and the body were so sweet when the body was so frail and subject to death, and the soul a spiritual and never-dying substance, what will it be when the body shall be made immortal and, in some sort, spiritual? Oh, with what pleasure will the body awake out of its long sleep and arise and shake off its dust and put on its beautiful garments of immortality and glory! With what delight and joy will it first open its eyes upon those beautiful and glorious objects which will quickly present themselves to its view? This much concerning the resurrection of the righteous bodies.

The second antecedent to the judgment of the righteous will be their meeting with the angels at their graves' mouth. Matthew 24:31: "He shall send His angels with a great sound of a trumpet, and they shall gather the elect from the four winds, from one end of heaven to the other." No sooner are they awakened and raised out of their graves but they are entertained by angels, those holy and excellent creatures who have such a dear love for them, and before have done many good offices for them though, when before in the body, they did not perceive it and were too low and unfit for their acquaintance; but they will then know them and be able to discern the beauty of those lovely spirits who, for so many years, have been beholding the face of their Father in heaven which will have cast a luster upon them that will be matter of their admiration; and these shall be part of their acquaintance and companions in glory. Instead of devils, those angels of darkness, which used to assault, buffet, and molest them when in the body before, they shall now have angels of light with them, and about them, to join together in the praise and love of the great Jehovah. The angels will be sent to call them and gather them, and we may rationally imagine that they will salute them at their rising and welcome them out of their graves.

We read of the angel Gabriel's salutation of Mary in Luke 1:28: "Hail, thou that art highly favored, the Lord is with thee; blessed art thou amongst women." And we find the same angel's word to Daniel in chapter 9:23: "Thou art greatly beloved." Such salutations, possibly, the angels may give to the saints at the resurrection: "Arise, you that are highly favored of God; come forth, you that are greatly beloved. Welcome, welcome, you happy ones; you that are blessed among the children of men. Your Lord is come down and stays for you. He has sent us to call you, to convey you into His presence, and bring you where He is that you may see and share in His glory." Oh, how will such words make their heart to glow within them! How joyful will such a message be unto them! Oh, happy they are that ever they were born; or rather that ever they were new born! Oh, happy they are that should live that they should be raised to see such a day as that will be! Oh, what looks, what speeches, what joys will they have, when they are entering by the angel!

The third antecedent to the righteous judgment will be their meeting one with another, Matthew 24:31. The angels will be sent to gather the elect together. 2 Thessalonians

2:1: "I beseech you, brethren, by the coming of our Lord Jesus Christ, and our gathering together unto Him." The saints will be all gathered together, and we shall be gathered with them, if we are found in that number. There we shall meet with Abraham, Isaac, and Jacob, and all the holy kings, prophets, apostles, martyrs, and holy men who have lived in all generations; and all these in another hue than when they lived upon the earth. They will arise like so many shining suns out of the earth. Oh, how shall we be delighted with the sight of such a glorious train and company, when we see the image and picture of the Lord upon them, drawn to life! What sweet greetings shall we have and mutual congratulations of our old acquaintances in the flesh who were with us acquainted with the Lord! And this is the end of our hearing, fasting, praying, self-denial, mortification, and the poor services we have done for the Lord. Is this the issue of our pains and labors? Oh, happy we are that ever we repented, believed, and closed with Jesus Christ! Oh, happy we are that laid up our treasure and waited for the glory and happiness till this time.

The fourth antecedent is that the righteous shall be caught up together in the air. All the righteous shall be caught up, they who are raised from the dead, and they that remain alive upon the earth on that day. 1 Thessalonians 4:16–17: "The dead in Christ shall rise first; then we which are alive and remain shall be caught up together with them to meet the Lord in the air."

We read of the two witnesses who were slain after

three days and a half: "The Spirit of life from God entered into them and they stood upon their feet and heard a great voice from heaven saying unto them, Come up hither, and they ascended up to heaven in a cloud," Revelation 11:11–12. In the morning of the resurrection, the Spirit of life from God will enter into the bodies of all the saints, and they will stand up and, possibly, they may hear a voice from Christ in the air, "Come up hither," and then they will be caught up and ascend into the air to meet with the Lord. Oh, what inexpressible pleasure and delight will they feel when they find themselves begin to move upward, when they are leaving the earth and wicked men, and so many glorious persons of them together ascending to meet their most glorious Lord!

The fifth antecedent to the judgment is their meeting with the Lord in the air. 1 Thessalonians 4:17: "Then we which are alive and remain shall be caught up together with them, to meet the Lord in the air." We have spoken of the meeting of the soul and the body, of the meeting of the saints with the angels, of the meeting of the saints with the saints, all which meetings will be very delightful; but the meeting of the saints with the Lord Himself will be beyond all. Oh, how sweet will the sound of Christ's coming be unto them before they see Him; when they hear the long-expected shout and the sound of the last trump! This, this will be music indeed in their ears; then, then they will lift up their heads with joy; and think how transporting the first glance of their eye will be upon the Lord Jesus Christ when they see

Him yet afar off clothed with such brightness and beauty! Never did their eye behold such an object before. They admired to see the saints, and to see themselves so transformed; but how will they admire to see the Lord in such glory? If so be that some of His disciples gazed after Him with wonder, when He was taken from them and ascended up into heaven, Acts 1:11, with what wonder will all His disciples, most of whom never saw Him in the flesh, none of whom saw Him in such glory, then gaze upon Him when He shall come down from heaven? "Ye men of Galilee, why stand ye gazing up into heaven?" say the angels. "This same Jesus, which is taken up from you into heaven, shall so come in like manner as ye have seen Him go into heaven." If you look and wonder at His going, how will you look and wonder at His coming, which will be as surely, but far more gloriously? But when they are come nearer to Christ, and have a fuller view of Him, oh, what thoughts! What affections! What joys will there then fill their souls! Oh, what workings, what beating of heart, what transports and ravishment of heart will they have! Oh, how would they be overwhelmed with His sight, and utterly unable to bear it, if they were not strengthened beyond their present capacity?

And is this the Savior and Redeemer of the world? Oh, glorious Sun of righteousness! Did this most excellent Person, who thus appears in the brightness of His Father, and is now come down from His glorious habitation, with such a glorious train of angels, once vouchsafe to dwell with men, and veil His glory in the flesh? Did this eternal Son of God stoop so low as to take upon Him our nature;

yea, to take upon Him the form of a servant? Did He
live in such meanness and obscurity and endure
such hardship, contradiction, reproach and injury,
when He was upon the earth? Oh, infinite conde-
scension! Did this Lord of life and glory, in the days
of His flesh, so weep and pray and cry, sweat, bleed,
and die, though with such pain, anguish, and disgrace, yet with such willingness and patience in our
steads that He might redeem us from sin and death
and wrath to come, that we might not perish but
have everlasting life? Oh, wonderful, inconceivable
love! What, so glorious a Person to be made man?
To be made a curse? To do such things? To suffer
such things? For such mean, vile, cursed sinners as
we are that we might be blessed and happy with
Him? Oh, surpassing superlative kindness! Is this
He who made choice of us when He chose so few?
That called us when most were passed by? That
pitched His love upon us when there was nothing
attractive in us, nothing to move Him but His own
bowels? That revealed His secrets to us when He hid
them from the wise and prudent? That brought us
nigh when we were afar off, and made us fellow citizens and fellow heirs with the saints, and of the
household of God, who were by nature the children
of wrath even as others? Oh, astonishing free grace!

Is this He who clothed us when we were naked,
even with the robes of His own righteousness? That
washed us when we were defiled, even in the foun-
tain of His own blood? That cleared us when we
were troubled, even with the comforts of His own
Spirit? That strengthened us when we were weak
even with His might and glorious power in our in-

ner man? Was it from this Person that we receive our pardon and peace, our supports, our graces, our encouragements, and all the sweet refreshments we have found in ordinances? Is this the Advocate whom we made choice of, relied and trusted upon for life and salvation? Is this the Master whom we have followed, and whose work we were employed about? Is this the Captain whose colors we wore, and under whose banner we fought? Is this the Lord whom we obeyed? The Friend, the Husband whom we loved? And is He so glorious? Oh, how will the saints be wrapped up in admiration and joy! Oh, how will they all be in a flame of burning love and affection when they come to behold the Lord Jesus Christ Himself; and, viewing Him in such glory as then He will be decked withal, when they come to see Him face to face, who has such loveliness in His face, and such love in His heart for them! It is said in 1 Peter 1:8: "Whom having not seen, ye love, in whom though now ye see Him not, yet believing, ye rejoice with joy unspeakable, and full of glory."

If so be that the saints now love Christ, whom they never saw, only have heard of, and believed the report of the Word, how will they love Him when they have a sight of Him, and see a thousandfold more beauty in Him than was reported or could be imagined? If so be that now sometimes they rejoice with glorious and unspeakable joy in believing, what will they do when they come to see Him in His glory? If they can now rejoice in tribulations, and take pleasure in the cross and reproach of Christ, what will they find in their Master's joy, and the crown that He now comes to put on their heads?

Oh, how glad will they be that they have been counted worthy to suffer anything for such a Savior! It will be a joyful time, indeed, unto the saints when they are caught up into the clouds to meet the Lord in the air.

And the joy of Christ will be no less to meet with them. Oh, with what an eye will He view them when they are arising and ascending with so much of His beauty and luster upon them! None can conceive the love and delight which the Lord Jesus will take in them in that day. He will look upon them as those that were beloved by the Father Himself from all eternity; as those who brought Him out of heaven before to redeem them, and now to glorify them; He will look upon them as the travail of His soul, as the price of His blood; He will look upon them as His jewels, as spoils taken out of the hands of His enemies. He will look upon them as plants grown up into perfection, as servants who have done their work, as those who have kept His honor in the world. He will look upon them as His dearest spouse and most beautiful bride, who now comes to be joined to Him more nearly, and to live with Him forever. Oh, the love and joy of Christ at this meeting!

If so be that Christ so dearly loved His spouse, and could delight in her too when she was black and sooty, when her clothes were black and sooted, when her affections were weak, low and inconstant, how will He love and rejoice in her when she is made perfectly like Himself and so beautiful with His comeliness? When her stains are all washed off, and she is presented before Him without spot, wrinkle, or blemish, or any such thing? When she shall be arrayed in white, and has put on her shining garments, and shall appear so lovely, and her love shall be so high, full, strong, and flaming? Never did lovers meet with such delight and joy on their wedding day as Christ and His spouse will meet at the day of His second appearance. Oh, the sweet smiles the saints will see in the face of Christ! Such smiles upon them, such glances of love, will sparkle forth from the eyes as will ravish their hearts. Oh, the sweet words they will hear! The welcomes He will give them when they first meet; when they are come, He will place them at His right hand. So much concerning the more immediate antecedents of the judgment of the righteous.

Chapter 5

The Judgment of the Righteous Continued

The next thing is to speak concerning the judgment of the righteous itself. And there are two things the Scriptures speak of which Christ will do at His second appearance in the judgment of the righteous:

He will take an account of them.

He will pronounce the sentence upon them.

Christ will take an account of the righteous. Romans 14:10, 12: "We shall all stand before the judgment seat of Christ, and every one of us shall give an account of himself unto God." Though the righteous shall not be brought to condemnation, yet they shall be brought into judgment, which will be for their Maker's honor and their own; especially of those who can give a good account of all the talents the Lord has entrusted them with.

I know it is a question among divines whether the sins of God's people will be mentioned and made manifest at the day of judgment. I shall not determine the question, since the Scripture is not so plain. Possibly the Lord, having pardoned them, covered them, and blotted them out of the book of His remembrance, will not mention them on that day; but sure I am that, if they should be mentioned, it will not be to their disgrace and grief, but to their more abundant joy in the Lord who has forgiven them. If they could read their sins in the book of God's remembrance, they will find them like so many debts crossed out with the red lines of Christ's blood. If the devil should be permitted to accuse them at that time, who is now the accuser of the brethren, and rip up their secret faults, the Lord Himself will stand up and plead for them. He will make known the sufficient value of His merit for their ransom, and publicly acquit them for all guilt and condemnation. "Who shall lay any thing to the charge of God's elect? It is God that justifieth: who is he that shall condemn? It is Christ that died for them," Romans 8:33–34. There are four things Christ will take an account of in judging the righteous.

Four Things Christ Will Take account of Judging the Righteous

First, He will take an account of their graces. The vessels of the virgins will be looked into, what oil they have gotten; the hearts of the saints will be looked into, what graces they have obtained. Christ will then take notice what godly sorrow they have had for sin; their secret weeping and mourning will then be made manifest. He will then take notice what humility and meekness, what self-denial and patience they have had, especially what faith, and love, and hope, and spiritual joy they have had, and all their raised affections towards Himself and heavenly things in His ordinances. And His judgment of grace will not be according to the appearance and show which has been, but according to truth; and then the saints shall be ranked not according to their esteem and dignity in this world, but according to the measure of the graces they have obtained.

Second, Christ will take an account of the improvement of the talents of graces and gifts and opportunities of service which He has entrusted them with, Matthew 25:19. And Christ will then take chief notice of those who have been most industrious, faithful, and instrumental for doing most good, and bringing much glory to His name and, though all shall have a full reward that are found truly faithful, and shall enter into their Master's joy, yet they shall have a more full reward and be capable of more joy and glory than the other.

Third, especially, He will take an account of their works of mercy. Matthew 25:35–36: "I was hungry, and ye gave Me meat; I was thirsty, and ye gave Me drink; I was a stranger, and ye took Me in; naked and ye clothed Me; I was sick and ye visited Me; I was in prison, and ye came unto Me."

It will even astonish and confound the righteous to hear such language as this from the Lord Jesus Christ when He appears in such glory. They will be ready to question, "When was He in any want and received relief at their hands?" Or, as Matthew says, "When saw we Thee hungry thirsty, or naked, and ministered any help?" "We received all from Thee, but we could give nothing to Thee! Thou didst relieve us and redeem us out of the deepest poverty and misery in which we were sunk, and should have perished without Thy help. But what relief hadst Thou from us?"

Then the King will answer and say unto them,

verse 40, "Verily I say unto you, inasmuch as ye have done it to one of the least of these My brethren, ye have done it unto Me." At such a time and such a time, the poor came to you for relief, making use of My name, whose back, for My sake, you clothed, and whose bodies you refreshed, and whose necessities you supplied, and that was done unto Me. Though they were poor, they were My brethren; some of My servants were brought into straits for conscience sake, and you received them, or sent to help them. You received Me then, or gave help to Me; that money was not thrown away, it was given to Me, and I am come to give you a thousand-fold reward.

Were this truth more effectually believed, what forwardness would there be in Christians to works of mercy? Surely they would look upon that part of their estate as best improved which in such works is bestowed. Christ does not mention any other use which they put their money to which, if worthy to be compared, would be made mention of. He does not speak of so much laid out in building, so much laid out in clothing, so much laid out for food, so much laid up in portions for children; all this the wicked can do; but so much laid out to the poor, and Me in them, which is the only part you have laid up for yourselves, and which I am now come to return to you with usury.

Fourth, Christ will take an account of the afflictions which the righteous have endured; especially of their suffering for His sake such reproaches, such losses, imprisonments, banishments, buffettings. If they have suffered death, with what honor will this be made mention of; with what great esteem will He receive and speak unto them which have come out of great tribulation! And oh, the joy in this morning after the tears of the night! Then they will find that their "light affliction which they have endured for a moment" has wrought for them "a far more exceeding and eternal weight of glory," 2 Corinthians 4:17.

The second thing in Christ's judgment of the saints is the sentence which He will pronounce upon them, which will be a most gracious invitation to them to take possession of the kingdom of heaven which He has prepared for them. Matthew 25:34: "Then shall the King say unto them on the right hand, Come ye blessed of My Father, inherit the kingdom prepared for you before the foundation of the world."

All Christ's invitations in Scripture are very sweet. "Come unto Me, all ye that labor and are heavy laden, and I will give you rest," Matthew 11:28. How sweet is this to a troubled conscience and an oppressed spirit, ready to sink under the burden of sin? "Ho, every one that thirsteth, come ye to the waters, and he that hath no money, come and buy wine and milk without money, and without price," Isaiah 55:1. Oh, what sweet words are these to those that are parched, pained, and ready to die with spiritual thirst, and can find nothing in the creatures which can give them any satisfaction or ease!

But of all the words that ever Christ spoke, of all the invitations that ever Christ made, this will be the sweetest which He will give to the disciples at the last day: "Come ye blessed of My Father, inherit the kingdom prepared for you from the foundation of the world." Come, you blessed and happy ones, however accounted miserable ones by men, yet blessed of My Father. Come, inherit the kingdom prepared for you from the foundation of the world. Take possession of your eternal inheritance. Come enter into the kingdom of glory which the Father has chosen and called you unto, and which I have purchased and now have fitted and made ready for you. Come along with Me and I will show you My glory; and 'where I am there ye may be also.' Come along with Me into heaven, and you shall live and reign with Me forever and ever. Come along and enter now into your Master's joy; come, and I will show you the Father, and bring you into His house and presence where there is fullness of joy, and pleasures forevermore."

And now, beloved, think with yourselves, what joys, what exaltations, what clapping of hands, what shoutings, what hallelujahs, what hosannas, what triumphing acclamations the saints will make upon hearing these words. But here words fail; conceptions fall short. Who can utter what the affections and behavior of the righteous will be when they have their sentence, and hear such sweet and gracious words from the mouth of their Judge and Redeemer?

This much concerning the judgment of the righteous.

Chapter 6

The Judgment of the Wicked

In treating the second appearance of Jesus Christ, I shall, as in the judgment of the righteous, speak of the immediate antecedents, and of the judgment itself.

The immediate antecedents of the judgment of the wicked will be:

The resurrection of their bodies from the grave. All the wicked that are dead shall be raised, though not so soon, yet as certainly as the righteous. John 5:28–29: "The hour cometh that all that are in their graves shall hear His voice, and not only they that have done good shall come forth to the resurrection of life, but also they that have done evil to the resurrection of damnation." When the wicked die, their bodies are clapped up in the prison of the grave where they rot and putrefy under the chains of death which are laid upon them, and their souls are shut down into the prison of hell where they are bound up in chains of darkness and woe, and are reserved unto the judgment of the great day. When the Lord Jesus shall appear to judge the world, He will bring the keys of death and hell along with Him and open both of these prison doors, not to give liberty and release to the prisoners, but, as prisons are opened at assizes, to bring them forth unto judgment. He will open the prison of hell, and all the souls of the wicked shall come forth like so many locusts out of the bottomless pit; and He will open the prison of the grave, and all their bodies shall creep like so many ugly toads out of the earth. And then soul and body shall be joined together again, and this meeting will be sad beyond expression.

The meeting of the souls and bodies of the righteous will not be more joyful than the meeting of the souls and bodies of the wicked will be doleful; possibly some of the wicked had no pains in their death, and their souls went forth out of their bodies without much pain or fear; but their entrance into their bodies again will be with inexpressible horror; and, if some of the wicked had their consciences awakened at death and they lay down with terror, when they awake and rise again from the dead it will be with far greater terror. The old world died in a fright with the deluge of water which overwhelmed them. Korah, Dathan, and Abiram, with their company, died in a fright at the cleaving and opening of the earth's mouth which swallowed them up. Judas and other despairing souls died in a fright at the apprehensions of the open mouth of hell ready to receive their guilty spirits; but none of the wicked could go forth of their bodies in such a fright as they will enter them again at the last day.

The damned souls have been lying in hell many years, full of anguish in their separation, and they know that their anguish will be increased by the torment of their bodies in their union; and no wonder if they are exceedingly unwilling and fearful to enter in their old lodging. Their bodies have been sleeping all this while in the dust and have felt no pain at all; and how unwelcome a guest will their souls be! Never was death so terrible unto them as life will be at that day; they would rather sleep still in their graves and continue in their rottenness and corruption; they would rather lie hidden forever in the dust of oblivion, or be quite annihilated like beasts, than to rise again to such torments as now they must undergo; but they must arise, willing or unwilling. It is said that the vile bodies of the righteous shall, at the last day, be fashioned like Christ's glorious body, Philippians 3:21. They shall be made like Christ's body in beauty and glory, but the bodies of the wicked shall have another hue and fashion.

If it were possible to fashion bodies like devils, those impure and foul spirits, such spiritual bodies the wicked should have. To be sure, their bodies shall have no glory put upon them, but they lay down vile bodies; they shall rise up far more vile. They lay down in dishonor and they shall be raised in far greater dishonor. Indeed, they will be raised incorruptible and immortal, but this will not be for their glory, but that they may be capable of the greater and longer torment and misery. Their bodies will be so far from being made beautiful like Christ's that, I believe, they will not regain that natural beauty which they had here upon the earth. Now, some of them outshine God's own children (whose chief beauty lies inward) in external comeliness; then, none but the bodies of God's children will shine. The bodies of the wicked, most probably, will be swarthy, black, ugly, monstrous bodies. If there is a ghastliness upon the bodies of the most beautiful when they are dead, what ghastliness will there be upon the bodies of all the wicked when the second death shall seize upon them? Were their bodies never so beautiful in themselves, yet their features would quickly be altered by the horrible passions of their mind; the blackness and dread of the soul would quickly appear in their countenance, besides the impressions which the fire of hell will have upon them. The soul will have nothing in the body which will give it any delight or ease or in the least contribute unto the assuagement of its anguish. It will return into the body as in a prison or dungeon where there no pleasure is to be found; and, if the body is black, how black will the soul be, after so long an abode with foul devils in the lower regions of darkness? And when such foul souls and such vile bodies meet, what a meeting, what a greeting will there be?

We may fancy a kind of language between the soul and the body: "Come out of your hole, you filthy, dunghill flesh, for the pampering and pleasing of whom I have lost myself forever; who has stolen my time and thoughts, and heart from God and Christ and heavenly things, to feed and clothe and cherish you, and make provision to satisfy your base deceitful lusts, when I should have been making provision for your and my everlasting happiness. Awake and come forth out of the dust, you bewitching dirty flesh, who lulled me asleep so long in your pleasing chains, until you suddenly opened your doors and thrust me out, where I was awakened in torment before I was aware. Now I must come into your doors again that you may share and taste of the bitter issue of sinful pleasures and delights."

And oh, how will the body be affrighted as soon as the soul is entered! Never did the soul taste so much of the body's delights as the body will then feel of the soul's anguish. The body will say to the soul, "And have you found me out, oh, my enemy? Could you not have let me alone to lie still at rest in the sweet sleep? Have you used me as a slave, and employed all my members as servants of iniquity and unrighteousness; and are you now come to torment me? And is this the fruit of all the pleasures we have taken together? Should you not have been more wise and provided better for yourself and me?"

Oh, what cries and shrieks will the tongue give forth as soon as it has recovered its use! Oh, what fearful amazing sights will there appear before the eyes as soon as they are opened, when they first peep out of the grave, and sinners see heaven and earth on fire about them, and Christ coming in flaming fire, to take vengeance upon them! Oh, how dreadful will the shout and the voice of the archangel, and the sound of the last trumpet summoning them to judgment, be unto the ears! Oh, how will every joint and member of the bodies of the wicked tremble when they are raised again at the last day!

The second antecedent to the judgment of the wicked will be their meeting with devils. The righteous will meet with angels to welcome them out of their graves; the wicked will meet with devils to entertain them at their resurrection. And then they will not appear unto them like angels of light, as sometimes here they have done, but like foul angels of darkness, as they ever were since their first fall. They will not then entertain the wicked with pleasing baits, and sweet alluring temptations, and pretend to be their friends who consult their good and satisfaction beyond God Himself, the chief good of mankind, as they did when their abode was in the world before; but they will spit forth their venom and malice then in their faces; possibly they may buffet their bodies and lay painful strokes upon them. Surely they will terrify their souls for those things which they have drawn them into the commission of.

Oh, how will they mock and deride their folly and madness for opening their ears to their whispers, for opening their hearts so freely when they have knocked at the door and enticed them to sin! Then the damned will perceive that the devil's design was their ruin and misery when the pretense and show were consultation for their good and happiness; that he labored to please and delight them not out of love, but malice, that he might undo them; that he lulled them asleep that they might not perceive their misery till it was too late; that poison was in his sweetest bait and that their softest pleasures were Satan's silken cords by which he was drawing them into endless woe and bitterness. Then they will perceive how the prince of darkness has blinded their eyes and deluded them; how the old Serpent has beguiled them through his subtlety and deceived them; how they have been gulled of a crown and a kingdom they had the proffers of and were in a capacity to obtain. Then they will perceive whose slaves they have been while they were serving divers lusts; that the devil was their lord and master, and led them captive at his will, and now they will meet with their masters whom they have served unto their terror and amazement. How will they be affrighted at the apparition of so many devils about them, when they shall throw into their thoughts such hideous apprehensions, and lash their spirits with horrible scourges, and they shall seize upon their bodies, and tear them, and drag them to the judgment seat, and there is none to rescue and deliver them!

The third antecedent to the judgment of the wicked will be their meeting one with another. As with the elect, so all the reprobates will be gathered together into one company. Oh, what an innumerable company of rebels and traitors and villains will then be gotten together! How fiercely and horribly will they look upon one another! And if they speak, what language of hell will issue forth from their lips! They may meet with their old companions and fellow sinners, but it will not be like such as they now call meetings of good fellowship when they get together in a tavern or ale house, or some house of wickedness, to drink and sing and dance and sin and make merry in the pleasing of their flesh. They shall not then have ale and wine and women and music, or any incentives to mirth and sensual pleasures. The last meeting will be no merry meeting, but sad and dismal. The pleasing affections which they formerly had for their friends will be changed; their love will be turned into hatred, and the joy they have found in them will be turned into grief and anger. Oh, the angry countenances the wicked will have on that day! It is said that the nations will be angry. Oh, the

angry speeches! How will they rage and storm at one
another; especially at those who have drawn them
into sin! Oh, how will they curse and damn one another! Oh, the horrible noise that will be among the
damned crew when they get together! It may be from
words they fall to blows and tear one another's hair,
and spurn at one another's bodies and bite one another's flesh, and even claw out one another's eyes;
we cannot conjecture so much of the misery of the
wicked as will be on that day.

*The wicked that are alive on the earth at the second ap-
pearance of Christ shall see the righteous that are dead arise
out of their graves with marvelous beauty and joy.* And
those that are alive will be wonderfully changed in
the likeness and fashion of Christ, and all of them
suddenly caught up together in the clouds to meet
the Lord in the air; which sight will be fearful and
amazing to them when they perceive themselves to
be left behind. We read in Revelation 11–12 of the
two witnesses, after they had lain dead for some
time, had the spirit of life put into them, and they
stood upon their feet and were called up and ascended up into heaven. It is said that their enemies
beheld them and great fear fell upon them; so, when
all the witnesses and servants of the Lord shall have
a spirit of life put into them, and stand upon their
feet, and are called up and caught up in the clouds
to meet the Lord, their enemies and the wicked on
the earth will behold them; and great fear will fall
upon them. But oh, the fear and trouble which will
be upon the spirits of those unbelieving, Christless,
graceless sinners whose abode shall, at that day, be

among the believers, and some of them linked in the nearest relations to them, when their believing relations shall be caught away from them and carried up into the air with the rest of the glorious train of saints, when they themselves shall remain below upon the earth. It is said that, at the time of Christ's coming, Luke 17:34–36, "Two men shall be in one bed, the one shall be taken, and the other left. Two women shall be grinding together, the one shall be taken, and the other left; two men shall be together in the field, the one shall be taken, and the other left." Friends may be together at that day, as at other times, not expecting Christ's coming, and, it may be, less expecting it than before they did; some will be in the fields together, some in houses together, some will be in beds together, some will be in churches together. It may be ministers preaching and people hearing, as you are hearing me this day.

Suppose that the heaven should just now open, and you should hear the sound of the last trumpet, and Jesus Christ should descend with a glorious train of angels into the air. Then all you that are believers, and have gotten an interest in Christ, would immediately be caught up in the clouds to meet with the Lord. But all you that are impenitent and unbelievers would be left behind; and think what terror would fall upon you to see us caught away from you. It may be some of you might come hanging about me and others, when you see us arrayed in shining garments, and suddenly changed into the glorious likeness of our Lord, and called by the angels to go up to Him. "Oh, take us up along with you; what, will you leave us behind?"

Alas, what can I do for you then? I must say, "I told you of this time and thing before, but you did not seriously regard it so as to prepare. I called you often to repentance, and preached Jesus Christ to you, showed you the way of salvation; but you would not accept Him. You refused Him and lived in the neglect of your own salvation. I told you that, if you did not forsake such and such sins, they would be your ruin; and yet you would not be persuaded to leave them. I forewarned you of the miseries which would come upon you at Christ's coming, but you would not take warning."

Fain I would have had you up all along with me to meet my Lord; and, if I could have been instrumental to convert and turn you unto Him, my joy and crown would have been the greater. Oh, how glad would I have been of your company in this triumph! Some hearkened and believed; some awakened when they were called, and repented and reformed their lives; some were wise and forethought, and made provision for this day; and now see how they shine. See the mirth and joy in their countenances; see the fruit of their tears and self-denial, of their faith and love and holy walking. Now, now, we are going together to our Lord whom we have sought, served, and trusted with our happiness; and oh, that you would have hearkened and been persuaded to have joined yourselves to our number that we might have gone together! Oh, that you would have joined yourselves to our Lord, and have had fellowship with the Father and His Son Jesus Christ, and broken off your fellowship with the unfruitful works of darkness and workers of iniquity! But you would go on in the broad way because it was easy; the way to heaven was too narrow and difficult for you.

If profession would have been enough, and externally joining yourselves to God's people would have brought you to heaven, this some of you could do with readiness sufficient. But when you must have a power as well as a form, and when you must mourn for sin, crucify the flesh, mortify the deeds of the body, deny yourselves, take up the cross, be so strict in your lives, make conscience of thoughts, words, and all your actions, this you could not do. You could brook to be religious sometimes by-the-by; but, when you had nothing else to do but to make it your business to be religious, you could not endure. You could put on a form and outward visage of godliness on the sabbath-day, but to be religious on weekdays, and every day, to be holy in all manner of conversation, this was too much, and a hard saying that you could not bear. And, if you did not like the terms of the gospel, and would be the servants of the devil, while you seemed to be the servants of Christ, and go on covertly in the way to hell, while you seemed to be going in the way to heaven, what can I do for you now?

I thought you would have shined and gone with us when you shined so much in profession; and are your lamps now gone out when the Bridegroom is come? Alas! Who can supply you now with oil? I have little enough for myself, and none to spare for you! And do you ask me for oil? Alas! If I had enough, I could not part with it and put any into your vessels. Now, now, it is too late; I came with oil often to sell from my Lord and Master, and you might have had it for nothing. You might have bought it without money and without price; but then you slighted and refused all proffers of grace which were made; you valued your lusts, which you have parted withal for it, at a higher rate. You refused the oil altogether, or at least took no more than would light your lamps. You would not receive any into the vessels of your hearts. And do you think I can supply you with oil now?

Some of you had convictions once in the time of the plague, when death raged among you, and some good work was beginning then in you. And is it now worn off, come to nothing, and dwindled into an empty profession? Alas! What shall I do for you now? You know I ventured my life for you, to preach to you when the arrows were flying so thick about you; ventured my liberty for you, my health for you, and was often spent for you, and among you that I might be instrumental to call and save you. But when the thunder of judgment was a little over and out of hearing, you quickly dropped asleep, and the voice of preaching could not enter your ears and awaken you. Alas! Why do you look upon me now with such rueful countenances, and stand with such trembling joints, and speak so earnestly unto me as if something might yet be done for you, and are loath to let me go from your company?

Alas! What can I do for you now? Should I stay and preach to you again, and call and invite you to Jesus Christ, and open the treasures of the gospel, and now you would open your ears and hearts to receive? Alas! Now the mystery of God is finished; the treasures of the gospel are shut up and sealed, and the day of grace is quite spent and gone and cannot be recalled. Could not you have opened before when you knew I knocked often and hard in my Master's name for entertainment? I called, but you refused; I stretched out my hand and lifted up my voice like a trumpet, but you did not regard and follow the counsels which were given unto you. And now my preaching work is done for ever.

Should I stay and pray with you, and for you, that God would pardon your sins or defer your judgment but a little while, if it were but for a week, or a day, that you may prepare your accounts? Oh, how presently would you make your peace with God! How readily would you accept Christ on any terms! Do anything, suffer anything, deny self, take up your cross! Oh, how diligent would you be in the service of God, and resist Satan, and take heed of sin! Alas, poor souls! All these desires are too late. I have prayed with you, and for you, and you have had warning and time to prepare for your accounts and have been called to these duties before. But now the oath is sworn by Him that lives forever and ever that time shall be no longer; now the ear of God is shut and no prayer can enter.

Now Christ is come down from the mercy seat, from the right hand of the Father, where He made intercession; and the throne of grace is now turned into a judgment seat. Now there remains nothing but a fearful looking for a judgment to devour the wicked. Alas! Why do you hang about me with tears and weeping? What can I do for you now? Can I carry you all up with me in my arms? Would not the load be too great for me? And if all of us together could hang and help some of you up into the air with us, and bring you into the presence of our dear and glorious Redeemer, with what confidence could you stand before Him? With what face could you look upon Him when you are so black and filthy, and have such guilt upon your consciences? Would not your looks betray you to be none of our number? Would not your black and trembling joints speak what you are? And would not Christ then frown you away from our company? And then we must, of necessity, let you fall from on high among your fellow hypocrites and unbelievers. If we could carry you up with us, if you should lay hold on us, would not the angels snatch us out of your arms, or would not devils tear you away from us? And could I rescue any of you out of Satan's hands when he comes to seize upon his own? Alas! What can I do for you at this time? I must go away and be gone, and bid you now adieu forever; the saints are all risen and have put on their glorious attire and we are called for. It is your own fault that you did not help to fill up this number. And when such of us as belong to Christ should be caught up in the clouds, oh, how dreadful will it be for you, and all that should be found in the number of them that are left!

The fifth, and most dreadful, antecedent to the judgment of the wicked, will be the sight of the Lord Jesus Christ Himself, who will be revealed from heaven at that day in flaming fire to take vengeance upon them, 2 Thessalonians 1:7–8. The sight of their Judge will affright them. Revelation 1:7: "Behold, He cometh with clouds, and every eye shall see Him, and they also that pierced Him, and

all kindreds of the earth shall wail because of Him.
Even so, Amen." Every eye shall see Him, not only
the righteous, but also the wicked, and they also that
pierced Him, that is, the Jews which crucified Him,
and He said, Matthew 26:64, "Hereafter shall ye see
the Son of man sitting on the right hand of power,
and coming in the clouds of heaven."

Oh, how fearful will the sight of Jesus Christ be
to Judas that betrayed Him, unto the officers that
took Him, unto the base servant that smote Him
with the palm of his hand, unto the people that
mocked and spit upon Him, unto the Pharisees that
accused Him, unto Pilate that scourged and condemned Him, unto Herod that scorned Him, unto
the soldiers that mocked and crucified Him, unto
the priests that stirred up the people and Pilate
against Him, and in the midst of His agony and anguish railed on Him? Though they did not see Him
come down from the cross, yet, when they see Him
come down from heaven, they will believe that He
was the Messiah, and oh, how will this sight terrify
them! Then they will smite their breasts, indeed,
and be filled with horror when they perceive that
this same Jesus was the Son of God and is now the
Judge of the world, and is to come to call them before His bar who then did stand before theirs.

The high priest that rent His clothes when
Christ called Himself the Son of God will be ready to
rend himself in pieces for not acknowledging it;
and with what face will Judas look his Master in the
face when he sees Him come in such glory? And if
some soldiers that kept Christ's sepulcher did so
shake and become like dead men at Christ's resur-

rection when they saw the angel whose countenance was like lightning, and with raiment white as snow, come and roll away the stone from before the door thereof, Matthew 28:2–4, oh, how will they all that had a hand in His death quake and tremble when they see the Lord Jesus Christ Himself come with such power and glory, and all the holy angels with Him, to call them to judgment!

Further, it is said that all kindreds of the earth shall wail because of Him. Matthew 24:30: "All the tribes of the earth shall mourn when they see the Son of man coming in the clouds of heaven." This we are to understand of the wicked kindreds and tribes of the earth; the sight of Christ will be matter of the greatest joy unto His disciples, but of the greatest sorrow unto the wicked world. See how the moaning of the wicked is set forth in Revelation 6:15–17: "And the kings of the earth, and the great men, and the rich men, and the chief captains, and the mighty men, and every bondman, and every free man, hid themselves in the dens, and in the rocks, and in the mountains, and said to the rocks and to the mountains, Fall on us, and hide us from the face of Him that sits upon the throne, and from the wrath of the Lamb; for the great day of His wrath is come, and who shall be able to stand?"

Then profane and wicked kings, who would not submit to the government of Christ, but broke His hands asunder and cast away His cords from them, shall see the King of kings and Lord of lords come down from heaven to judge them. And oh, with what fear would they then run and hide themselves in dens, or under some great rocks and mountains, if they could, from the face of Him who will then sit upon the throne of judgment! And with what trembling will they stand among the meanest of their subjects, divested of all their power and dignity!

Then the nobles and great men of the earth who, having been lifted up above the ordinary degree of men, have lifted up their hearts also with pride and haughtiness above measure, and let loose their reins to lasciviousness, and wallowed in filthy delights and pleasures, shall see the Son of Man coming in the clouds. And oh, how will their proud hearts then be brought down, and their haughtiness laid low, and their sweet sinful delights be turned into gall and wormwood! Then will they cry to the rocks to cover them and the mountains to hide them, if they can find any such place to receive them in this terrible day.

Then the chief captains and the mighty men, who employed their force and strength under the banner of the devil, and endeavored to promote the interest of his kingdom in the world, and rebelled against the Lord of Hosts, shall see the heavens opened and this mighty Captain come down with the armies of heaven attending upon Him in white, to execute vengeance upon them! And then their courage will fail them, and the wrath of the Lamb will make them tremble, and they could creep into a rock or any hole to hide them.

Then the rich men, who have placed their hearts and confidence in their riches, especially those who have heaped up riches by unjust and unrighteous practices, shall see the Son of man coming against them; and they will weep and howl for the miseries that are come upon them, and their riches will be so far from profiting them in the day of wrath that they will be witnesses to accuse them and aggravate their condemnation. Then every bondman and every free man that are slaves to the devil and their own lusts shall see the Son of man coming to judge them, and be in the number of the mourners crying to the mountains to fall on them.

Then there will be distress upon all nations, and great perplexity, sea and waves roaring, and men's hearts failing them for fear when they are looking up into the clouds and see the Son of man coming down, His throne prepared for judgment. The heathen nations will mourn to see Him, but especially the wicked who have had the name of Christians upon them and have sat under the light of the gospel. Oh, how will their faces be filled with shame and confusion, and their hearts with terror and astonishment, when they behold the face of the Lord Jesus Christ shining with such beauty and glory; but looking on them with anger and disdain!

"And is this glorious King that Jesus Christ whom we heard so much spoken of when we lived upon the earth? Was He indeed so great whose command we disobeyed, whose threatenings we slighted, whose grace we abused, and whose wrath we disregarded? Was it so excellent a Person who was described and set forth to us by ministers in such superlative expressions, all which He exceeds, and yet we could see no form nor comeliness in Him, nothing for which we could desire Him? Was this the Savior that was preached to us and offered to us? Is this that Jesus Christ that we were pressed so frequently, and so earnestly, to get an interest in, with so many powerful arguments, and yet could not be moved and persuaded? Was it this Person that called us, and stretched forth His hand all the day long to us, that wooed us and entreated us by His messengers to accept pardon, grace, and salvation, and knocked at the door of our hearts again and again by His Word and Spirit for entertainment? And did we shut our ears and our hearts against Him, and refuse all the gracious tenders which were made unto us? What, did we hearken to the devil when he tempted us to sin, that he might destroy us, and not hearken to Christ who would have persuaded us to faith and obedience, that He might save us? Could we harbor base lusts, which were like so many vipers in our bosoms, and give no entertainment to Jesus Christ who would have brought riches and glory with Him? Oh, what fools and mad men and women have we been! How have our cursed hearts deceived us and the devils deluded us! How have we been bewitched to prefer the vanities of the world, and the satisfaction of the desires of our flesh, before an interest in such a Savior! Woe! Woe! Woe! be unto us, for now the great day of the Lord is come and who is able to stand?"

This is the fifth antecedent to the judgment of the wicked; they shall see the Lord Jesus coming in the clouds, be summoned to the bar, and be placed at His left hand.

The sixth antecedent will be their seeing the judgment and hearing the sentence of the righteous: "Come, ye blessed of My Father, inherit the kingdom prepared for you from the begin-

ning of the world." And oh, how will they grind and
gnash their teeth, and their hearts be ready even to
burst with envy and indignation, to see these poor
mean Christians, whom some of them have separated from their company, and accounted as the off-
scouring of the earth, and not worthy to sit with the
dogs of their flock, exalted to such dignity, shining
in such glory, and adjudged to such happiness,
when they themselves are looked upon with such
contempt and standing waiting for the judgment
and final doom to torments and eternal misery!
These are the antecedents of the judgment of the
wicked.

Chapter 7

The Judgment of the Wicked Continued

I shall here speak of:
1. The Judge.
2. The Assessors.
3. The Malefactors.
4. The Crimes.
5. The Accusers and Witnesses.
6. The Conviction.
7. The Sentence.

1. The Judge of the wicked, as of the righteous, will be the Lord Jesus Christ. It is said in Romans 3:6: "God will judge the world"; but it will be God in Christ, reconciling the world (of the elect) unto Himself, 2 Corinthians 5:19. And God in Christ will judge and condemn the world of the reprobates. "The Father hath committed all judgment to the Son," John 5:22. "And He hath given Him authority to execute judgment, because He is the Son of man," verse 27. The same Jesus whom the wicked would not submit unto, and take for their King to rule over them, they must submit unto and have for their Judge to examine and condemn them. The properties of this Judge are worthy here of our observation.

Christ will be a most glorious Judge. Never was there such a Judge seen on the earth; it will be the greatest judgment. There will be a general assize of the

whole world, and Christ will be the greatest Judge,
the greatest for dignity and glory, that ever eye beheld. Christ will be most glorious with regard to His
person. He will appear to be the Prince, the Lord of
glory, and be admired not only by the saints, but
also by the wicked among whom, before they saw
Him, He was despised. The despisers shall behold
the luster of their Judge and wonder and perish, as it
is said in another case, Acts 13:41. Christ will be
more glorious with regard to His retinue; all the
holy angels, those glorious spirits who are about the
throne of God, shall attend upon Him. Matthew
25:31: "When the Son of man cometh in His glory,
and all His holy angels with Him"; yea, all the holy
saints also shall attend upon Him in the judgment
of the wicked. Jude 14–15: "Behold the Lord will
come with ten thousand of His saints, to execute
judgment upon all the ungodly," yea, and He will
come with all His saints, 1 Thessalonians 3:13. The
whole innumerable company of saints shall attend
upon Christ in white shining garments, with bodies
like Christ's, more beautiful and glorious than the
most splendid attire can make them; and Christ will
then be admired in all the saints and believers by
the wicked which shall behold them; and Christ will
sit upon the throne of His glory, Matthew 25:31. "I
saw a great white throne, and Him that sat upon it,
from whose face the earth and the heavens fled
away," Revelation 20:11. We read of a glorious throne
which Solomon made in 1 Kings 10:18–20, but the
throne and tribunal seat of Christ will be far more
glorious than Solomon's, or any monarch's who
ever lived upon the face of the earth.

Christ will be a most powerful Judge. He will have power to raise all the wicked out of their graves unto life again, which requires as much power to effect as giving them their being and life at the first. He will have power to bring all the wicked to His foot, and keep them in awe that they shall not stir, nor lift up the hand in the least in a way of rebellion, which is more than the most potent prince that ever lived could do. He will have power to execute vengeance upon all the wicked together and inflict an infinite punishment upon them. And He will put forth no less power in the destruction of the wicked at that day than was put forth in the first creation of the world, wherein He will make His power known, Romans 9:22. The wicked "shall be punished with everlasting destruction from the presence of the Lord, and from the glory of His power," 2 Thessalonians 1:9.

Christ will be a most knowing Judge. He will know all the persons of the wicked; not one shall escape His eye. He will not know them in any way of nearness and familiar acquainting Himself with them; but He will know them in a way of perfect cognizance of their persons. He knew them when they lived and rebelled against His laws, and He will know them again when they are raised. He will not only have a general knowledge of them, but He will know them particularly; none of the ancient rebels shall be able to hide themselves either under rocks or mountains or in the crowd and throng of the wicked which shall be gathered together before Him on that day. Christ will find out all His enemies and He will know all their crimes, He will read them all written

in the book of God's remembrance; and, the book
of their own consciences being then opened, He
will present all their sins to His view. The eye of the
Judge will be a piercing all-seeing eye which cannot
be blinded. And, therefore, there will be no mistake
or error in the judgment through ignorance, or
false information, as there may be in the courts of
judicature upon the earth.

Christ will be a most holy Judge. He will be without
the least stain of sin. He was so when He lived
among sinners on earth and, surely, He will be so
when He descends from the holy of holies in
heaven. Some earthly judges are guilty in the same
way as the malefactors who are brought before them
so that, while they judge others, they condemn
themselves; but there will not be the least mote of
sin in the eye of Christ, not any tincture of defilement; and, therefore, as it will be impossible to
blind Him because of His knowledge, so it will be
impossible to bribe and corrupt Him in the judgment because of His holiness. And by consequence:

Christ will be a most impartial and strict Judge. He will
be most impartial with regard to the persons whom
He will judge; the high degree and quality of men
upon earth will be of no account with Him; the rich
will be of no more regard than the poor, nor the
highest princes more than the meanest of their subjects. Death levels all men and puts a conclusion to
all earthly dignities; and, in the resurrection, all will
stand upon even ground. Now, some lords and great
men may murder and oppress and break laws and,
through favor, may escape punishment; which
crimes, if meaner persons had been found guilty of,

would have cost them their lives. But Christ will have
no more favor for a lord or a knight or a gentleman,
no, nor a king or queen, or greatest lady, than for
the most contemptible beggar. He will not accept
the persons of any and connive at the sins of some,
which those that should reprove them now can wink
at as if there were no faults because the faults of
such persons as are high, whose favor they desire,
and in persons from whom they might receive damage and disesteem should they be plain and faithful.
But Christ will neither need the favor, nor fear the
danger of any; and He will not court and flatter any
because of their nobility and greatness, but will im-
partially judge the highest and greatest by the same
rule as He will do the lowest and meanest.

And Christ will be a more strict Judge with regard to crimes. He will bring forth all the sins of the
wicked to light; not one sin which they have committed from the day of their birth to the hour of
their dissolution but shall be had in remembrance
and be brought into public view when the Lord
shall enter into judgment with the ungodly world.
Some of the wicked now sin more secretly; they have
sweet morsels rolling under their tongues which are
not perceived. They have their Delilahs in corners
which are not known. They shroud themselves under the shadow of the wings of the night that they
may conceal some of their wicked lewd practices
which, should they be found in, would fill their
cheeks with shame and blushing; but Christ will call
them at the last day to a strict account, and bring to
light the hidden things of darkness, 1 Corinthians
4:5. And oh, the contempt and confusion which they

will be covered with when all their shameful and abominable sins shall be made manifest!

Christ will be a most righteous Judge. He will judge the world in righteousness. Some of them will be found to have been unrighteous in their judgments, and others unrighteous in their dealing, and all of them unrighteous in their state; but Christ will judge them all in righteousness. He will judge them according to their works. As He will be righteous in not inflicting upon them a greater punishment than their sins have deserved, He will not punish lesser sinners with more stripes and greater sinners with fewer stripes; so neither will He be unrighteous in inflicting upon them a lesser punishment than their sins have deserved, but will proportion their punishment to their offense. Revelation 18:7: "How much she hath glorified herself, and lived deliciously, so much torment and sorrow give her." Christ will be exactly righteous in His judgment, severely righteous without the least mixture of mercy. The wicked shall have from Him the *summum jus*, and that *fine ula injuria*; they shall have the highest right and justice, without the least injury. God's justice requires satisfaction for their sins, and Christ will satisfy the demands of justice to the full upon the ungodly by distribution of such punishments as are the just desert of their sins. Christ will even all scores that day between God and sinners; at the last He will begin to take the payment of that debt from them which they owe for sin which they will be paying unto all eternity. Christ will come with the balances and sword of justice in His hand. He will come to take vengeance upon disobedient children.

Christ will be a most furious Judge. He will be most gracious towards the righteous, but most furious against the wicked. "He will come in flaming fire to take vengeance upon them," 2 Thessalonians 1:8. He will come in flames of love towards His people, but in flames of anger against His enemies. A fire shall devour before Him, and it will be very tempestuous round about Him. See Isaiah 66:15: "Behold the Lord will come with fire, and with chariots, as with a whirlwind, to render His anger with fury, His rebukes with flames of fire."

We read of such wrath on that day in the Lamb as makes the kings and great men of the earth to tremble, and call to mountains and rocks to fall on them and hide them from it, Revelation 6:15–17. Never were there greater love and more tender compassion and pity than are to be found now in the Lord Jesus Christ toward all those who apply themselves unto Him under a sense of sin for salvation here in this world; and never were there greater wrath and revengeful fury than will be found in the same Lord Jesus Christ when sinners shall come before Him to be judged at the last day. He will be very furious, ten thousand times beyond a bear when she is bereaved of her whelps, or a lion when she is hunger-starved. How fiercely will Christ look upon the wicked! What scorn and contempt of them will they see in His face! What dreadful frowns in His brow! What fiery anger will sparkle from His eye in His looking upon them, as if He would look them dead, or look them into hell, before He has pronounced the sentence! How fiercely will He speak unto them? There will be terror in His looks and there will be terror in His voice! He will speak to them in His wrath, and vex them in His hot displeasure. His anger then will break forth into a flame. He will appear to be jealous and very furious when He comes to execute vengeance on His adversaries, and punish His enemies for their sins.

Christ will be an inexorable Judge. None is now more easy to be entreated as a Savior; whosoever comes unto Him may be welcome to Him; He has promised in no wise to cast out such, John 6:37. The most rebellious sinner may find entertainment with Jesus Christ now, and prevail with Him to procure pardon, peace, and salvation upon their repentance of their sins; but when He is come down from heaven to judge the world, He will be inexorable. No prayers, no entreaties, no tears, no arguments will in the least move Him to take any pity on such as shall then be found in their sins. When the wicked, at the day of judgment, shall have their eyes opened to behold the Lord Jesus Christ in His beauty, then one smile of His countenance will be really accounted of more worth than the whole world; and to be made like such a Person and dwell forever in His love and joy, they will then clearly see to be inconceivably beyond all the enjoyments of the creatures in their fullest delights. And to be thrust out of His presence, they will account their chiefest misery; then they will have other apprehensions of hell's torments, when they are just ready to be cast into the burning lake.

When they are awakened in the morning of the resurrection, they are brought to Christ's bar and perceive how near they are to execution; and great distress will be upon them when they look about them, and all refuge fails, and they see no way for them to escape. If now, with their cries and supplications, they might prevail with the Judge for some commiseration; if they had but the least hopes of obtaining the favor and admission into the inheritance of the saints, oh, how would they all fall down upon their knees before Him with the lowest submission and reverence! How would they cry and weep, entreat and beseech! How would they kiss His feet, wash them with tears, and wipe them with their hair! How earnest and importunate would they be with Him for a pardon, if importunity would prevail! If there were but one promise left in the whole book of God for them which might possibly bring unto them some relief, how greedily would they all catch at it, and humbly woo the Lord for mercy! No, the Judge will be then inexorable; they may cry, but it will be to no purpose. He will shut His ears against their prayers and hide His eyes from their misery; they had promises enough while they lived, but they did not regard them. They did not believe and apply them. And now, nothing but threatenings belong to them and remain for them. Christ often cried to them by His ministers, and moved them by His Spirit, to open the doors of their hearts and give Him room and entertainment, but they shut their ears and hearts against Him. And now, Christ will shut His ears and the door of mercy and heaven against them. He will be inexorable. Thus concerning the Judge of the wicked.

2. The assessors, or those who shall sit with

Christ in the judgment of the wicked, will be the righteous. This promise the Lord makes particularly, and especially to the twelve apostles in Matthew 19:28: "Verily I say unto you, That ye which have followed Me," who have denied yourselves, parted with all, taken up your cross and followed Me in the regeneration or restitution of all things, when the day of the resurrection comes, and the Son of man shall sit on the throne of His glory, when I shall sit upon My judgment seat and gather all nations before My bar to receive their doom, "Ye shall sit on twelve thrones, judging the twelve tribes of Israel"; and though the apostles of Christ will be especially honored and exalted in the day of judgment, and have seats, or degrees of dignity above others; yet this honor also shall all the saints have, to sit with Christ in judgment. 1 Corinthians 6:2: "Do ye not know that the saints shall judge the world?" They judge and condemn the sins of the wicked world now by their holy conversation, and they will judge and condemn the persons of the wicked at the last day by their approbation of Christ's judgment. The crimes of the wicked will be scanned before the righteous, their secret sins will be ripped up and made manifest unto them; they will not only be brought in as accusers and witnesses against some of the wicked, of which I shall speak by and by, but also they will join with Christ in the examination of the wicked; and they will also approve of Christ's justice and righteousness in the condemnation of sinners for their sins.

And when Christ pronounces the sentence of condemnation upon them, "Depart from Me, ye cursed, into everlasting fire, prepared for the devil and his angels," they will join with Him and approve of this sentence. It may be they will, with one voice, say, "Even so, Amen"; or, with a loud shout, accompany Christ's words saying, "Depart, ye cursed, into everlasting fire." A strange turn and change of things will be there at that day. Felix, who sat on the judgment seat when Paul was at the bar, will stand at the bar when Paul will sit among the judges. The Lord will bring down the mighty from their seats, and all wicked princes and judges of the earth shall be dethroned, when the righteous, though of a low degree, shall be exalted to sit as judges upon them.

3. The malefactors who shall be judged will be:

First, devils, 2 Peter 2:4. The angels which fell are said to be delivered into chains of darkness and to be reserved unto judgment. They are punished in part now, but their punishment is not yet complete. When Christ came the first time in the flesh and began to dislodge the devils from their habitation in those persons whom they had got the possession of, they were afraid that He would have completed their torment presently and, therefore, they cried out, "Art Thou come hither to torment us before the time?" Matthew 8:29, and "Let us alone, art Thou come to destroy us?" Luke 4:34. But when Christ comes the second time in His glory, then He will judge and condemn the wicked angels, and the saints shall join with Him therein. 1 Corinthians 6:3: "Know ye not that we shall judge angels?" Then the measure of their sin will be completed, and the time of their torment will be come, and their punishment will be completed too; the way and manner of their judgment is not spoken of in Scripture, and therefore I shall not speak of it. But that they shall be judged to everlasting fire is evident from the sentence pronounced on wicked men in which it is said that everlasting fire is prepared for the devil and his angels.

Second, all wicked men and women who ever lived, or shall live on the earth, from the beginning of the creation unto the dissolution of the world, that have no interest in Jesus Christ, will be the malefactors which shall be judged at the last day. This day is called the day of judgment and perdition of the ungodly. 2 Peter 3:7: "And the unjust are said to be reserved to the day of judgment, to be punished." And the Apostle Paul tells us that "the Lord Jesus should be revealed from heaven, in flaming fire, taking vengeance on them that know not God, and obey not the gospel," 2 Thessalonians 1:7–8.

By "them which know not God" we may understand the heathen and the Gentile nations, this being the character given of them. 1 Thessalonians 4:5: "Not in lusts of concupiscence, as the Gentiles which know not God." And the Ephesians, while heathens before the gospel came among them, were strangers to the covenant of promise, having no hope, and without God in the world, Ephesians 2:12. All the heathen nations shall be judged by Christ, but I shall not speak of their judgment in which we are not so much concerned.

By "them which obey not the gospel" we are to understand all those nations upon whom the light of the gospel has shone and unto whom the sound of the gospel has come, but yet have not yielded obedience thereunto, so as heartily to accept Christ for their Savior upon His own terms. All Christless, graceless persons who have heard of Christ and enjoyed the means of grace will be the chief malefactors in the day of judgment. I might here give a catalogue of sinners which shall be judged; take one in 1 Corinthians 6:9–10: "the unrighteous, fornicators, idolaters, adulterers, effeminate, abusers of themselves with mankind, thieves, coveteous, drunkards, revilers, extortioners, and all other unjustified, and unsanctified sinners." But more of this when I come to speak of the conviction of the wicked.

4. The crime for which the wicked shall be judged and condemned by Christ will be sin; first, sin against the law, and that in two kinds.

They will be condemned for sins of omission. Matthew 25:42: "I was hungry, and ye gave Me no meat; I was thirsty, and ye gave Me no drink." They will be condemned for sins of commission, and that in three kinds:

They will be condemned for sins of thought and heart. 1 Corinthians 4:5: "when the Lord comes, He will make manifest the counsels of the heart." He will condemn men for their wicked thoughts and contrivements, for their sinful lusts, desires, and delights.

They will be condemned for sins of word. Matthew 12:36–37: "But I say unto you, that every idle word which men will speak, they shall give an account thereof in the day of judgment; for by thy words thou shalt be justified, and by thy words thou shalt be condemned." If men shall be judged for idle words, much more shall they be judged for taking God's name in vain, for hideous oaths and blasphemies; if for unprofitable speeches, much more for corrupt communications, for lying, slanderous, bitter, reviling speeches.

Christ will judge the wicked for their sins of deed. Romans 2:6: "He will render to every one according to their deeds," and verses 8–9, "to them that obey unrighteousness, indignation, and wrath, tribulation and anguish upon every soul of man that doeth evil, of the Jew first, and also of the Gentile."

Second, the sins against the gospel will be the chief condemning crimes of the wicked. No sins against the law will be found so heinous, but if sinners are found, after the commission of them, to have obeyed the gospel, to have repented and believed, and yielded the fruits of new obedience, they will have all pardon and absolution on that day; but final disobedience to the gospel will be unpardonable. Final impenitence and unbelief in those which have been called to repent and close with Jesus Christ will certainly bring men under the sentence of condemnation. I might here give a more particular catalogue of the sins which the wicked shall be judged for by Christ, but something more of them under their conviction by Christ.

5. The accusers of and witnesses against the wicked being the same, I shall join together, and they will be God, men, devils, and themselves.

God will accuse the wicked.

God will be an accuser of, and witness against,

the wicked at the day of judgment.

God's justice, to speak after the manner of men, seeing this judgment is set forth in such a manner for our better apprehending of it, because we are not able to conceive in this state the way exactly of God's proceeding against sinners in judgment on that day, will arraign the wicked before the judgment seat of Christ, and draw up, as it were, a bill of indictment against them, "Whereas these men and women, who lived in such and such places, and times, though they were My creatures and subjects, were made by Me and for Me, and I gave them My holy, and righteous, and good law to be the guide and rule of their life and actions; yet, having no fear of Me before their eyes, they cast My commandments behind their backs and lived in a course of rebellion and disobedience against Me, committing such and such sins. And I sent My Son into the world to die for sinners, who gave Me sufficient satisfaction; and I made Him known, and the way of salvation by Him, and offered Him unto them, and entreated them by My ambassadors to be reconciled; but they shut their ears, and hardened their hearts, and refused My Son, trampling upon His blood; they grieved My Spirit and neglected the salvation of their own souls. Therefore, I now require satisfaction from them and that a suitable punishment be inflicted upon them for their disobedience."

God's goodness, bounty, and patience will accuse them when they are thus arraigned and indicted by His justice, which will aggravate their sins. "I nourished and brought up these creatures like children, and yet they rebelled against Me. I spared them as a

man spares his son who serves him, and yet they had
no regard of Me. I delivered them in six troubles,
and in seven, recovered them often upon a sick bed,
and brought them back from the grave when they
were ready to go down into the pit; yet they knew not
that I healed them, and were so much the more disobedient unto Me. I loaded them with mercies and
yet they loaded Me with iniquities; I would have led
them to repentance by My patience and goodness,
but they were the more impenitent and hard-
hearted, and resolved to do evil. I stretched forth My
hand all the day long to these disobedient and gain-
saying creatures, and would have received them had
they returned into the arms of My mercy; but nothing would win and persuade them to leave their sins
and come unto Me. And now My patience is spent;
long-suffering is at an end, and compassion is shut
up against them forever. And now, let them smart
for all their abuses, affronts, and contempts which
they have offered to Me."

God's omniscience will be a witness against the
wicked at the day of judgment. Their sins have been
all committed under the view of God's all-seeing eye,
and they have been noted down upon the book of
His remembrance; and God will witness against
them. "I saw these wretched sinners when they were
born, and traced all their steps. I compassed their
path and their lying down, and was acquainted with
all their ways. I set them behind and before, and My
eye was continually upon them; I perceived the first
sproutings and buddings of sin in their tender
years. I took notice of their disobedience to their
parents when they were young; of their lies and

pride and vanity, of their idleness and sloth and misspending their precious time. I was an eye-witness to all their sins from their youth to their dying hour. I beheld them when no eye was upon them. I saw their privy lewdness, and all their deeds of darkness, which they committed in dark corners. When I kept silence and did not speak, I was not blind so as not to see; and, although I did not smite, I did note, and what one of them has the confidence to deny any one of their sins which I have been a witness unto?" The first accuser and witness against the wicked will be God Himself.

Men will accuse the wicked.

Men, both godly and ungodly, will accuse and witness against the wicked at the day of judgment.

The godly include both godly ministers and godly friends. Godly ministers will be the accusers and witnesses against the wicked. Ministers must give an account then to their Lord of the souls which He committed to their charge, Hebrews 13:17. And, in some of their flock, they will rejoice because their testimony concerning Jesus Christ was believed, because the gospel which they preached among them was obeyed, because the Word was received as the Word of God. They will rejoice in those who have been effectually wrought upon by their ministry; in those who they have been instrumental to regenerate and espouse unto Jesus Christ, to persuade to leave their sins and submit themselves to the yoke and scepter of the Lord. Such will be the joy and crown of rejoicing to their ministers on that day; of whom, with unspeakable comfort, they will say to their Lord, "Behold the children which Thou hast given us. Thine they were, and are, and Thou didst give Them unto us, and they have believed and kept Thy word. And now, as they have shared in Thy glory, let them with us share in, and participate in Thy glory."

But alas! What a sad account will they have to give of others of their flock, who have not believed and yielded obedience to the gospel which they have preached. It will be sad for them when they must bring in heavy accusations against them. "Lord, Thou didst send us upon Thy ambassador unto them; but they regarded neither messenger not message. We preached often in Thy name, but either they would not hear when they might, or they would not believe and yield obedience when they heard. We often told them of their sins and foretold them of their danger if they did not repent and reform; but they would not receive conviction nor be persuaded to repentance and reformation. If we spoke of sin more generally, they did not look upon themselves as concerned, and made no application unless it was to others. If we came more home and close, they shrouded their sins as close as they could under the veil of some thin excuses. They shut their eyes and would not see; and, if the beams of light broke in upon them and in start they opened their eyes a little, they were either offended that we should disturb them in their sleep, or they quickly shut their eyes again and dropped asleep faster than before and soon wore off the convictions and troubles of mind which sometimes they have had under the light and alarm of the Word.

"We often showed them their face in a glass, but they have gone away and forgotten what manner of men and women they were. We have told them of the works of the flesh which should certainly exclude them from the kingdom of heaven, that no unrighteous persons, nor unclean persons, nor drunkards, not covetous persons, or revilers, nor extortioners, could be saved without repentance and sanctification. And yet they would not leave their sins; they would be unjust and unclean still; they would be covetous and revilers still; they would wallow still in their filthiness and hold fast their sins, whatever we could speak against it. We preached unto them of the day of judgment, and foretold them out of Thy Word of these very things which are now come to pass; but they did not believe it, nor consider it, nor take any care to prepare for this day. They thrust the thoughts of judgment out of their mind and put the evil day far from them. We preached unto them the gospel, opened the rich treasures thereof before them, made known the exceedingly great and precious promises of the covenant of grace, the inestimable privileges and unspeakable benefits which belong to those that belong to Christ, and offered all unto them in Thy name if they would accept them and yield obedience unto them; but all these things were slighted and undervalued by them. We called and cried, we beseeched and entreated them that they would be reconciled unto God; but they would not give ear unto us.

"We held forth Thee, O Lord, to them, and studied to set Thee forth in the best words we could think of. We told them of Thy beauty and love and desireableness above all persons and things in the world; told them of their need and that they were undone without Thee. We tendered to them Thy blood, and the purchase there of pardon and peace and happiness forever; but they were like the deaf adder which will not hear. They were like rocks unmoved; they refused Thee and Thy treasures, trampled upon Thy blood, and put both us and Thee to shame by their refusal. We invited them unto the marriage feast, but they would not come. All excused themselves with one excuse or another. One had bought a farm, and he must go see it; another was engaged in a great trade, and he must follow it; another had married a wife and he could not come, and none of them would come and taste of the banquet. The cares of the world, the deceitfulness of riches, the pleasures of this life, and the lusts of other things, so overcharged their thoughts and hearts that the gospel and rich provisions thereof lay by disregarded."

Such will be the accusations of some ministers; such witness they must give at the last day against those of their flock who shall be found in the number of the wicked and disobedient to the gospel. Then their sermons, now forgotten, will be remembered, and will be so many evidences against them. Oh, that our people would remember them now! Oh, that they would now consider and believe, turn and live, and avoid the accusations and witness, which otherwise we must be forced to give in against them.

The godly friends of the wicked will be their

accusers and witness against them. Some of them are linked in near relations to the godly who now are endeavoring to be instrumental for their salvation. But, if they do not prevail, they will hereafter be their accusers and witness for their condemnation.

The believing husband will then accuse and witness against the unbelieving wife. "Lord, she lay in my bosom and was beloved by me as myself. I cherished her and was as tender of her as my own flesh, according to Thy command; but all my love and kindness to her could not win her heart for Thee. I told her often of Thy beauty and Thy love, which was a thousandfold beyond what I, or any man alive, could possibly express; but she was stupid and unbelieving, and wholly disregarded both Thy Person and Thy love. I covered her faults with love as much as I could from others, and used many entreaties and loving persuasions to draw her to amendment, telling her the danger and destructive issue of a sinful course; but she would not hearken to amend. Her heart was set upon sin and vanity; she was proud and foolish; she was wanton and froward and would not be reclaimed. She saw my grief and sorrow for sin, she was a witness to my tears and mournful complaints; yet she could bear up under greater guilt without any sense. She saw me often retire into my closet, and knew that I spent time daily between Thee and me alone; and yet, though her need was as great, she would not be persuaded to an imitation. I have often, in the secret silent night when sleep has fled from both our eyes, taken advantage of such opportunities to discourse with her about her soul affairs, told her of the sleep of death which ere long would seize upon us, the night we must spend in the grave. I told her of the morning of the resurrection, of the second coming and our appearing before the tribunal seat; but nothing would quicken her to make preparation for death and judgment. She heard as if she were asleep, as indeed she was asleep while awake and dead while she was alive; asleep and dead in sin and security."

The believing wife will then accuse the unbelieving husband: "Lord, Thou knowest how I loved, honored, reverenced, and obeyed him in lawful things, and was faithful to him according to my duty; but he would not love and honor Thee. He was unthankful and would not obey Thy more reasonable commands, unto whom he owed a greater subjection. I have often sat alone like a widow at home when he has been reveling abroad with his companions. I have been pouring forth tears for him at the throne of grace in my closet when he has been pouring in wine and strong drink in taverns and ale houses. I have been troubled for him when he has stayed out so late, and troubled more with him when he has come in so full of drink and passion, and with much patience have endured his foul speeches and behavior which he has used. I have watched the most fit opportunity I could take to put him in mind of his sin and danger, and I have done it with the greatest humility, meekness, and tender affection I could. But either he has not regarded my words, or flown out into a rage against me. Oh, how fain would I have persuaded him to draw in the same yoke of Christ with me, but he would draw another way, do what I could! None of my prayers, nor tears, nor arguments, no, nor the love of Christ, nor the love of his own soul could prevail with him to change his course; he would not leave his drunkenness and adultery, his worldliness and injustice, his lying and overreaching, his swearing and bitterness against Thy people. By no means he would be persuaded."

Believing parents will then accuse and witness against their unbelieving children and servants. "Lord, we endeavored to bring them up in the nurture and admonition of Thee; we labored to put good principles quickly into them; we dropped many wholesome instructions upon them; we prayed frequently for them and with them, and spoke plainly and earnestly to them about their soul concernment. We told them of the immortality of their souls, the preciousness of their time, the evil of sin, their need of Thee, the excellency of grace, their danger of hell, the way to escape it, the glory of heaven, the way to attain it. But alas! To the grief of our hearts, they shut their ears against all our instructions, and would take none of our reproofs or counsels; they would go foolishly and stubbornly on in a course of sin, and neither Thy law nor Thy fear would restrain them." Thus these and other godly relations would rise up in judgment, and witness against the wicked.

The ungodly friends and companions of the wicked will at that day be their accusers and witness against them; especially those who have been drawn by them into sin. However now they are very well pleased with them, and delight in their company because sin pleased them, and they do not feel nor believe the bitterness which will be consequent; yet, when they come to be judged and punished for those sins, they will with rage and madness accuse and curse those wicked persons who were their first tempters. Drunkards will accuse them that drew them first into taverns and ale houses, and persuaded them by toasts and otherwise to drink beyond their measure. Adulterers and adulteresses will accuse those that first enticed them to private lewdness. Ungodly servants also will then accuse their wicked masters, and ungodly children their wicked parents, who have been drawn into sin by their example. Thus men will be accusers and witnesses against the wicked.

The devils will accuse the wicked.

Devils will be accusers and witnesses against the wicked. They are now accusers of the brethren; then they will be accusers of the wicked. They accuse the brethren falsely, they will accuse the wicked truly. Now they please and flatter the wicked, and persuade them to sin; then, they will accuse them for these very sins which they have persuaded them unto. They have done the devil's drudgery all their days and have been his faithful slaves. And this is his recompense: he will be their accuser at the last day.

The wicked will accuse themselves.

The wicked will be accused by themselves. Their own thoughts will accuse them in the day when God will judge the secrets of men by Jesus Christ, Romans 2:15–16. Their own consciences will accuse them and be as a thousand witnesses against them.

They will find all their sins registered in that book, and that book will then be opened and they will not be able to deny one word of what they find there recorded. Thus of the accusers and witnesses against the wicked.

6. Here I shall speak of the conviction of some particular sinners; especially of such who have lived in the days and places where the gospel has been preached, whom the Lord Jesus Christ, with up-braiding, having so full evidence, will convict of their sin.

To set this out in a more lively way, suppose that this very day was the day of judgment, and in this very church was the judgment-seat; that here was a great white throne, and the Lord Jesus Christ Himself sitting upon it in His glory with millions of holy angels about Him, and all the saints in white at His right-hand. On His left are all the wicked gath-ered together into one body, as it will be at the last day; and the Judge should cry with a loud voice, "Bring the prisoners to the bar; bring the sinners to judgment!", and so summon and convict particular sinners.

1.) *Come forth, all you ignorant persons who have not known the Father nor Me, nor the mysteries of salvation, how-ever clearly revealed in My Word, who lived in darkness and loved darkness, and hated the light, lest your deeds should have thereby been reproved.* What, dark in a Goshen? Ignorant in London? In a place of so much knowl-edge and instruction? Did not your parents teach you when you were young? How is it that you would not be taught? If parents neglected to instruct you, had you not ministers who were ready to do it? How is it that you have not learned? If knowledge did not offer itself to you, why did you not seek after it? Why then did you not learn of yourselves? Was there anything in the world that concerned you more to know? Was not knowledge of Me and My ways worth the looking after? Had you a capacity for other knowledge and not for this? Have not others learned who were naturally as dull and had as few helps as you? Had you time to spend about other things, in sports and sins, and not time to spend in getting knowledge? Had you an ear and yet did not hear so as to learn? Had you an eye, and yet did not see so as to understand? And if you were naturally blind, had I not eye-salve? Could I not have opened your eyes? Was I not willing? Did not I stand in the gates to call upon you? "How long, ye simple ones, will ye love simplicity? and fools hate knowledge? Turn unto Me, and I will pour out My Spirit upon you, and make known My words unto you," Proverbs 1:22–23. Have you neglected Me through ignorance? Is not your fault double, because you neglected knowledge too? Have you committed many sins through ignorance? Is not this an aggravation of your sin? Did you not hate knowledge and, therefore, disregard it? Haven't you loved sin and, therefore, shunned the light which would have revealed it and disturbed you in your wicked courses? Have you liked darkness so well? And is it not fit then that you should go to the place where there is blackness of darkness forever? Take them devils, bind them hand and foot.

2.) *Come forth, all you slothful and unprofitable per-*

sons. Did you not have talents committed to you for My use and service, and what have you done with them? Did you bury them in the earth or lay them up in a napkin? What, could you lie down and slumber when you had so much work to do? Could you trifle away so many hours when time was so precious? Could you sleep in the day, in the day of grace, sleep in the harvest which was so rich and plentiful where you lived? Could you stand idle all the day long in the marketplace? Were you born for nothing, that you lived so unprofitably and were good for nothing? Would not religion have found you sufficient employment if you had followed its directions? Did the difficulties of duties discourage you; and, therefore, you would let them alone though they were so necessary? Had the command of God no force with you? Would not your own good and happiness move you at all to diligence? Did the fear of men, and suffering damage in the world, keep you off from zealous profession and a strict course of life? And should not the fear of God and the danger of hell have kept you from sin and stirred you up unto the most difficult and hazardous duty? Was there a lion in the way to heaven? And were there no lions in the way to hell? Did not some sins cost you pains and labor? Did you find no difficulty in the service of the devil and your own lusts? And was not holiness more worth your pains to get?

Would not I have proved a better Master had you been diligent in My service? Could you be diligent in your callings, to get a livelihood for yourselves and children, and neglect the life and salvation of your precious souls? Would not My work have

brought wages with it? Was there no sweetness mingled with the difficulty, and would not the fruits
have been sweeter? Would not a crown and kingdom, a weight of glory and eternal pleasures, move
you to undergo some difficulty? Was there so much
difficulty in obedience to My commands, which are
not grievous to a spiritual heart, and is there not
more difficulty in suffering what you must unavoid-
ably suffer for your neglect? If My yoke was painful to
an unaccustomed neck, could not I have fitted your
neck to it and made it easy? If My burden was heavy
to a weak back, could not, would not I have put under My shoulder and helped you to have borne it?
Were not the most difficult duties I required for your
own good, and so many privileges, and the best work
you could be employed in? Were any of My servants
so weary with My service, with the hardest work I set
them about, as you were wearied with your idleness
and doing nothing? Did not the earth groan under
such unprofitable burdens? Did not hell gape for
you long ago, and devils long for this time when you
should be delivered into their power? Take them,
devils, bind them hand and foot.

3.) *Come forth, all you that have neglected family
worship, and never sought after God in your closets.* Were
not you creatures, and did the law of creation require no worship? Were not you subjects, and should
you not have shown homage to your Sovereign? Did
you not live upon God's feeding and bounty every
day, and should not you have acknowledged depen-
dence? Did not God bring you into your family relation, and did He require no duty? Did not He
threaten to pour out His wrath upon irreligious fam-

ilies, and yet would not you set up religion in yours? Had you any business to do in your houses of that consequence as worshipping God in your houses? If you did not have the ability to pray at first with others, might not you have attained it had you prayed by yourselves? Would not God have helped you had you been willing to have been helped? Had you been sensible of sin, would you have wanted words in confession? Had you been sensible of your wants, would you have lacked expressions to make them known? Was it curiosity and elegance of words that God so much looked for? Would not sighs and groans have been understood? Would not the Scriptures have furnished you with expressions had you read them? Would not sermons have furnished you with matter and expressions had you repeated them? Had you need of such and such things for your families, and had you not need of God's blessing? And could you hope for His blessing if you did not worship Him? Might you not have prospered more in the world if you had prayed more in your houses? Might not you have had more comfort in your relations if you had daily engaged with them in the duties of God's worship? Might not family prayer have prevented much sin and sorrow which you brought upon you? Did not you fall into many snares daily for want of the armor of prayer?

Had your children and servants no need of religious education? Were they likely to be obedient and faithful to you if you did not teach them to be obedient and faithful unto God? Had not you the charge of their souls put into your hands, and what account can you give? Have not you brought their blood upon your heads? Have not you contracted to yourselves the guilt of their sins? Can you endure to hear their curses, and damning of you, for neglecting to give them such religious education as might have been the means of their salvation?

And you that were under government of families which had no religion, could you so willingly imitate the governors, and the rest, in the neglect of God's worship? Could you contentedly go to hell for company? Is it an alleviation of our grief and horror that all your family is together? Can your masters or fathers answer for themselves or you? Had not you a greater Master in heaven whom you should rather have obeyed? Did not you understand your duty? And, if you could not worship God more publicly, should not you have sought out retiring corners? If others would not pray with you, should not you have prayed alone by yourselves? What if you had no example for it in your house, had you no precepts for it in the Word? What if you were under command, and much business was required of you, and you were discouraged in such duties, could not you have found some time when business was over, or before business began? Could not you have redeemed time from sleep and recreations rather than have neglected God's worship daily? Would not God have encouraged and rewarded you? What if you had been scoffed at and reproached for this, would not the favor and smiles of God have compensated the gloats and scorns of men? Would not heaven have been worth all the reproaches you would have undergone? Could you eat and drink and sleep, and not pray to God, which was more necessary than anything which is most necessary for your bodies? And, if there was no worship of God at home, could not you have looked abroad? Were there none that lived near you, and who would have been glad of your company in the worship of God and way to heaven? Could you find out no religious young men or young women suitable to your degree who would have quickened you and heartened you against discouragement? Did not you devote yourselves rather to the service of some lusts, and were glad of any excuse when conscience would have minded you of your duty towards God? Take them, devils, bind them hand and foot.

4.) *Come forth, all you sabbath-breakers, you who have spent the day in sleeping, in eating, and drinking to excess; who, instead of holy meditations, have been thinking and contriving your worldly business.* Instead of religious conference, you have discoursed only of earthly matters; instead of going to church to worship God, you have walked into the fields and spent the time in recreation; or, if you have seemed to give God a half-day service by your presence at church one part of the day, yet you have worshipped Him only with your bodies, when your hearts were removed far from Him. Had not you an express command for the sabbath's observance? And, if the day of the first institution was changed, was the day and worship thereof laid aside and ceased to be a duty? If the Jews were obliged to keep a day holy, were not the Christians much more? Was not the sabbath made for man? Was it not for his privilege to take that time for holy rest and worship? And did the gospel limit men's privileges? Did not the moral law, of which sabbath observance was one precept, bind throughout all generations? Could you call other days holy which the Scripture gives no warrant for, and not observe that holy day which you were enjoined? Did not God allow you six days for labor in your calling, and was it unequal for Him to take one day for His own worship? Had He eased you of the burdensome ceremonies under the law? Was the sabbath so burdensome to you? Could you reasonably hope to enter into eternal rest, and keep a sabbath in heaven, if you would not celebrate the appointed sabbaths on earth? Were not the works of creation and redemption worthy of your memorial? Was not communion with God in ordinances desirable? Had you no need of these spiritual provisions which God used to deal forth on the sabbath days to them that waited upon Him for them? What, not worship God either in your houses nor in His house, neither on work day nor on sabbath day? Could your sometimes cold and formal services be counted worship? Did you think that lip service could ever be heard by God, who searches and requires the heart? Did you think that sermon, unminded and unremembered, which you neither believed, nor were affected with, would be effectual to save you? Take them, devils, bind them hand and foot.

5.) *Come forth, all you swearers and profaners of the name of God.* Did you never read nor hear the third commandment, which forbade this sin? Did you never hear My strict injunction that you should not swear at all in your discourses, but that your communication should be yea and nay? Were you never told that swearers would fall into condemnation?

Was the great and dreadful name of God of so little regard that you could not only use it irreverently so frequently, but also even rent it in pieces by your oaths? What profit did you get by your swearing? And are you likely to sustain no loss? What pleasure did you find in your swearing? And are you not likely to reap bitterness? Was it for your honor to swear by the name of God? Or rather was it not for your dishonor? But how did you dishonor God? What an affront did you offer to Him hereby? You called upon Him sometimes to damn and sink you. Can you speak in that language now, now that damnation is so near you? Worms! Could not God have trodden you under His feet, or crushed you as easy as you do a fly, every time you profaned His name? And, because He was patient, would you presume? Because He did not presently punish, did you dare Him, and fly in His face to provoke Him to fury? You who have sworn in your folly and have not repented, God has sworn in His wrath, and will not repent, that you shall never enter into His rest. Take them, devils, bind them hand and foot.

6.) *Come forth, all you scoffers at religion and the zealous professors thereof, who taught and spoke of religion as if it had been a fancy and cunningly devised fable, and of most holy, humble, and self-denying Christians as if they were the most mean-spirited, foolish, and contemptible people upon earth, and have used the name of a saint in derision and proverb of reproach.* Have you the same mind now that religion was but a fancy? Is your resurrection and My appearance but a fancy? Is your eternal punishment in hell likely to be but a fancy? Had you not sure ground and bottom for your faith in the Scriptures?

Could you have desired more reasonable evidence of things done before your age? Could you laugh at Scripture threatenings? And can you laugh now that you are come to execution? Could you condemn gospel promises? And are they so contemptible now in your eyes when you now see the accomplishment of them before you? Against whom was it that you opened so wide a mouth? Who was it that you flouted and scorned? What, My disciples, because they were meek and humble and did not take the pleasure of sin with you, and were strict in their profession and conversation? What do you think of them now? Were they so mean-spirited and contemptible? Were they so foolish, who made so wise a choice? Did they do well or ill in staying till the time of their happiness? Look upon the persons now whom once you scorned and thought unworthy of your company. Was it as ridiculous a thing to be a saint as you imagined? Was not shining with them in glory at all desirable? Would not you be glad to be numbered among them now? Why do you not laugh and sneer at the saints now? You fools and blind sots, do you know what you scoff at? Could you see no excellency in holiness and the divine nature, in My image, which was engraven upon them? Did any man of understanding laugh at the light of the sun? They were lights in the dark world where they lived. What, mock at holiness! Hereby you mocked at God Himself, who is so infinitely glorious in His attributes and, hereby, distinguished from all His creatures. Vile wretches! Take them, devils, bind them hand and foot.

7.) *Come forth, all you persecutors of My disciples.*

Was it not enough for you to mock them, but you must persecute them too? Was it not enough for you to persecute them with the tongue, but you must persecute them with the hand? What, could you betray them like Judas for a piece of money, or out of malice, which is worse? Could you disturb them in their service and worship of Me when they were praying for your conversion and salvation? Could you hale and drag them to prison, who endeavored to keep you out of the prison of hell? Could you seek the ruin of such as were the best friends of your souls, when you never received injury from them? Could you be so envious of them?

Do you know whom you persecuted? It was Me. It was Me whom you persecuted when you persecuted My disciples. It was Me whom you wounded through the sides; it was Me whom you betrayed in betraying them. It was Me you spurned at when you lifted up the heel against them. And did you ever think to prosper in this way? You, you have been, above all other persons upon earth, My professed enemies, and most like your father, the devil. Come, you wretches, gird up your loins like men; gather your forces together; put on strength and courage, if you have any, and lift up your hand, if you dare, against Me. Do you find strength to fail you now, and your forces too weak to make resistance? And were you so foolish as to engage in battle, where you might have known you should certainly be conquered at the last? Does your courage fail upon the sight of the Captain? And should you not have been afraid to touch any anointed ones, My enlisted soldiers? You served the devil and fought under his banner against Me and Mine, and can he deliver you now out of My hand? Can He defend you against My rage and fury? Or would he do it if it lay in his power? Had you ever more spite and malice against My people than the devil had against you in setting you about this persecuting work? Did not he design your ruin thereby? Did not he think of this day and, on purpose, draw you to this sin that you might be the more horribly tormented? And do not he and his angels wait now for you that they may drag you into torments? Take them, devils, bind them hand and foot.

8.) *Come forth, all you intemperate and licentious persons, who have indulged your flesh and laid no restraint upon your sensual appetites; who have made provision for your flesh to fulfill the lusts thereof, but made no provision for My glory and took no care to fulfill My commands.* Did you never hear of such a duty as self-denial, which I required of all My disciples and followers? Were you never told that, if you followed the inclinations and obeyed the commands of carnal self, it would be to your ruin and destruction; that bitterness and sorrow would be the issue of flesh-pleasing; that lust, if conceived, would bring forth sin, and sin, when perfected, would bring forth death? Did you never read that if you lived after the flesh, you should die, and that you must, through the Spirit, mortify the deeds of the body, otherwise life and happiness could not be obtained? And yet, could you lay the reins on the neck of your lusts? If you had no faith, had you no reason either to keep you from intemperance? If you did not live like Christians, could you not live like men? Would you need be brutes and live as if you were all body and had no souls of such high capacities? Were you so blind as not to see afar off before this day of judgment, when I should call you to an account, or see a little before you to the day of your death which would put a conclusion to all your sensual pleasures? Could you bribe and muzzle conscience, and lay it asleep, while you took your pleasures? Could you tread reason under foot and resolve you would not be controlled by any light, or law, or government, from your eager prosecution of your carnal delights? Take them, devils, bind them hand and foot.

9.) *Come forth, all you gluttons, who have pampered flesh with delicious food, but never had the least regard to feed your souls which had more need;* who have spent many hours and days in feasting your bodies, nourishing yourselves against the day of slaughter, but, when you were invited by My messengers to the marriage feast, to the feast I had prepared for you, of the richest and most costly spiritual dainties, you had no stomach, no appetite, and could not, would not come. What, did you indeed make your belly your god, and can such a god save and make you happy? Did you think food which perishes could give happiness to a never-dying soul? Did you not know that both meat and belly would be destroyed, and that your bodies would become food for worms? And yet, could you make it the chief business of your lives to feed your bodies? You are allowed food convenient, and sometimes for delight, that your bodies might serve your souls with strength and vigor, and both their Lord and Master; but excess you were forbidden, which distempered both body and mind, and made you unfit for the service of the Lord, and yet would you overcharge yourselves? Now, reap the fruit of this intemperance, and taste the gall and wormwood which your sweet baits are turned into. Take them, devils, bind them hand and foot.

10.) *Come forth, all you drunkards, who, if you have not overcharged your bellies with excessive eating, have often intoxicated your brains with the fumes of excessive drinking; who have drowned your understanding, wit and fancy, your natural parts and ingenuity, which might have rendered you useful in the church or commonwealth where you lived, and made yourselves mere sots by drunkenness.* And what account can you give of the talents you were entrusted withal? What excuse can you give for this sin? Were you enticed to it and overtaken before you were aware? But who would entice you to drink a potion which would kill your bodies? And was not the death and damnation of your souls more to be avoided? Would you be enticed to that unto which every beast will *not* be enforced? But were you not forward of yourselves to the sin? Did you not like the company well that joined with you therein? Did not you overtake the sin by your desires? Did not the liquor please your appetite? Did you not swill it in without persuasion? If you had been overtaken would you have been so often guilty? Would you have come so often unto the places and company where you fell into it? Was not your chief mirth among your cups, and drunken companions? Were you not melancholy and troubled when your meetings of good fellowship were disappointed? You would have your sups, and drink wine in bowls, and strong drink without measure, and now also you shall have a cup to drink of, even a cup of the wine of the wrath of the angry, almighty God. Now you shall drink of the dregs of this cup which has ten thousand times more bitterness in it than your other cups had sweetness. Take them, devils, bind them hand and foot.

11.) *Come forth, all you adulterers, you who have neighed like full-fed horses after your neighbors' wives, and assembled by troops in harlots' houses;* or if not so, have committed this in secret corners. Was there no shame in you to keep you from this nasty, filthy sin? Could you delight so much to wallow in mire and dung? Was there no fear in you to restrain you? Did not conscience check and rebuke you when this lust first conceived in you? Did you never hear that "whoremongers and adulterers, God will judge"? And did not you think you should be called to an account for this sin? Could you melt in filthy, sinful pleasures for the flesh, and not consider how you should consume in torment? Were your short pleasures comparable to an eternity of pain and misery? Were there no pleasures of a higher nature, and sweeter relish attainable in life if you had foregone and denied yourselves unlawful pleasures? Have you not lost them, and the unspeakable eternal joys of heaven, by your intemperance? Take them, devils, bind them hand and foot.

12.) *Come forth, all you covetous persons, whose treasure and heart, hope and confidence, have been in earthly things;* who have made the world your god, desiring and loving and delighting and trusting in your wealth and riches, as if they could yield the most contentment and be the best defense unto you;

whose greatest thoughts and care and labor have been spent about getting and keeping an estate and portion in the world, with little heart to use it for yourselves, and much less for the good of others and glory of God that gave it. Did you not know that covetousness was idolatry? And that no idolater should have any admittance into the new Jerusalem? Did you not know that the love of the world was inconsistent with the love of the Father? Had you such mean thoughts of God that you chose the world before Him? Were the riches of grace of so small esteem that you preferred earthly riches? Had the treasures of heaven no more worth in your account that you should neglect and disregard them, and make choice rather of treasures on earth? When you had tried the world, and found it vain and empty, would you still set your heart upon it? When you felt such thorny cares and piercing sorrows in your eager prosecution of this world, could not this damp and deaden your affections to it? When your own and others' riches sometimes suddenly took flight as upon an eagle's wing, did you not foresee how naked and bare death would strip you of all? And yet, would nothing wean your whorish hearts from the love of the world? Were you never told that riches could not profit you in the day of wrath? Is not all your wealth consumed now? Treasures there are indeed prepared for you, but they are treasures of wrath which you have deserved. Take them, devils, bind them hand and foot.

13.) *Come forth, all you unmerciful persons, whose bowels have been shut up against the poor and needy, who have spoken churlishly to the poor, looked upon them afar off.*

Or, if you have spoken to them fair, and said to the naked and destitute of daily food, "Depart in peace, be ye warmed, and be ye filled," yet have not given unto them things needful for the body, whatever abundance you had by you, you have had no pity on My distressed members, so as to contribute any relief to their necessities. "I was hungry, and ye gave Me no meat. I was thirsty, and ye gave Me no drink. I was naked, and ye clothed Me not. I was a stranger, and ye took Me not in. I was sick, and ye visited Me not. I was in prison, and ye did not administer unto Me." Did you not understand it was your duty to relieve the poor? Had you not your riches given to you for this end? Was not this the best use you could put them unto? Would not works of mercy have brought unto you the best returns at last? Might you not hereby have laid up for yourselves a good foundation against this day? If you had laid out your estates according to My prescriptions, might not you now have laid hold on eternal life? Were you never forewarned that such should have judgment without mercy that did not show mercy? And you that have had no mercy to forgive, that knew not how to pass by real or conjectural injuries which you have received, that were ready to take your brother by the throat for a hundred pence when you might have been forgiven your ten thousand talents which you owed unto God, were you never told that the King of heaven would deliver you unto the tormentors if you were unmerciful? Take them, devils, bind them hand and foot.

14.) *Come forth, all you unrighteous persons, who have wronged widows and orphans, who have overcharged*

your neighbors in your dealings; who have overheaped an es-
tate together by unrighteous practices; who have squeezed and
oppressed the law of right written upon your hearts. Did you
not read it more plainly in the Word? Did not men
condemn you? Did not your own consciences secretly condemn you for your own unrighteousness?
And did not you think that the righteous God would
condemn you much more? Did you know that no
unrighteous person should inherit the kingdom of
heaven, that the Lord would avenge Himself upon
you for this sin? Did you wrong others so much as
you have hereby wronged yourselves? Is the gain of
the world comparable to the loss of your souls? Is a
little silver or gold, now taken away from you, comparable to the loss of heaven and eternal glory? Did
you think such faults would be winked at? Did you
not expect to hear of them again at the day of judgment? Is it an unrighteous thing to punish you for
your unrighteousness? Take them, devils, bind them
hand and foot.

15.) *Come forth, all you liars, who have taught and*
accustomed yourselves to this sin, who have not only reported
lies but also made them, whose words have been feigned and
deceitful. Did you not know that God who made you,
and to whom you owed all subjection and obedience, was a God of truth, and the Truth requires
truth? That every man should speak truth to his
neighbor; that He abhorred lying lips, and that He
threatened to punish liars with the second death,
and give them their portion in the lake of fire? And
had you no fear of God, nor fear of future judgment,
to restrain you? Might you not as easily have spoken
truth as uttered falsehood? Would you not hereby

have gained more credit in the world? Would you not have been more fit for society? Would you not have had more peace in your consciences? Did you excuse faults by your lips? But was it not a greater aggravation of them? If you hide them by lies from men, could you hide them from God who searched your hearts? Did you show kindness to any by your lies? And did you not injure yourselves a thousand times more? Did you harm others by your lies so much as yourselves? Did you not know that the devil was the father of liars? And were you so desirous to be like him? Take them, devils, bind them hand and foot.

16.) *Come forth, all you slanderers and backbiters, who have walked about with slanderers, and carried about tales unto the reproach and injury of your neighbor's good name.* Did you not know it was your duty to endeavor to preserve your neighbor's reputation as carefully as your own? Were you not commanded to speak evil of none? Could you flatter others before their faces, and alter your speech so much when their backs were turned? Did not your own self-contradicting words condemn you? Did you find good in back-biting and speaking evil of others? Did you gain reputation by wounding others' reputations? Or rather, did you not give occasion to others to speak as reproachfully as you? Did you not alienate affection and separate near friends by your slanders? Did you not know many things to be false which you spake to others' disparagement? Could you, with confidence, have averred the same thing to the persons themselves? Would they not easily have disproved you and put you to shame? And, if you were privy to some real faults of others, should you not have concealed them? If you had real love, would not you have covered them? Did you do as you would be done by? Had you not great faults of your own? And could you be content to have them blazed abroad? You have accused others falsely, and now you are accused truly, and you shall be punished justly. Take them, devils, bind them hand and foot.

17.) *Come forth, all you proud and ambitious persons, you that have built your nests on high, that have taken many dirty steps to get into the seats of honor.* Come, all you whose hearts have been lifted up with high towering imaginations and conceits of your own excellencies unto the scorning and contempt of others; who have had proud hearts, proud looks, proud speeches, and proud carriage towards others, especially towards them that have been of meaner degree; who have looked upon others afar off and have disdained the conversation and company of some of whom the world had not been worthy. Were you acquainted with no higher honor and dignity than the world could give unto you? Might you not have had seats in heavenly places if you had looked after them, and less after the other? Did you not know that the highest places on the earth are the most slippery places? Did you not foresee the turning of the wheel upon you? Did you not believe that God would cast down the mighty from their seats? That the higher you were lifted up in dignity, if your hearts were lifted up with pride, the lower and greater would be your fall? And was the favor and applause of men so desirable? Was it not an empty breath, an inconstant wind? If you had been ambitious, should you not have been ambitious for the favor of the kingdom of glory, which would have been so beneficial and lasting? And are you the persons that once were so proud and scornful? You proud! Had you such reason? Proud when creatures! Depending creatures who had nothing but what was borrowed and received from God! Proud when such mean creatures! Proud when fallen into the dirt and so defiled! Proud when sinners so vile! So full of sores! When you had such loathsome spirits! When you had such leprous souls! Could you lift up the plumes when you had such black feet? Could you be proud when you had lost God's image, and were so like unto foul devils? Proud when such beggarly sinners clothed in such filthy rags! Proud when such slaves and vassals to the vilest and basest tyrants! Proud in chains and fetters of Satan and lusts! You had reason indeed to be proud, and look so high, and speak so big when you were so odious to God, and such low, mean-spirited, miserable wretches, who were drudging in mire and dirt, and were led by the devils in chains like dogs towards the prison of hell. You scorned the company of My disciples, as if dirty dunghill-beggars should scorn the company of highborn noble princes. But now you shall be debased and laid low indeed. Take them, devils, bind them hand and foot.

18.) *Come forth, all you envious and malicious persons, you that have grieved at the good of others, which they have had or done.* Come, you who have grieved at the good estates of others, and that they have thrived faster than you in the world; who have grieved at the sweet and comfortable relations of others, and that yours have not been like to them; who have grieved

at the beauty or strength of body, the gifts and en-
dowments of mind of others, beyond what you yourselves have had; who have grieved at the honor of
others, who have been esteemed and preferred before yourselves; who have grieved because others
have done more good, and been more useful than
yourselves, and hence have secretly hated them and
borne malice towards them in your minds, and have
entertained thoughts of doing some mischief, and
were glad when any mischief befell them. You, you
have been children of the devil indeed, and the
likeness and lusts of your father you have had. Was
your eye evil because God was good? Did not God put
the difference between them and you, and should
not you have been contented? Was not God good to
you, and had you not reason to be thankful? Did not
you put a stop to the current of God's goodness by
your envy? Did not you lose the comfort of the good
things you had by this sin? Did not you hereby lose
the benefit you might have had by the good things
of others? Should not you have rejoiced in their
good things? If you had loved them indeed, would
not you have done it? Did not you rack and torment
yourselves by your envy? Had you been humble,
would you have been troubled? Had your affections
been set upon things above, would this sin have so
much prevailed? Had you been sincerely desirous to
promote God's glory, would you have been so much
concerned that your glory should be clouded when
God's glory was advanced, though by others more
than yourselves? Were you not warned to lay aside all
envy and malice if you would be Christians indeed?
If you had put your spirits under My government,

would not I have conquered, by My Spirit, their inordinate motions? Should not you have found sweetness and comfort and love if you had labored after and lived in the exercise of this grace? Did you not know that these were works of the flesh which would exclude you from the kingdom of heaven? Take them, devils, bind them hand and foot.

19.) *Come forth, all you wrathful and contentious persons, you that have had fiery spirits and fiery tongues.* Come, you whose tongues have been like swords, wherewith you have lashed and wounded others in your reproaching and reviling speeches; who have had the poison of asps in your hearts and lips, which has vented itself in virulent language; whose words have been bitter and clamorous, full of anger and wrath and contention; who have been incendiaries in the place where you lived; who have disturbed the peace of your families and turned all things into uproar and confusion. Did you not know the precepts of the gospel which commanded peace, gentleness, meekness, and easiness to be entreated? Did you disturb others' peace by your contentions, and did not you disturb your own? Did you raise an uproar in your houses, and was there not a greater uproar in your hearts? Did not you take bitterness of such a conversation and yet would you persist therein? Did not you receive some blows and wounds by your contention sometimes, and yet would not hearken to such rebukes? Were you angry with others without just cause, and was there not good reason that God should be angry with you? Was not the fire of your tongues kindled by the fire of hell? And is it unreasonable that you should be

thrust into the place of burning for your contention? Take them, devils, bind them hand and
foot.

20.) *Come forth, all you civil and moral persons who
have had moral righteousness, and have been upright in your
dealings, but wholly strangers unto the power of godliness.*
Come, you who have observed some precepts of the
second table of the law in reference to yourselves
and others externally, but have grossly neglected the
duties of the first table, which have had reference to
God; who have had no knowledge of God, nor fear
of Him, nor love for Him, nor delight in Him; who
have never sanctified His name nor day in your
hearts, nor worshipped Him in a spiritual manner
according to the prescriptions of His Word; who
never yielded obedience to the gospel, never saw
your need of Him, obtaining interest and acquaintance with Me, whatever calls and opportunites you
had. And do you think I should know you and own
you now when you are none of mine? Will your
moral righteousness stand you now in any stead,
when you are to give so strict an account? Did not I
tell you in My Word that unless your righteousness
exceeded the righteousness of the scribes and
Pharisees you could in no wise enter into the kingdom of heaven? That you must be born again or else
you could not be saved? That you must be holy or
else you could not be happy? Did you not hear of the
young man who had as much moral righteousness
as you, and yet missed heaven because he would not
obey My other commands? Has your moral righteousness been so perfect that it has had no flaw?
Have you lived free from sin, with regard to the sec-

ond table of the law, besides your breaches of the first? Will not conscience tell you of some slips, some stumbles and falls, as to your own external walking? Were you never guilty of unrighteous dealings? Never lustful and wanton? Never told any lies nor uttered any slanders? And even if you had been fair in your outward carriage and conversation, have you not been foul inside? Had you not need of pardon for your sins, and My blood to wash you from your filthiness?

Have not the best of your works been sinful, with regard to the principle and end and manner of performance? Did you think the works of nature would save you when the works of grace cannot, without the imputation of My righteousness, because of their imperfection? Must not God's justice be satisfied for your sins? And how do you think it should be done but by your eternal punishment in hell? Had you believed in Me, and yielded obedience to Me, My righteousness should have been yours, and then you might have held up your heads with joyful expectations of glory on this day; but you cleaved to your own righteousness, and were well and whole, and did not see your need of Me to be your Physician and Savior, and would not submit unto and accept My righteousness; and what have you to say as to why judgment should not pass upon you? Did you think such words as yours would satisfy justice when, if you had done better and kept the whole law for the greatest part of your lives, yet, you had but done your duty, and the sins of your youth were enough to sink you to hell; but was any of your righteousness perfect? Did you think to merit heaven by such works?

Do you think you deserve a crown of glory for your civility or morality? Where have you a promise of it? And if you had no promise, could you think ever you should attain it? What, is your mouth stopped, and are you speechless now? Take them, devils, bind them hand and foot.

21.) *Come forth, all you hypocrites, who have made a show of holiness, and have borne the name of zealous professors of religion, but have been actuated by carnal designs and principles.* Come, you who have used religion as a cloak for your covetousness; who followed Me only for the loaves; who have been hollow at the heart, rotten at the core, painted sepulchers, blazing comets, wandering and falling stars, for whom the mist of darkness is reserved forever. What do you mean by your shows and outward appearance of worship and service? Do you think that the all-seeing and heart-searching God judges according to outward appearance? Did you think that lip service and bodily exercise would be accepted by Him? Or was it an acceptance only with men which you sought after? That reward you had, and can you expect any other reward when you did not desire nor design it? And what does it? Can it now profit you that men accounted you religious? Will their esteem of you procure pardon and salvation for you? Could you be content to cast away and lose all your external service for want of sincerity and an internal living principle? Did you not think that all your services would rise up one day in judgment against you? Did not you affront the highest Majesty by that mockery of your show-worship? Did He not very well understand which way your heart went when you seemed most devout? Was not He acquainted with secret lusts which you harbored in your hearts, and secret ways of wickedness which you walked in when you made a show of mortification and self-denial, and a holy and strict conversation? Were you not warned against hypocrisy, and told how odious it was unto God, and that hypocrites' portion would be in utter darkness where there is weeping and wailing and gnashing of teeth? Take them, devils, bind them hand and foot.

22.) *Come forth, all you backsliders and apostates from Me and My ways.* Come, you who turned back to ways of profaneness and open wickedness after some time of profession and joining yourselves with My people. Was My service so burdensome that you could endure it no longer? Was the way to heaven so unpleasant that you would walk no longer therein? After some trial in show of Me, did you prefer and make choice of the devil before Me? After some washing of yourselves, would you wallow in the mire again? After having some vomit off your stomach, would you again lick it up? After some sweeping and dressing, would you open the door and let in seven worse spirits to defile your hearts? After you seemed to be escaped, were you again entangled? Would you put your foot again in to the snare, and bind yourselves even in the fresh bonds of sin? Did you prefer the company of the wicked, which were going hellward, before the company of My people, which were going heavenward? Could you now wish that you had held on, and held out with them unto the end? Would not you have rejoiced if you had been now found in their society?

Did you repent of your repenting, and do you not now repent of your backsliding? Were not you told that, if you drew back, My soul would have no pleasure in you? And you that have turned aside from Me and My ways into the ways of error, that sucked in damnable heresies from false teachers, did you not know that there were damnable heresies as well as other damnable sins? Were you not warned that Satan sometimes appeared as an angel of light? Would you so quickly turn aside after some workings and striving of My Spirit with you, and some hopes which you gave of your conversion and reformation? Did not you perceive how Satan lay upon the catch as soon as you began to be awakened, to prejudice you against the truth and draw you aside unto another way to serve him? If you had heartily loved the truth, as it was with Me, would you have been so deluded? Was not deep humiliation and mortification of every lust too hard a doctrine; and, therefore, you chose such as would give you more scope and liberty, and shroud your lusts under some other name, and term your hatred and anger against My people by the name of zeal for My glory?

Did you think that if you gave Satan just one hold it would not be sufficient to undo you? Had you stuck close to My ministry and ordinance, would you have been so deluded? Did you think yourselves wiser than My ministers? As soon as you got a glimmering of light, could you so readily open your ear to slanders, and receive prejudices against them through Satan and his instrument's persuasions, to the shipwrecking of your own souls? Did you not find how wavering and unsteady you were, how like children tossed to and fro with every wind of doctrine, when once you forsook My ministry, which I had appointed for your establishment? Did you think that you might live above ordinances in the world? Did you imagine to get into a higher form when you went forth of My school? And, when you expected perfection most, were you not more imperfect than before? When you fancied a clearer light, were you not most full of darkness? When you thought yourselves so holy as none but you, and none must be holy but those of your way, were you not most unholy and like smoke in My nostrils? Could I accept your worship out of the way of My ordinances and institutions? When you thought yourselves most guided and acted upon by the Spirit, was it not a spirit of delusion? Did My Spirit lead you and act upon you in a way which My Word did not allow for? Were not you the renders and tearers of My church?

Was it not by reason of you that the ways of truth were evil-spoken of by evil men? Were not those without prejudiced against My very ways because of your delusions, which made so forward a profession? Suppose I permitted some of Mine to mistake in circumstances; was this a just excuse for your errors in fundamentals? When the Word was opened for you to inform yourselves in the truth, did not you wrest the Scriptures to your own destruction? Suppose you denied yourselves something; were they those things that I commanded? Suppose you suffered something in your way; do you hope for a reward for suffering which I never called you unto, and which did but much the more harden your party and promote your delusion? Did you know what a snare you were hampered in as soon as you put your foot in the way of error, and turned aside from the old strait and narrow ways of My Word and ordinances which have brought so many to heaven? Were not you in a greater unlikelihood of being called effectually than drunkards, adulterers, and the most vicious, who lay more naked to the blow of the Word and were more ready to receive instructions? You were more forward to reprove My ministers than to receive My ministers, and convictions from them; you could call them anti-christian and false prophets, though they adhered to and maintained nothing but the truths of My Word; and, when I gave them so many seals of their ministry in the conversion of so many souls, you could call them self-seekers and hirelings, though they gave such evidences of self-denial, and many of them forsook all that they had rather than make a breach upon their conscience. You could, some of you, entrench upon their office, though you had no call or commission from Me. You had the Scripture to reveal to you the right way, but you shut your eyes against the light and chose the ways of darkness; and it is now fit that you should go to the place of darkness. Take them, devils, bind them hand and foot.

23.) *Come forth, all you impenitent and unbelievers, all you who have been called to repentance by ministers and the Spirit in ordinances, and when a stiller voice was not heard, were you not called by a louder one by God in His judgment?* Did you not know that unless you repented, you would certainly perish? That iniquity would be your ruin unless your hearts were broken for it and from it, and yet you, though you lay under the guilt of so much sin, could be so impenitent and hard-hearted? Were you not called to Me by the voice of the gospel? Did not I call you and stretch out My hand all the day long to you? Did not I stand at the door of your hearts, and woo hard for entry, and yet could you shut the door against Me, though you had so much need of Me? Had you not commands and encouragements to believe? Could you rationally desire firmer ground and footing for your faith? Did you give God the lie by your unbelief? Have you not hereby fastened the guilt of all other sins upon yourselves which I was willing to take off from you? Would any sin against the law have condemned you, had you turned from it and yielded obedience to the gospel? Were you not foretold of the wrath to come, and yet you would not flee from it? Were you not offered a Savior, and yet would you not accept Him? Had not you treasures opened before you, and would you not look after them? Were you not shown the way to heaven, and would not you walk in it? How can you escape that have been guilty of disobedience unto the gospel? Take them, devils, bind them hand and foot.

Christ, at the day of judgment, will convict the whole ungodly world, especially those who lived under the sound of the gospel; their crimes will be made manifest and evident, and every mouth will be stopped when they are found guilty before Him, and they cannot deny it. Then the wicked will be speechless and stand, after their full conviction, like so many rogues in chains before the Judge. And think now with yourselves what the behavior of the wicked

will be when they are thus convicted of their sins
and are ready to receive their sentence. I believe
some of you have seen malefactors at the bar, when
the jury has found them guilty, and the judge has
been proceeding to give the sentence of death. How
their countenance has changed and their joints
trembled, and inexpressibly horror seized upon
them; but oh, the dread and terror that will be upon
the spirits of the wicked when they are convicted of
sin by this Judge! And with what trembling expectations will they wait for their sentence!

7. And this is the seventh particular to speak,
concerning the sentence which the Lord Jesus
Christ will pass upon the wicked in judgment. See
Matthew 25:41: "Then shall He say to them on His
left hand, Depart from Me, ye cursed, into everlasting fire prepared for the devil and his angels."
Depart from Me, you who have formerly said in your
hearts unto Me, "Depart, we will not have Thee to
reign over us"; who have said to My ministers,
"Depart, we will not hearken to your words"; who
have said to My Spirit, "Depart, we will not yield to
Thy motions."

Now, depart, depart, from Me, you that would not
come unto Me. You have been often called and invited to come, but you refused. Now depart. You
would not have one call more; you shall not have
one offer of grace more forever. Depart, never shall
you hear My voice any more; never shall you see My
face any more.

Depart, be gone out of My sight. Depart from Me,
you cursed; as you cared not for blessing, so shall it

be far from you. As you loved cursing, so shall it be unto you. Depart with the curse of the law, with the curse of the great God upon you. Let the curse of God clothe you like a garment and bind you like a chain; let it enter into your flesh and bones like oil to enrage so much the more the flames of hell about you; and let it pierce into your soul and fill you with horrible anguish. "Depart from Me, ye cursed, into everlasting fire." You shall not depart into your old habitations, to spend an eternity in sinful, sensual pleasures; no, depart into torments, depart into fire, into the fire of hell, into the burning lake, into Tophet ordained of old for you, into a stream of fire and brimstone enkindled by the breath of God. Depart into everlasting fire; go dwell with devouring fire, and inhabit everlasting burnings. Depart into everlasting fire prepared for the devil and his angels. You served the devil and divers lusts while you lived in the world; now go and live with the devil and his angels in hellfire forever; partake of the torments primarily prepared for him, and which belong also to you, because you belonged to his kingdom.

And, when the sentence is irreversibly pronounced by the Judge upon the wicked, O what direful shrieks will they give forth! With what horror will they cry out, "How shall we be able to endure the devouring flames and everlasting burnings in hell?"

Thus have I done with the judgment itself, both of the righteous and the wicked, at the appearance of Jesus Christ.

Chapter 8

The Sentence of the Wicked

The next thing is to speak of the execution of the sentence pronounced upon both in the judgment, which you have spoken of together. Matthew 25:46: "And they shall go away into everlasting punishment, but the righteous into life eternal."

Concerning the execution of the sentence on the wicked, they shall go away into everlasting punishment. Here I shall speak, first, of the wicked going away; and, second, of their going into punishment. The former implies the punishment of loss, the latter the punishment of sense.

When the sentence is pronounced, the wicked shall go away. Here I shall show from whom they shall go away; from what they shall go away; and the aggravations or vexing considerations which gospel sinners will have in their going away.

The wicked shall go away. From whom the wicked shall go away?

They shall go from Jesus Christ. The righteous are at His side and shall remain with Him, but the wicked shall go away from Him. The righteous shall go with Him and abide with Him; where He is, there they shall be also. They shall be forever with the Lord, but the wicked must go away and be eternally separated from His presence. The righteous shall behold His glory and share in it; they shall see the smiles of His face and be entertained by Him with inexpressible love, but the wicked shall be thrust out of His presence with frowns and indignation. It will be one great part of the misery of the wicked that they shall go away from so glorious a Person as the Lord Jesus Christ.

They shall go away from the saints. Now some of them are mingled with God's people, as the tares and the wheat grow up together, the sheep and the goats feed in the same pasture. And, though it was bitter for the wicked to dwell with the righteous, because of the contradiction which was in their lives to their lusts, yet then it will be more bitter to them to be excluded from their society because then they will perceive their excellency with admiration. When the righteous seem to shine with such beauty, and rejoice with songs of triumph, and the wicked must be gone away from them, this will fill the hearts of the wicked with racking envy and torment them unspeakably.

From what will the wicked go away? They shall go away from happiness, from the happiness of heaven, and the doors of heaven shall be shut upon them. They shall see Abraham, Isaac, Jacob, and many come from the east, the west, the north, and the south, even an innumerable multitude of all kindreds, nations, and tongues, and enter in and sit down in the kingdom of God, and themselves thrust out and thrust down to hell.

Next, I shall speak concerning the aggravations or vexing considerations which gospel sinners will have in their going away. As the sin of those is more heinous who sin against the light of the gospel than of those who sin only against the light of nature, so their punishment will be more severe; all shall be beaten, but those persons with many stripes. As there will be degrees, some will have a larger capacity. So there will be degrees of torment and misery. All shall be filled with torment, but some will have a larger capacity. Gospel sinners especially will have stings beyond what heathens will be capable of in their punishment of loss when:

1. They shall have a clearer discovery of the glory and happiness which they have missed. Now they hear of heaven and the happiness which the saints shall have in the vision and fruition of God; but there is a veil of unbelief upon their minds that they do not apprehend such a happiness as is spoken of. They have mean thoughts of God and of heaven; they think there is no heaven like the earth and no happiness like the fruition of the creatures; no glory like the glory of the world, no treasures like earthly treasures, and no delights like those which they find in the objects of their sense. But when their portion in this life shall be spent, and the good things which they enjoyed shall be taken away from them, when their honors shall vanish like smoke or a thin vapor, their riches shall fly away like an eagle or sail like a ship out of their sight; when the sensual delights and pleasures shall fail them and die like sweet flowers in their hands; when the bright cloud of earthly things, which shadowed the glory of heavenly things from their view, shall be blown away and the veil shall be torn in pieces which was before them, and hindered them from looking into the

holy of holies, and the scales fall off from their eyes; in a word, when the heavens shall pass away with a great noise, and the elements shall melt with fervent heat, and the earth with the works thereof shall be burned up, and they shall be awakened out of their sleep in their graves, and shall be summoned before the tribunal seat of Christ, and stand there stripped and quite naked of all their enjoyments in the world which they have set their hearts upon, and they shall be examined and condemned for their sins; then, then their eye will be opened, and they will clearly see their mistake of happiness. Then they will perceive, and be fully persuaded of, the fullness of joy and unspeakable pleasures at the right hand of God, the least taste of which would ravish their hearts ten thousand times more than all the full drafts which they have taken in the sweetest of all their sinful delights.

I say, they shall see this happiness, and that which will vex them to the heart will be that they shall only see it, not enjoy the store in it. Oh, what high apprehensions will they then have of the glory of heaven! They will see the crown which will be put upon the head of the righteous, which will have more worth then in their esteem than all the crowns and scepters of the greatest kings upon the earth; then they will be clearly convinced that the chief treasures were in heaven and the sweetest delights were to come; and the thoughts of missing this crown and glory, such treasures and sweetness, will tear their very hearts. They must go from heaven and happiness.

2. In going away, they shall remember the capac-

ity which they had once of obtaining this happiness. If they had been brutes indeed, and had capacity for a sensitive life only, and grace and glory had been removed so far beyond their reach that it had been impossible for them to attain it, it would not so much trouble them to lose it, whatever other miseries they should endure. But they were capable of the beginning of heaven in the life of grace, and the completing of their happiness in glory; they will remember that they had souls endued with reason and hereby were advanced to a higher capacity than beasts; that they had minds capable of divine contemplation and hearts capable of divine affection; that they had wills which might have chosen God for their portion and heaven for their inheritance; that they had desires, loves, hopes, and joys which, if they had wrought Godward and Christward as they did towards the creature, if they had wrought upward and heavenward, as they did downward and towards the earth and earthly things, they might have been happy forever. They will see that others who had the same nature as they had, and were guilty at first of as great sins as they had committed, yet repented and turned and believed and reformed, were changed and saved; and with inexpressible vexation they will think that thus it might have been with them, if they had not been fools; if they had seriously endeavored to fill up the capacity which God had given them.

3. In going away, they will remember the offers which they had of this happiness; that they lived in places where the light shone and the gospel sounded, and Christ was preached and tendered with all the benefits of His purchase; and they will

remember how often they were called to repent, how earnestly they were entreated to be reconciled. They will remember the discoveries which were made to them of future glory, and the invitations which they had to come unto Christ, that they might have pardon and life, all which was little regarded by them. They would remember how long and how loud Christ knocked at the door of their hearts for entrance; that He knocked by such a sermon, by such a motion of the Spirit, by such a judgment, such an affliction, such a deliverance, and yet they barred the door and deafened the ear; and, if they did not fully resolve to keep Him out, yet they put Him off with so many tedious delays until, all of a sudden, death knocked at their door, broke it open, and dragged them away to hell before they had given entrance to Jesus Christ, and had provided an eternal habitation for their souls.

They will then remember the opportunities and seasons of grace which once they enjoyed; that once they had a day, a day of grace, and that, with some of them, it was a long summer's day. They will remember that they had calls at the first hour, and the third hour, and the ninth hour, and at the eleventh hour; and then, all the day long, God stretched forth His hand unto them, but they did not know the day of their visitation. They were more foolish than the crane and the stork and the swallow; they did not understand their appointed time; they did not mind the things that belonged to their peace until they were hidden from their eyes. They slept in the harvest, and loitered and sinned away their time, wasted their day in which they should have made provision for their souls. Oh, how will they then be ready to tear themselves in pieces that they should have neglected so great salvation in the day when salvation was attainable! Yea, that they should refuse the offers of grace and pardon and peace and life and happiness which, in that day, were so frequently and earnestly made unto them. Then they will wish that they had opened their ears and hearts, that they had regarded and accepted such gracious offers, whatever they had neglected or parted withal. Then they will wish they had embraced and improved the opportunities which once they had for prayer and hearing and attending upon God's ordinances; that they had been in the church when they were in the ale houses; that they had associated themselves with God's people, when they frequented the company of the lewd and ungodly; that they had been upon their knees, with grief confessing sin, when they took so much delight in the commission of it; that they had taken time from their sports to make their peace with God; that they had worshipped God in their closets, and worshipped God in their families, and laid up for themselves treasures in heaven. And horrible will their vexation be that they did not do so.

4. In going away, they will remember for what it was that they refused this happiness; that it was only the satisfaction of some foolish and unprofitable lusts. If two kingdoms of equal worth and glory were proposed to a man's choice, it would not trouble him that he had refused the one to obtain the other; but if a man were to choose whether he would be a king or a slave, if he should refuse the former and choose the latter, when he came to feel the misery of

his bondage, this would trouble him more than the bondage that he might have avoided; that he has chosen this thralldom and parted with a kingdom for it. They will then perceive that they have chosen to be slaves unto sin and Satan rather than to be heirs unto the kingdom of glory. I know that though now they are slaves and serve divers lusts, and though their bondage is a thousand times worse than if they were vassals to the cruelest tyrant upon earth, yet they are not sensible, neither are they weary of their bondage, because their wills are in thralldom and their affections are captivated; and though entrance to the glory of heaven is the choicest privilege upon earth and most desirable, yet they do not desire it, but prefer their slavery before it because they are blind, unbelieving, besotted sinners, and judge things according to sense. Yet, on the day of Christ's appearance, all things will appear with a new face, and they will look upon things with a new eye. They will then perceive that they were slaves all their days, and there was no such drudgery as that which they were employed in; and that there is no such glory and happiness as that which they refused and foolishly cast away. Then it will sting them indeed to remember that they have chosen rather to do the work of the devil and yield obedience to the basest lusts, for which they must now be repaid with the wages of death and eternal misery, than to do the work of the Lord, who would have rewarded them with eternal life and a crown of glory and immortality. Then they will say, "What profit have we gotten by these things whereof we are now ashamed? What fruit do all our labor and toil in the world yield unto us? What are we the better for our riches and great estates on the earth, for our labor and high esteem among men? For our lascivious pleasures and delights, now vanished and gone, which we bought at so dear a rate, at the loss of our precious and immortal souls, and forfeiture of an inheritance in the kingdom of heaven?" Then they will cry out, "O bewitching world! O deluding devil! O deceitful heart and lusts! O what fools and mad men have we been that we should trample jewels under our feet like swine and, instead of them, put dross and dung into our cabinet? That we should so sweetly drink the poison of sin to the bane and ruin of our souls, and refuse to taste of the cup of salvation which all our days was held forth unto us?" Then they will cry out of their voluptuousness, their covetousness, their pride and haughtiness and the like lusts which have kept Christ out of their hearts, and keep them out of the kingdom of heaven.

5. In going away, some of them will remember how nearly they missed their happiness; that they were almost persuaded to be Christians in deed as well as in name, and to accept Christ upon His own terms; that they were not far from the kingdom of heaven; that they were come even within sight of the heavenly Canaan, and yet died in the wilderness; that they were come even to the gates of the new Jerusalem, but, finding it too strait for them and the luggage of their sins together, there they stuck and could not enter in; that they climbed up a great way the hill of Zion, but did not reach the top and, tumbling down, their fall was the greater. They will remember the means of grace which they enjoyed, the

ordinances which they sat under, and the entreaties
which the Lord made with them by His Word and
Spirit about their life and salvation, and the carriage
of their heart towards the Lord in these entreaties.
Some of them will remember what convictions the
Lord wrought in them of sin, and what troubling of
conscience for fear of hell and wrath to come; and,
if they had followed their preparative work, they
might have quickly been acquainted with Christ and
escaped the misery which they feared; but they shut
up their eyes against the light, stilled the noise of
their consciences, and calmed their spirits with the
delights and pleasures of the world, and so grew
more hardened in sin than before, and gave such
repulses to the Spirit that the Spirit quite departed
from them.

Others will remember that they were persuaded
to ascend some steps higher under the ministry of
the Word. They were reproved for such and such
gross sins which they lived in the practice of, that
they could have no ease in their consciences until
they had broken off that wicked course; that they left
off their drunkenness and their swearing, their uncleanness and unrighteous dealings, and were, in a
great part, reformed in their lives; but there were
some lusts in their heart which they hugged secretly
and delighted in, and would not be persuaded to
leave, which were their undoing. Pride, revenge, un-
charitableness, covetousness, and the like remained
in their reigning power, which were inconsistent
with the power of godliness.

Others will remember what profession they
made, and that they went with some kind of glad-

ness in the company of God's people, into His house and ordinances, and heard the Word, and received some impressions thereof; yea, obtained some kind of righteousness, repentance, faith, desire, love, joy, hope; that they had some tastes of the heavenly gifts and the powers of the world to come, and thought themselves as fair for heaven as the best, and whoever missed, that they could not miss glory; but oh, the confusion and vexation which will be upon the spirits of these persons when the Lord Jesus will disown them and shut them out of His kingdom! Oh, what tearing of heart will they have when they perceive that they were mistaken, and find themselves disappointed of the happiness which they had such hopes of, and confident expectations to obtain; when they find that their silver was but dross, and their graces were but counterfeit and not of the right stamp; that they had not the image and superscription of Christ upon them; when they remember that they had a righteousness, but it was like the morning cloud, which the wind of affliction or temptation had driven away; that they had some repentance, but it was legal, not evangelical; that the tears they had sometimes shed for sin were like the early dew, which the bright sun of prosperity quickly dried up; that they had a faith, but it was a temporary faith, which wanted deep rooting in the heart, and whatever flourishing fruit it quickly sent forth, yet the hot sun of persecution withered it so that it came to nothing when they were put upon the trial; that they had desires after Christ, and the favor of God and spiritual things, but they were but faint wishes.

They were like the untimely birth of a woman which never came to any perfection. They had love to God in show, or it may be at some time a passionate glow of heart upon an ordinance which was not kindled by a spark falling down from heaven upon them, blown up by the Spirit of God, but a false or more inferior fire which arose from a sympathy with ministers or other Christians in the more inferior working and impressions of their love which was indeed sincere and arose from a right principle; they had some kind of hope, but it was like a spider's web, broken quickly to pieces or swept down with the broom of destruction with them into hell. They had some joys, but they were fleshly and ungrounded; some tastes arising from misapprehensions of gospel privileges, and misapplication of gospel promises, all which quickly vanished and came to nothing. They will find (if not before, then surely at that day) that they were mistaken and have lost all their pains and labor for want of a thorough work of grace, for want of soundness at the root, for want of hearty sorrow, deep humiliation, well-grounded, deep rooted faith, supreme love, well-bottomed hope, universal reformation, and mortification of the deeds of the body; that none of their actions were accepted by the heart-searching God for want of a right principle and end.

And when these persons are sentenced to hell, are going away from Christ, and the glory which once they had hopes of, and were so near unto, and, had they gone but a step or two further, they might have attained, oh, what inconceivable grief and cuttings of heart will there be! They will remember then that they did not enter in at the strait gate, and they will wish with all their hearts that they had striven, that they had taken more pains, that they might not have missed and fallen short of salvation. Possibly, then, with unutterable anguish, they may say, "There is a glorious inheritance in heaven which we are now departing from; we often prayed for it when we were upon the earth, and, if we had been sincere and fervent, if we had resolved to take the place by storm and would not have been denied, we might have gotten it. We have read of it in the Word, and heard of it in the sermons, and it has been offered to us freely, and, if we had renounced the world, forsaken sin, and chosen it for our portion, we might have had it. We parted with some sins; if we had left all, it should have been ours. Once we had some hopes of it, when we had some taste of it, and had done some things to obtain it, and, if we had gone a little further, we might have indeed obtained it. If we had taken pains with our hearts before God, to get them raised to things above; if we had denied ourselves, and mortified our members upon the earth; if we had put away all our transgressions, cast away our own righteousness, rolled ourselves wholly upon Jesus Christ, and acted faith upon Him and the promises and His kingdom, and walked in the narrow way, which we seemed to walk in, we might now have been made possessors hereof, and shined among yonder glorious saints, some of whom were our companions, and hoped for our company, and wonder to see us separated from them. But alas! We were slothful and careless; we were unwatchful and idle. Our pains were more to *appear* religious than to *be* religious. We had some lusts which lay nearer to our hearts than Jesus Christ. We did some things with seeming vigor, but carnal motives were the chief incentives to our duties. And however lifeless, faithless, and empty of true grace they were, yet we trusted in them and made them our savior, and never were brought clear off from our own bottom unto a closure with Jesus Christ. We have fooled away our salvation and made ourselves unworthy of eternal life. Deservedly, deservedly do we lose this crown for our own folly. Oh, that we had been sincere and thorough Christians!"

6. In going away, it will sting the wicked to think that now the happiness of heaven is irrecoverable. Once they might have obtained it, and that upon easy terms; yea, after some refusal of it, they had fresh offers and invitations. The door of mercy and the gate of salvation and glory stood open a long time, but now the door is locked upon them and will never be opened again. They must go away without any hopes of ever entering upon the new Jerusalem, or obtaining the least degree of the happiness of the saints; they must bid adieu to joy and comfort forever. These considerations will sting gospel sinners in their going away. Thus concerning the first particular in the execution of the sentence of the wicked, they shall go away.

The Punishment of the Wicked

They shall go into punishment, and here I shall speak, first, of the punishment they shall go into; and, second, of their entering into this punishment.

1. Concerning the punishment which the wicked shall go into. Take two or three places of Scripture which set forth this punishment. Matthew 25:41: "Depart, ye cursed, into everlasting fire." Mark 9:43–44: Then go into hell, where the worm dieth not, and the fire is not quenched." Revelation 14:10–11: "They shall drink of the wine of the wrath of God, which shall be poured out without mixture, into the cup of His indignation, and be tormented with fire, and brimstone, and the smoke of their torment ascends up for ever and ever." The punishment then will be God's wrath which the damned shall drink of, so as to feel the immediate impression thereof upon their souls, and fire and brimstone kindled by the breath of God, the impression whereof they shall feel upon their bodies.

But what tongue can express the punishment of the wicked in hell? If some expressions in Scripture concerning it are metaphorical, surely they fall short of what real punishment will be. The drops and sprinklings of God's wrath here are but small in comparison with the ocean which the wicked will be cast into; the top of the cup has nothing of the bitterness which they will find in the dregs. Never was there such a fire on earth as the fire of hell; never was there such a pain endured by those which have undergone the most exquisite torments as the pains and torments which shall be inflicted hereafter upon the damned. Yet, though we are not able here to conceive how dreadful this punishment will be, we may conceive it to be inexpressibly more dreadful than any punishment upon earth if we consider:

The Inflictor of the punishment;
The subject of the punishment; and
The properties of the punishment.

The Inflictor of the punishment.

Consider the Inflictor of the punishment which the wicked shall go into; and that will be the most holy, just, powerful, and sin-avenging God. The wicked will then fall into His hands immediately, and oh, how fearful a thing will it be to fall into the hands of the living God! Hebrews 10:31. Wicked men now have no fear of God before their eyes, though their sins and affronts to God are great; yet, because His goodness and patience towards them are also great, because He keeps silent and does not speedily execute His vengeance upon them, therefore they are secure and insensible of His displeasure, and have lighter thoughts and lesser fear of Him than of weak dying worms like themselves.

But when their eyes shall be opened at the last day, and a discovery of God shall be made unto them in His infinite majesty, greatness, power, holiness, and fiery indignation against them, oh, how fearful then will it be to fall into His hands! It will be very sweet to fall into the arms of His love, but very dreadful to fall into the hands of His displeasure.

When God executes His vengeance Himself, He will do it very terribly, especially if we consider that He will glorify His infinite wisdom in the punishment of the damned, which will contrive such tortures for them that if all the men in the world would join their wits together, and take to their help all the devils in hell, they could not invent the like.

Dreadful ingredients will His wisdom find out to put into the cup which He will put into the hand of the wicked to drink.

He will glorify His infinite power. He will make bare His arm and smite with infinite force. The blow of a child will make little impression, but if a Goliath smites with a Goliath's sword, he will smite to the ground. The weightier the hand, the heavier the stroke. There is more difference between the power of God and the strongest creature than between the strongest creature and the weakest child. It would be dreadful to be delivered up to the power of some strong and fierce cruel creature; what will it be to be delivered up to the power of the omnipotent and most furious God? God will glorify the power of His anger in the destruction of the wicked. Romans 9:22: "What if God willing to show His wrath, and to make His power known. . . ." God will show what His power can do in punishing the wicked. His last work of power in punishing will be as glorious as His first work of power in creating. And He will glorify the power of His anger in hell as He will glorify His goodness and love in heaven. In heaven He will open the treasures of His love, and in hell He will open the treasures of His wrath. God will inflict the punishment.

The subject of the punishment.

The subject of the punishment which the wicked shall go into will be both soul and body.

The souls of the wicked will be punished not only with the loss of the glorious and comfortable presence of God, and the happiness of heaven, but also I conceive that they will be filled with anguish through the impression of God's wrath upon them. They will be filled up to the brim with the wrath of God; the arrows of the Almighty will be shot up to the head in them and pierce them through and through. We read in Romans 2:8–9 of indignation and wrath, tribulation and anguish, which at the day of wrath will be upon every soul that does evil.

The impression of God's indignation and wrath on the soul will effect tribulation and anguish; such wounds they will have in their spirits as will be insupportable, such tribulations as will be horrible, such anguish as is inconceivable, when the hand of the Lord is upon them, when they see the frowns of His brow, when He strikes them with anger. Christ tasted the bitterness of God's wrath in His soul for the sins of others which caused His bloody sweat in the garden and such roarings upon the cross. Oh, how bitter will the wrath of God be to the wicked when their souls taste it for their own sins. It will be God's wrathful presence which the souls of the damned will feel, the impressions of which will make hell to be hell, as it will be the glorious and comfortable presence of God which the souls of the righteous will feel the impressions of, which will make heaven to be heaven.

The bodies of the wicked shall be punished; they have been sharers in sin and they must share in torment. They must lie in the lake of fire and brimstone, Revelation 20:10. The torment of the bodies of the wicked will be dreadful; besides the impression which the anguish of the soul will make upon them, they will have their own proper torment through the sense of the fire which will be kindled about them and burn more horribly than did the London fire when it got into the heart of the city. Their torment will be greater than if scalding lead were poured in their bowels, than if they were torn in pieces with wild horses, than if their breasts were ripped up and their hearts plucked out of them with burning pincers. It will be worse than if they were cast into a cauldron of boiling pitch or lead, or put into Phalaris's bull or Nebuchadnezzar's fiery furnace. The torture of the damned bodies will be far beyond the sharpest pain now incidental to human nature by racking diseases or that has been inflicted upon any of the children of men by the most cruel tyrant. The bodies of the wicked, when raised again, will be strengthened unto a greater capacity for punishment when they will be made incorruptible and immortal, and punishment will be the end of their resurrection; but more of this punishment under the properties.

The properties of the punishment.
It will be universal. It will not only be in soul and body, but also in every part of both, in every faculty of the soul, in every member of the body. Oh, the black thoughts, the dismal apprehensions, the grisly fancies, the heavy griefs, the sinking fears, the dreadful terrors, the hellish grips, the utter despair, the horrible anguish and confusion which the soul will have when the wrath of God shall be poured in upon it like water. The wicked will not only be in hell, but they will have a hell in themselves; in their consciences they will have a never-dying worm

which will gnaw and tear them; they will have a storm in their spirits, raised by the wind of God's wrath, which will blow most fiercely upon them. Every faculty of the soul will be afflicted according to its capacity, and every member of the bodies of the wicked shall be tormented. Oh! How will their eyes glance, their tongues roar, their hands and feet fry, their flesh roast! No part will be free from the devouring flames of this horrible burning fire. There are many diseases to which the body is exposed in this world, but very seldom do they meet together in the same subject; if the head aches, the members may be free; if the foot is pained, the hand may be at ease and ready to contribute some relief upon the pained parts. And if the body is sick, the soul may give some consolatory arguments to alleviate the irksomeness of the disease; but in hell, the punishment of the wicked will be universal; it will be in every member of the body and every faculty of the soul.

The punishment of hell will be extreme. The souls of the wicked shall be filled with anguish, as full as they can hold. Their capacity will be larger, and they will be filled up to the height of their capacity; and their bodies also will have the most exquisite pain it is possible for them to endure. Their sense of pain will be quicker, and their strength to endure pain greater, and their pain will be in the utmost extremity. Some pains of the body here are not very acute, and some troubles of mind may well enough be borne; but any disease in extremity is very irksome. The pain of the head or the tooth in extremity, the gout, stone, colic in extremity, especially the troubles of the mind in extremity, will make a man weary of his life; but to have every part afflicted in extremity, and the uttermost extremity, and that beyond our own capacity or conception, will be very dreadful.

The punishment of the wicked will be continual, without any intermission or alleviation. The wicked will have no rest day nor night, Revelation 14:11. There will be nothing but weeping and wailing and gnashing of teeth, Matthew 22:13. The most painful diseases here have fits which do not continue long; the diseased find, after their fits, some ease and assuagement. They have intermissions sometimes, some light intervals; but the wicked in hell will have no ease or assuagement, no light intervals of their grief and pains. There will be no mixture of comfortable ingredients in the cup of God's wrath, which the damned must drink of. There will be but one fit in their disease, and this fit will always be at the height. They will not have the least drop of water to cool so much as the tip of their tongue, which shall be tormented in flames. Their grief will not have any allay; they will not have one comfortable thought; no eye to pity them, none to bring any relief unto them. Oh, how bitter will their sins be unto them! Here they are but bitter sweets; then they will be nothing but bitterness, and gall and wormwood unto them. Their punishment will be continual.

The punishment of the wicked will be without remedy. There will be no escaping or flying from the wrath of God. Now sinners may flee from the wrath that is to come; but, when it has once come and has gotten hold of them, it will hold them down so that they shall never get loose from it. Now they may agree with their adversary upon the way; they may make their peace with God in the world. There is no sin for which they may not obtain a pardon but the unpardonable sin against the Holy Ghost, which carries men away from God; but, hereafter in hell, there will be no more sacrifice for sin. The Savior of mankind will be their Judge and pass an irreversible sentence of condemnation upon them. It is possible now for the wicked to be delivered from this punishment, but it will be impossible then to be delivered out of it; their punishment will be without remedy.

The punishment of the wicked will be eternal. Hellfire will be unquenchable, Matthew 3:12, and everlasting, Matthew 25:41. The smoke of their torment will ascend up for ever and ever, Revelation 14:11. This eternity of punishment will be a fearful aggravation of it. If you saw a malefactor torn to pieces with wild horses, or thrown down in a fiery furnace and there burned to ashes, you would say that either of these were dreadful punishments, though the pain possibly might not endure a quarter of an hour, for death concludes all bodily pains here. What then will it be to endure the torments of hellfire forever? A small pain, if it should last long, would be very irksome; much more such racking pains by the stone, bladder disease, gout, colic, and the like, if they should continue for a month or a year together. How miserable would they make life to be?

Yea, if a man should hold but one of his fingers in the fire but for a day, it would afflict him more than all outward comforts could delight him. The torments of hell will not be in one part only, but in every part; not in a weaker degree, but in the greatest extremity; not for a day, or a month, or a year, but forever. The wicked will be always dying, never dead; the pangs of death will be ever upon them, and yet they shall never give up the ghost. If they could die, they would think themselves happy; they will always be roaring and never breathe out their last; always sinking and never come to the bottom; always burning in those flames and never consumed. The eternity of hell will be the hell of hell.

When our Savior endured equivalent punishment to this of hell for His people, it had not this circumstance of eternity in it, there not being that need, because of the excellency of His person. Though the pains of hell got hold of Him, yet they could not keep Him in hold. He broke through and triumphed over them, and could say in the conclusion, "It is finished." But the damned will not be able to break through their punishment; they will be compassed about with it, and hedged in and shut down, and never be able to lift up the head. Never shall they say of this punishment, "It is finished," for their pains will always be, as it were, beginning; when they have spent the time of as many years in hell as there are stars in the firmament, sands on the seashore, and motes in the sun, their torment will be, as it were, beginning, and no nearer a conclusion than the first day they were cast into that place. Who can express this eternity? When we launch forth our thoughts in the considerations thereof, we lose them quickly, it being such a depth which cannot be fathomed, such a vast ocean which cannot be measured. Yet, to extend your thoughts a little in the consideration of the eternity of the wicked's punishment, I shall, by one or two suppositions, illustrate something of the vastness thereof.

Suppose that this globe of the earth on which we tread were hollow, and that it were filled up with great folio books as full as it could hold; and, moreover, there were books heaped up upon it to fill the whole circumference of the air round about it; yea, that the whole space to the place of the utmost verge of the heavens were filled with books, and all this vast number of books were filled with figures in the highest degree of multiplication. Oh, what a number of books would there be in the whole space! What a number of figures in these books! And what a vast number would there be deciphered by these figures? A bit of paper half as broad as a half-penny will hold the figures of the number of as many years as has been since the creation of the world. What then would a whole leaf of a great folio-book? What would a folio-book hold? What then would a room full of folios hold? Now if, at the end of time, when the wicked go to hell, God should fill the whole space of the world full of folios full of figures of numbers, and tell the wicked that every thousand years one of these numbers should be subtracted, and promise them when all the numbers were subtracted out of all these books, they should have a release out of their torments, they should have a small spark of hope that after the subtraction of so many millions, millions, millions of innumerable number, in the revolution of so many millions, millions,

millions of innumerable years, yet at last there
would be an end. There would be time then set, and
a wearing towards an end. Yet if we could cast our
thoughts so far on this number of years to think
that if every thousand years one was subtracted yea, if
they were all subtracted as many thousands of times
as the number of the figures in all these books, yet
even then the punishment of the damned would be
as far from ending as at the very first beginning of
them.

Yea, suppose further that there were as many
worlds as the number of the books before supposed
would arise unto, and these worlds should continue
as many years as by this account there would be
worlds; and all these worlds were filled with angels
and men, and all these angels and men should be
employed in nothing else from the beginning of
these worlds unto the end of them but in conceiving
numbers of years unto the uttermost conception
which they could have of numbers. What an inconceivable number of years would there be conceived
by so many angels and men, in so many years, in so
many worlds! Yet if all that vast number of years were
joined to the end of the time, wherein all the numbers in the figures of so many afore-mentioned
books were subtracted by one in a thousand years,
and these multiplied as many thousand times as
numbers were conceived; such a vast number of
years would reach a great way, but they would not be
so much as a hair's breadth in the measure of eternity. And if you would suppose the space of all these
years too to be spent by the damned in torments!
Even then their torments would be as far from a

conclusion as they were upon their first entrance into hell. O eternity! Eternity! Eternity! How vast is eternity! How infinite and immeasurable! How horrible will the thoughts of eternity be unto the damned, to be punished so extremely, and that without any intermission or hopes of conclusion, to fall into such a horrible pit and fiery lake, and there burn forever without any possibility of ever getting forth. O dreadful! O blind world! O sottish sinners! that take no more care now to avoid and get deliverance from such a punishment as this which they are exposed unto, and will be the certain consequence of sin, without repentance. Thus concerning the punishment which the wicked shall go into.

Their entrance into this punishment.

When the whole crew of wicked and ungodly persons, together with the whole flock of devils, are departed from the presence of Christ and the glorious saints, and heaven is now upon their backs and hell before their face, and they are now come to the very mouth of the bottomless pit, unto the doors and great gates of hell, and now they are opened before them and unto them and for them, and they shall see the black smoke ascend up from thence and smell a horrible stink of the sulphurous fire which they must be thrown into; and when they behold the horrible flames of fire flashing forth from the furnace of hell, ten thousand times more dreadful than those which were seen to arise from London on that Monday night, and now begin to feel the heat and see others tumbling in before them, and they following them; and when they begin first to put their

hands and their feet into the fire, and now they are
in and covered with flames and begin to boil and
fry; and when they perceive the gates of hell to be
shut upon them, and great stones rolled before
them, which can never be removed, and great bars
put upon them, which can never be broken, and
they are out of all hopes of ever breaking prison and
getting forth—oh, how will they shriek and roar and
cry out in the anguish of their souls, and torture
their bodies!

"Woe, woe unto us miserable sinners! And is this
the hell which the ministers warned us to flee from?
And yet would we run ourselves into such flames? Is
this the wages of sin? Have our drunkenness, swearing, whoring, lying, and unrighteous dealing such a
dreadful consequence as this? Is this the company
we must take up our dreadful abode with? And is this
the place of our eternal habitation? Must we then
dwell in this devouring fire and inhabit these everlasting burnings? Oh, miserable, miserable, forlorn
wretches we! Would to God we had never been born!
Oh, that we had been dogs or swine! Oh, that we
had been serpents or toads! Oh, that we had been as
the meanest worms, or stones, or any thing without
souls, who are now annihilated! Oh, that we had
been nothing or might be turned into nothing! Oh,
that we could recall our time; how would we improve
it! Oh, that it were with us as once it was, when our
being and abode were upon the earth; when the day
of grace shone upon us and the means of grace were
offered to us! How would we pray, hear, watch, strive,
and live! How would we forsake sin, and accept
Christ, and deliver up ourselves unto universal obe-

dience! But alas! Time is fled; the day is spent; the door is shut; we are bound up in chains which cannot be remedied, and now are extreme and will never be ended! Oh, the pain of my eyes! Would I had none! Oh, the pain of my tongue! Would that it were out and I were dumb! Oh, the torture of my hands and feet! Would that they were off and my whole body were consumed! Oh, I am sick! I am sick! And here is no physician! I am sad! I am sore troubled! And here is none to pity me! Oh, my heart burns! My head aches! Oh, the terror which I feel! Oh, the gripes and tearings of the never-dying worm within me."

But who can conceive what the thoughts and complaints of the damned will be at the first entrance into the punishment of hell? Thus concerning the execution of the sentence pronounced by Christ upon the wicked.

Chapter 9

The Sentence of the Righteous

The next thing is to speak of the execution of the sentence pronounced by Christ upon the righteous. Matthew 25:46: "These shall go away into everlasting punishment." There is the execution of the sentence upon the wicked. "But the righteous into life eternal." There is the execution of the sentence on the righteous. And here I shall speak:

Of the righteous going away.

Of the righteous going into life eternal.

Concerning the righteous going away.

The wicked shall go away, and the righteous shall go away too. The wicked shall go from Christ, the saints, and the happiness of heaven; and the righteous shall go away from devils, wicked persons, and the misery of hell—a going away which, with some considerations, will be unspeakably comfortable unto them.

The righteous shall go away from devils. Christ here redeems and delivers them from that tyranical power which the devils had over them before conversion; yet they are not wholly freed in this life from all their assaults, baits, and snares. Some of them are much buffeted and oppressed by them most, if not all, their days; but, at the last day, they shall go away from Satan. The devil and all his angels will be locked up in the bottomless pit and the righteous shall never be molested with any of them any more. However, the righteous sometimes are foiled by Satan here, and receive some wounds in the spiritual combat; yet, then, they will be victorious and triumph over principalities and powers, and leave them bound in chains behind them. They shall go away from devils.

The righteous shall go away from all wicked persons. Some of the wicked separated themselves from their company while they lived on earth; now God will separate them from the company of all the wicked. They were hated and troubled by the wicked, and some of them suffered much under their reproaches and persecutions. The wicked will cease from troubling them any more. Their hearts were grieved with their oaths, filthy lewdness, and ungodly conversation in the world; but now they will go away from the wicked; no devils or wicked persons shall be admitted into their society or have any room in the place where they are going.

The righteous shall go away from the place and state of misery which the wicked shall go into. They shall be delivered from the damnation and punishment of hell, and all the fears of it forever. And herein their joys will be inconceivable in that:

They will have deeper apprehensions of the punishment of hell than ever entered here into their hearts to imagine. They were told by the Word and ministers what a dreadful punishment was prepared for the damned, and they believed it and feared it and fled from it, but the one half was not told them! The fire which they conceived was but, as it were, a painted fire in comparison to that which they will see the wicked cast into. The pains they fancied were but flea bites in comparison with those which they will see the wicked undergo; they guessed something of the wrath of God by the little scorchings thereof in the first conviction of and contrition for sin. By the sweetness of God's smiles of love afterwards, they judged that His displeasure and fury would be insupportable; but their thoughts were mean and short of that fiery vengeance and dreadful wrath which will then break forth into a flame to consume the ungodly. As the wicked will have high apprehensions of the glory and happiness of the righteous beyond whatever entered into their hearts to conceive here in this world; and it will be their unutterable grief to be deprived thereof and shut out forever from the kingdom of heaven which the righteous with joy and triumph shall go into; so the righteous shall have deep apprehensions of whatever they imagined here. And it will be no small part of their joy that they were delivered from this misery, and saved from the torments of hell, into which they shall see the wicked go with such dread and horror. Lazarus will see Dives to be tormented; the other Apostles will see Judas thrust into hell; and all the righteous will be spectators of the vengeance which the Lord Jesus will execute upon the ungodly world. And oh, how will they then adore God's electing love? How will they value the blood of Christ which was shed for the redemption of them? How will they bless God for pardoning mercy? How will they hug the feet of the Savior who has delivered them from this so dreadful wrath and fearful torments, which they will see inflicted upon the damned?

Especially when they consider in the going away that they were by nature children of wrath even as others, Ephesians 2:3; that they had as foul natures as the vilest; that they had as leprous, poisonous, odious hearts until they were renewed and sanctified as those which they shall see condemned and tormented; that they were sometimes foolish, disobedient, serving divers lusts and pleasures, hateful and hating one another, until the kindness and free love of God were manifested in the regeneration and renovation of them by the Holy Ghost, Titus 3:3–5; that they were dead in sins with others, and walked according to the course of the world, according to the prince of the power of the air, who wrought in them, as in other children of disobedience, so that they were as forward as others to fulfill the lusts of the flesh, and of the mind, and ran with others into the same excess of riot until God, who is rich in mercy, for His great love wherewith He loved them, quickened them and saved them by His grace, and hereby put a difference between them and the wicked, who went on to the end of their sensual course, in which sometimes they were running with them in company, Ephesians 2:1–4.

Yea, some of them will remember how they outstripped others in sin, and were guilty of more gross breaches of the law than many millions of the wicked whom they will see condemned; and that they should escape, and be awakened to repent, and enabled to believe and reform, and that they should obtain pardon and salvation through Christ when others were passed by and let alone to perish under smaller sins, this will fill them with astonishing admiration and wondering joy, when they see some of their near relations going to hell; their father, their mother, their children, their husbands, their wives, their brethren, their sisters, their intimate friends and companions. However they are grieved now to see them take such courses and walk in the way to hell, and they labor to pull them out of that way, and would fain persuade them to walk with them in heaven's way, and are troubled to think of the torment which they must endure if they go on; yet hereafter relative ties and those affections which now they have to relations out of Christ will cease, and they will not have the least trouble to see them sentenced to hell and thrust into the fiery furnace, but will rejoice in the glory of God which will be manifested upon them in their destruction. And oh, the joy that they will be filled with to think that they were not passed by with the rest of their relations; that they were not under the same deserved condemnation with them; that God would choose but one or two in many families, and they should be in the number of the chosen ones; that when His chosen were comparatively so few, and the reprobates so many, they should be elected when there was no motive in them to incline God to the choice of them; that He should choose them freely! If He had not chosen them, if they were to change places with some of their wicked relations going to hell, this would be dreadful. But that they are going from hell, when their relations are going into it, this will fill them with joy unspeakable.

Especially when they consider in their going

away that they were sometimes so near hell; that while they were in a state of nature, and under the guilt of sin, some of them were so near to death that they were brought to the sides of the pit, to the doors of the grave, to the very brink of hell, before they repented and accepted Jesus Christ. Some of them will remember how near they were to death when they were young; how near they were to death by some casualties; how near by some diseases. Some of them will remember the great plague of London which swept away so many thousands, how ill they were provided for death at the beginning thereof; how nearly they escaped the disease, and some of them, which had the disease, how nearly they escaped death by it; and if they had died then, they should have certainly gone to hell. Oh, how will they remember the providence of God in keeping them alive, notwithstanding the many dangers they were in of death, all the days of their unregeneracy! And when they moreover consider how they tried God's patience and trampled upon it by their heinous provocations, how they abused His goodness and turned His grace into wantonness; how they hastened in the ways of sin towards hell and were come even to the end of the line; that some of them were drunkards, sabbath-breakers, profane persons, swearers, unclean persons, and persecutors of the people of God, and were arrived even to the height of wickedness, and lacked but a step or two of falling into hell, and yet that the Lord should meet with them with flaming sword in the way of sin they were driving on so fast and furiously in, and stop them, turn them, change them, and bring them

home to Himself; yea, when they had deafened their
ears against many calls, and stifled many convictions, and often quenched the motions of His Spirit,
and were so unwilling to leave their sins and come
out of the way of destruction, and were so desper-
ately bent upon their ruin, that yet He should
knock, and call again and again, and follow them
still by His Spirit; that He should lay hold on them
as the angel did on Lot, and bring them out of
Sodom even by force, and overpower the contrariety
of their stubborn wills, and break open the door of
their hearts, and overturn the strongholds of sin
and Satan, and set up the throne of His Son within
them; that He should snatch them like firebrands
out of the fire, and pluck them out of the snare of
the devil that had almost dragged them into hell!

Oh, how will they be astonished to remember
God's infinite pity and love, and the power of His
rich grace that worked salvation for them!
Especially when they perceive how dreadful the misery is which they were hastening into. I have heard
of a man who, in the night, galloped over a high
bridge, which was broken down all but a narrow
plank which God's providence directed his horse's
feet upon which, if he had slipped never so little on
the one side or the other, horse and man would
have fallen into the deep stream and been drowned,
which the man did not know till the next morning;
but, when viewing the place, and considering the
danger he had so narrowly escaped, was struck with
such astonishment at it that he fell down dead in
the place.

When some of God's people shall go away from

hell at the last day, and look behind them into the
bottomless pit, and take a view of the streams of fire
and brimstone which are running in the burning
lake, and remember how they have galloped over
those streams when they were in the career of their
sins, and by how narrow a plank they passed over
them, that if they had slipped but a little aside they
would have fallen into the lake from whence they
could never be got out; when they shall remember
how near they were to hell, and how narrowly they
have escaped such horrible torments, surely they
will be struck with such admiration and joys which
now they could not bear, but would overwhelm their
spirits and bring immediate death upon them! But
then their nature will be strengthened to bear this
joy which might be enough to sweeten an eternity, if
they had no other happiness than the consideration
of the misery from which they have been so wonderfully delivered. Thus concerning the going away of
the righteous from the wicked, and the miseries
which they shall endure.

Concerning their going into life eternal.

Eternal life is taken in Scripture, frequently, for
the life of grace, but chiefly, and so here, for the life
of glory. By eternal life we are to understand the
glory and happiness which the righteous shall have
in heaven; of which happiness in heaven I shall
speak subjectively, objectively, and formally.

Subjectively. The subject of the happiness in
heaven will be both the bodies and the souls of the
righteous.

1. *The bodies of the righteous will be the subjects of the*

happiness of heaven. They shall be most glorious bodies, 1 Corinthians 15:43. They were sown in dishonor when they died; they shall be raised in glory at the resurrection. Some glory and majesty is put upon the bodies of men now, in comparison with the bodies of inferior creatures; but the bodies of the righteous shall then be made a thousandfold more glorious. There is not so great a difference between celestial bodies and terrestrial bodies, between the body of the glorious sun and the body of the meanest fly or worm, as then there will be between the bodies of the righteous on earth and in heaven. They will be celestial bodies; they will shine like stars, Daniel 12:3; yea, like the sun in the kingdom of their Father, Matthew 13:43. The bodies will be transformed whereby their dirty hue will be changed more than if all the stones in the street were turned into diamonds, Philippians 3:21. Their vile bodies will be fashioned like unto the glorious body of Jesus Christ. Now their bodies are vile, being so frail, especially as they are the instruments of sin; they are earthly as they bear the earthly Adam; then they shall be glorious, because they shall bear the image of the heavenly Adam. The bodies of some now shine with gold, pearls, and costly apparel which are about them and, yet, under all, their bodies remain vile bodies; but, hereafter, the bodies of the righteous shall shine with marvelous brightness and glory through the qualities which shall be in them, beyond what the richest attire can give.

2. *And, by consequence, the bodies of the righteous shall be most beauteous bodies;* they shall have a perfect beauty, beyond whatever eye beheld in the fairest woman

that ever lived upon the face of the earth. Their bodies shall have the most exact symmetry of parts; those which were misshapen here shall then be healed of that imperfection in their bodies. The crooked back shall then be made straight; the members which are now wanting shall be supplied, and the parts which are now dislocated shall be put into the right place and joined so exactly together; especially the lineaments of their face shall have such figure and composition as shall render their features most lovely and graceful beyond what the greatest observers and admirers of beauty can conceive in their fancy.

Moreover, the bodies of the righteous shall have a most sweet mixture of colors. There will be no black skin, no swarthy complexion, no pale face, no wan look. Their color will be most lovely, without change or fading; there will be no wrinkles of old age, but they will be always young, fresh, and blooming. If the composition of the elements, which are so dreggish, gives forth some such loveliness of color, what will the more refined compositions of the bodies of the righteous do when the Lord will fashion their bodies after the pattern of His Son's body? And, therefore, I conceive further that the bodies of the righteous shall have a most comely stature, not dwarfish, nor gigantic, but according to the measure of the stature of Christ.

And, lastly, to complete their beauty, I doubt not but they will have more graceful gestures and sparkling motions in their countenances; they will have no grief to deaden their beauty, no anger, no envy, or the like to change or transform their vis-

ages; but love and joy will continually look out at
their eye which will marvelously add to the luster
and sweetness of their beauty; they shall have most
beautiful bodies.

3. *The bodies of the righteous shall be most strong that they*
may be suitable to their great soul, and fit for such works as in
heaven they must be employed in. Were they weak as now
they are, they would never endure such works and
motions; they would tire and faint; their spirits
would quickly be spent; but in heaven there will be
no laziness and weariness, no fainting nor failure of
spirits; all their motions, though never so great and
continual, will be sweet and delightful; and, therefore, their bodies must be strong that they may be
suitable hereunto. Moreover, the glory of heaven
which they will have in their eye will sink in a weak
body; and the ravishing joys and love, the transports
of their souls in the visions which they shall have,
would crack a vessel to pieces. They must be strong
to bear the glory of the place, and when besides they
must endure to all eternity, and all this without
reparation by meat, or drink, or sleep. I conceive
that no bodies visible to us are made so strong as the
bodies of the righteous will be at the last day.

4. *Hence it follows that their bodies will be most healthful*
bodies; they will be free from all pains and disease
which may in the least weaken them; the tempera-
ture of their bodies will be so exact that there will be
no fighting of contrary qualities within them, no
flowing of ill humors. In heaven, there will be no
plague, nor ague, nor fever, nor gout, nor bladder
disease, nor any distemper; no need of food to preserve health, nor physic to recover it.

5. *The bodies of the righteous will be spiritual bodies, 1 Corinthians 15:44.* Not absolutely spiritual, for then they would cease to be bodies, but comparatively to what they are now, they will be spiritual. That is, I conceive that they will be quick and nimble in their motions like spirits. Now they are dull, slow, heavy, and a clog to the spirits. I conceive that, hereafter, they shall be like angels for quick and nimble motions; they may be so qualified as, in a moment, to move many thousands of miles. Why may not they move as quickly then as the sun and other stars in the firmament do now, which are bodies of many thousand times greater magnitude?

6. *The bodies of the righteous will be incorruptible and immortal.* 1 Corinthians 15:42: "It is sown in corruption, it is raised in incorruption." Verses 52–53: "In a moment, in the twinkling of an eye, at the last trump, the dead shall be raised, incorruptible; for this corruptible must put on incorruption, and this mortal must put on immortality." And verse 54: "Then shall come to pass the saying which is written, Death is swallowed up in victory." Now death is unavoidable, and unto some very terrible; death has all the children of men in the chase, and shoots his arrows at the righteous as well as the wicked, and though they are delivered from the sting of death, which is sin, yet they are not delivered from the stroke of death. But however death plays the tyrant here on earth and spares none, yet he will have no footing in heaven. The bodies of the righteous, when raised up again, will be impassible and immortal; immortality will swallow up life, and the life of the body as well as the soul will be everlasting.

7. *The souls of the righteous will be the subjects, and the chief subjects, of the glory and happiness of heaven.* If their bodies shall be glorious, their souls shall be much more glorious as being their most excellent part, and capable of more glory than their bodies will be. We read, Romans 8:18, of the glory which shall be revealed in us, that is, in the soul; and the Apostle tells us that the sufferings of this present time are not worthy to be compared with this glory. The greatest sufferings and calamities in this world have not that evil and misery in the least shadow of comparison with the happiness of the glory which shall be put into the souls of the saints; indeed, the Apostle compares them, and see how he makes his future glory to outbalance. 2 Corinthians 4:17: "These light afflictions, which are but for a moment, do work for us a far more exceeding and eternal weight of glory." The afflictions are light, but the glory will be weighty; the afflictions are but for a moment, but the glory will be eternal; the weight of glory will be exceeding, more exceeding, far more exceeding.

Here the Apostle lays one high expression on the back of another, and another upon that, like so many great mountains upon the back of one another; and, when he had gotten to the top of the highest of them, yet he is too low to look into the glory of heaven, and his expressions and apprehensions fall short of the glory which shall be revealed in the soul when it shall be received into the new Jerusalem, for it is yet to be revealed. And, therefore, as the Apostle John said, 1 John 3:2, "It doth not yet appear what we shall be, but when Christ shall ap-

pear, we shall be made like Him." Not only the body
shall be made like His glorious body, but also the
soul will be made like His glorious soul, for we shall
see Him as He is. As the eye conceives the image of
the object which it looks upon, so the soul, in its vision of Christ, shall receive the image of Christ and
have a perfect similitude and likeness unto Him.
The soul will be made most beautiful; the perfect
lineaments of Christ will be drawn upon it. If grace
makes the soul to shine here, how much more will
glory, which is grace in the perfection of it, make
the soul to shine in heaven? And, therefore, grace is
called glory; it is glory begun. 2 Corinthians 3:18:
"We all with open face, beholding as in a glass the
glory of the Lord, are changed into the same image,
from glory to glory, as by the Spirit of the Lord."

The veil which was over the law is now taken
away and, with open face, we behold the glory of the
Lord; that is, I conceive, the Lord Jesus Christ who is
the glory of the Father, the brightness of the
Father's glory, which glory was more dark to His
view under the law, represented by the cloud which
filled the temple; but now there is a more clear revelation of Christ without the veil and cloud of types
and figures, whom we now see in the glass of the
Word and ordinances, and hereby we are changed
into His image and receive from Him impressions
of grace which is glory begun, through the operation of His Spirit in His ordinances upon us. Yet still
we see Him in a glass and, therefore, there is darkness through this interposition; and the eye of our
faith, which looks through this glass upon Christ, is
weak and, therefore, our graces are imperfect and

our similitude to Him is imperfect. But when the glass shall be removed and, instead of the sight of faith, we shall have an immediate vision, then our souls will be changed into a perfect conformity unto His image; and it will not be from glory to glory, from one degree unto another, but glory will be arrived unto its height, and the souls of the righteous will be made perfectly glorious. There, souls will then have perfection of holiness, without the least remainders of sin, which in this world the most holy persons are not wholly free from.

Their thoughts shall be holy. No blasphemous thoughts shall then arise in their minds, no filthy thoughts, no envious nor malicious thoughts; yea, they shall not have the least vanity or impertinence in their thoughts; all their thoughts shall then be brought into perfect obedience unto Jesus Christ.

Their understandings shall be holy. There shall not be the least mist or cloud of ignorance to darken and sully them when they appear before the glorious Sun of righteousness. The brightness which will issue forth from His face will dispel all clouds, and they shall have a clear understanding of all things which they will need to know to make them happy. God will then unlock His treasures, open His books now sealed, and open their understandings too, that they may conceive those mysteries of His Word and that manifold wisdom of God which now exceeds their comprehensions.

Their memories shall be holy. They shall be strengthened to retain and bring forth continually out of their treasures whatever things, new or old, shall tend to feed them with love and joy, and elevate their souls in the praises of God.

Their wills will be perfectly holy. There will be a sweet harmony between their will and the will of God, a perfect compliance with the sweet law which they shall be under without the least contrariety or contradiction. They shall not have any evil motion or inclination to evil in heaven.

Their hearts and affections shall be perfectly holy. The inner room of their hearts shall then be swept clean of all cobwebs; the least dust of sin shall not remain; the roots of bitterness will be plucked up then, and the stains which are now upon them will be washed off. All the disorders and distempers of their affections shall be removed; yea, some affections which now they have, and are suitable to this estate of sin and imperfection, shall be removed in their estate of glory, such as grief, anger, fear, and the like. They shall have no bitterness upon their spirits, no sorrow in their hearts, no sinking and fainting of spirit, no discouragement and despondency, no terror or perplexity, no anguish or anxiety; all these shall flee away like a cloud. Yea, they shall have no hope in heaven, nor desire, as I conceive, because these affections suppose the chief good to be absent and imply imperfection; but there they shall have a perfect enjoyment and rest of soul in the chief good, which is the next thing to be spoken of, namely the object of the saints' happiness in heaven.

Objectively. The object of the happiness of the righteous in heaven, or the chief good which will make them perfectly and completely happy, will be God, who is infinitely good in Himself and infinitely blessed in the enjoyment of Himself; and in Him will the happiness of the righteous consist. That which fills the ocean, surely, will fill a bucket or nutshell. God will be the happiness of the righteous for ever; it is but a thin and subordinate happiness which is here to be found in the creature. It is but an imperfect happiness which is here to be found in God because of our blindness, sin, and incapacity; but, in heaven, God will be a perfect happiness unto the saints. It is said in 1 Corinthians 15:28 that then shall God be all in all. God will be the whole happiness of the righteous; God in Himself, God in His Son, God in the angels, God in other saints, God in themselves, God will be all in all, the only object of their happiness.

Formally. The happiness of the righteous in heaven will consist in the union of the subject and object together. God will be united to their minds by vision, and to their hearts by love, from whence will spring unspeakable joy.

1. *The minds of the saints will have a perfect vision of God, which will infinitely transcend all the visions and sweetest discoveries of God which they have, or are capable of, in this world.* Hereafter their capacities will be enlarged and their minds will be elevated. Here they see God darkly; there they shall see Him clearly. Here they see Him afar off; there they shall see Him nearly. Here they see Him as He is represented; there they shall see Him as He is. Here they see Him as in a glass; there they shall see Him immediately. Here they see something of God; there they shall see God. Here they see His footsteps, some impresses of God upon the creatures, especially upon His children;

chiefly they see His image in Christ whom they view by faith in the glass of the gospel, as was said; yet the uttermost they can here attain unto is to see His back parts; but in heaven they shall see His face; they shall see Him face to face; they shall see Him as He is. This will be the happiness of the righteous in heaven, to have the immediate sight, the beautiful vision of God.

2. *The hearts of the righteous shall be joined to God, who is their chief good, by love.* But who can utter the love which the saints shall have unto God in heaven? It will exceed our narrow conceptions; much more will it exceed the love which those of the most intimate acquaintance with God here attain unto. That it will be heightened beyond what now it is, we may apprehend if we consider:

The righteous will have an immediate vision of God, as has been shown. Now they live in a dark world, and have a cloud upon their minds, and see but a little of God through the perspective glass of His ordinances; a little in the works of His hand and in the works of His Spirit upon the hearts of His children; and if, when they see and know Him so little, they can love Him so dearly above the whole world, how will they love Him when they behold His face, when the clouds shall be dispelled and the sun breaks forth? When they behold His beauty, and the transcendent excellencies which are in Him, beyond whatever they could here imagine, how will their hearts be ravished with love for God in the face when they see Him in Himself, when they see Him in His Son, when the divinity of Christ shall appear in Him, and shall shine so gloriously before them, when they see the angels so full of God, and the saints so full of God, and everything in heaven represent the glorious Jehovah unto them?

The love of God will heighten their love for Him. To be loved by such an excellent person, with such a superlative love, oh, how will this inflame their hearts with love for Him when they take a review of the past expressions of His love, and the love of God in many things, which they did not mind when they were in the world! And when they see a thousand-fold more love in those things which they took notice of, but with low apprehensions and dull affections, how will it raise their hearts when their apprehensions of His love shall be raised! They will admire electing love so free towards them without any provision of merit in them. They will admire His love in sending His Son to redeem, and in sending His Spirit to convert them, His love in pardoning their sins, in adopting them to be His children. Now they admire His love sometimes. "Behold what manner of love is this, that we should be called the children of God," 1 John 3:1. Then they will admire it ten thousand times more. They will see God's love in all His fatherly provisions and protections, yea, in His chastisements and corrections and all His providences working for their good. But oh, what love will they see in His special distinguishing mercies beyond what now they apprehend! God's past love will have a present and deep impression upon their hearts.

Further, they will see the treasures of His love opened, the heart of God opened, and the glory which, in heaven, He will confer upon them, of which they shall never be deprived. And what a demonstration of God's love will this be unto them! Moreover, then they shall have no doubtings of His love, which here dampen their affections. They shall know assuredly that He has loved them, does love them, and will love them unchangeably and eternally; and, withal, they shall have a full sense of His love upon their hearts which will make such an impression as to raise their hearts to an inconceivable height of love.

3. *The righteous will have a higher capacity for love in heaven than here they have;* and they shall be filled with love unto the height of their capacity. They will be able to love a thousand times more than now they can do, and they shall love unto their utmost ability. They will see perfection of loveliness in God and all that are about Him, and they shall have perfection of love. Here their love is sincere and growing up, but it is weak and imperfect; hereafter, it will be grown up to the full height of it, and perfect love will cast out all torment. Here their love is mixed; the stream is divided; it runs and wastes itself in many small rivulets which empty themselves upon the creatures; but when the whole stream will run forth unto God undividedly, not a drop of their love shall be spilled on the ground. God will be the sole object of their love. Here their love is uneven and unconstant toward God; sometimes it ebbs and sometimes it flows. Sometimes they have a high spring tide of love for God; but, at other times, it is low water. Hereafter, then, love for God will be even and constant and always at the greatest height.

4. *And oh, what joy will there be in their hearts through the*

union which the righteous shall have unto God their chief good, when their minds shall be joined to Him in immediate vision and their hearts in perfect love! Oh, how sweet a fruition of God will this be! What delight will spring from hence! If the saints can now rejoice exceedingly in God, when they see Him so little, and their love is so imperfect, what will they do when they see and love Him perfectly and fully? If they are now exceedingly glad sometimes with the light of His countenance, though they have but a glimpse thereof, what will they be when they shall have a constant view thereof, and live eternally under the beams of that light? Their love for God is sweet now, though it is weak; but what will it be in heaven when the conjuction of their hearts to God by love will be so near and close? If the saints can now rejoice in hope of the glory of God, what will they do in possession thereof, when faith shall be changed into vision and hope turned into fruition?

Oh, how will the saints joy and triumph when they have sailed quite through the tempestuous sea of this world and are landed safely in heaven, where there is rest and peace without any windy storm? When they have gotten the victory over the devil and sin, and are now placed out of the gunshot of temptation, and have conquered, through Christ, the grave and death, and are out of fear of his arrows; when they have escaped the terrible wrath of God and find themselves in the arms of His love; when they perceive that they are in heaven now indeed, notwithstanding all their sins, doubts, and fears, and now they have the blessed vision of God which they so much desired, and the full fruition of God's love, which they hoped for; when they look about them and see so much glory about them, and shall look within them and see so much glory there revealed beyond whatever they could imagine, oh, how will they be transported with joy! Then, they will have fullness of joy in the presence of God, and their pleasure and happiness will be perfect without interruption or possibility of a conclusion. And the eternity of their happiness will be the heaven of heaven, as eternity of misery will be the hell of hell.

Thus concerning the happiness of the saints, or the eternal life of glory which they shall enter into.

Concerning the righteous entering into eternal life.

The righteous, after the pronouncing of their sentence, and their seeing the execution of the sentence of the wicked, shall pass away from them and go with Christ into eternal life. They shall go with singing to the Zion which is above, and with everlasting joy upon their heads. They shall obtain joy and gladness, and sorrow and sighing shall flee away, Isaiah 51:11. It will be a most glorious train, such as you never have seen, which will go together unto heaven. The Lord Jesus Christ will be in the head of His glory; all the holy angels will be with Him, and the whole company of the righteous will be together that ever lived in all generations. And oh, with what mirth and gladness will they move towards heaven together! With what shoutings and hosannas will they attend upon the glorious triumph of our Savior into the new Jerusalem! But when they are come to the gates of heaven, and the everlasting doors shall be lifted up to them, and they look into the place prepared for their eternal abode; when the Lord Jesus shall bring them into the glorious presence of the Father, and they shall have the beautiful vision of His face, and see the smiles of His countenance, and are received into the embraces of His love; then, then they will find themselves to be happy indeed. Then their hearts will be filled with joy and their tongues with singing; then they will sing the new song, the song of the Lamb, which now cannot be learned. Then they will sound forth the praises of God and cry out with a loud voice. Revelation 7:10, 12: "Salvation to our God, who sitteth upon the throne, and to the Lamb." And worshipping God they will say, "Amen, blessing, and glory, and wisdom, and thanksgiving, and honor, and power, Amen." And here they shall reign and live forevermore.

Thus concerning the execution of the sentence on the righteous, and concerning the second appearance of Christ, and the end thereof.

Chapter 10

The Certainty of Christ's Second Appearance

Concerning the certainty of Christ's second appearance, I shall prove this by several arguments.

ARGUMENT 1. If the Scriptures have clearly revealed and foretold Christ's second appearance to judgment, and the Scriptures are certainly true, then the second appearance of Christ is certain. But the Scriptures have clearly revealed and foretold this second appearance of Christ to judgment; and the Scriptures are certainly true. Therefore, the second appearance of Christ is certain.

1. *The Scriptures have clearly revealed and foretold Christ's second appearance to judgment.* It is not a truth written in the book of nature; it is not to be found in the writings of the philosophers, and those who have had the highest speculation of natural causes, and effects, and products; this is a mystery which the world, by wisdom, never could find out. It is a secret which has been hidden in God, and is revealed by the Spirit in His Word. This coming of Christ was foretold by Enoch in Jude 14–15: "And Enoch also the seventh from Adam prophesied saying, Behold the Lord cometh with ten thousands of His saints to execute judgment upon all." So it is an ancient revelation. The first coming of Christ was foretold to Adam in the promise that the seed of the woman should break the serpent's head. And the second

coming of Christ was foretold to Enoch. It is foretold by the angels, Acts 1:10–11. While the disciples
looked steadfastly upon our Savior in His ascension,
two angels said unto them, "Ye men of Galilee, why
stand ye gazing up into heaven? This same Jesus,
who is taken up from you into heaven, shall so come
down in like manner as ye have seen Him go into
heaven." However, devils are liars, and the father of
lies and liars; yet the good angels are true, and ministers of truth, and this is a true testimony. Further,
this is foretold by the Apostles who were employed
to be the penmen of part of the Holy Scripture, and
were guided by an infallible Spirit. The Apostle Paul
speaks often of it. Especially see his testimony in 1
Thessalonians 4:15–17: "For this we say unto you by
the word of the Lord, that we which are alive, and
remain unto the coming of the Lord, shall not prevent them which are asleep; for the Lord Himself
shall descend from heaven with a shout, with the
voice of the archangel, and with the trump of God;
and the dead in Christ shall rise first. Then we
which are alive and remain shall be caught up together with Him in the clouds, to meet the Lord in
the air; and then we shall be ever with the Lord."

Thus He sets forth Christ's coming in a comfortable manner unto His people; and, therefore, he ex-
horts Christians to comfort one another with these
words and hopes of Christ's glorious appearance,
when they should be caught up to meet with Him
and be with Him forever. And He sets it forth in a
dreadful manner, with regard to the wicked, in
2 Thessalonians 1:7–9: "The Lord Jesus shall be revealed from heaven with His mighty angels, in flam-

ing fire, taking vengeance on them that know not
God and obey not the gospel, who shall be punished
with everlasting destruction from the presence of
the Lord, and from the glory of His power."
Moreover, this coming of Christ is spoken of by the
Apostle in every chapter of both these epistles. First,
Chapter 1:10: "And to wait for His Son from heaven."
Chapter 2:19: "What is our hope or joy, or crown of
rejoicing? Are not ye in the presence of our Lord
Jesus Christ at His coming?" Chapter 3:13: "To the
end He may establish you unblamable in holiness at
the coming of our Lord Jesus Christ." Chapter 4:16:
"The Lord Himself will descend from heaven with a
shout." Chapter 5:23: "I pray that your whole spirit
and soul and body be preserved blameless unto the
coming of our Lord Jesus." 2 Thessalonians 1:10:
"He shall come to be glorified in His saints."
Chapter 2:1: "Now I beseech you, brethren, by the
coming of our Lord Jesus Christ, and by our gathering together unto Him, that ye be not soon shaken
in mind." Chapter 3:5: "And the Lord direct your
hearts into the love of God and patient waiting for
Christ."

I might turn you to other testimonies of His.
Titus 2:13: "Looking for the blessed hope and glori-
ous appearance of the great God, and our Savior."
Hebrews 9:28: "Unto them that look for Him shall
He appear the second time unto salvation."

We have also the testimony of the Apostle Peter.
1 Peter 5:4: "When the Chief Shepherd shall appear,
ye shall receive a crown of glory which fadeth not
away." 2 Peter 3:10: "The day of the Lord will come as
a thief in the night."

Of the Apostle John, 1 John 3:2: "When He shall appear, we shall be like Him, for we shall see Him as He is." And in the Book of Revelation frequently, such as Revelation 1:7: "Behold He cometh with clouds, and every eye shall see Him, and they also that pierced Him; and all kindred of the earth shall wail because of Him: Even so, Amen."

To conclude, we have the testimony of our Savior Himself while on earth to His disciples. Matthew 24:27: "As lightning, so shall the coming of the Son of man be." Verse 30: "They shall see the Son of man coming in the clouds of heaven." Verse 31: "and He shall send His angels with a great sound of a trumpet, to gather the elect from the four winds." Consider also Matthew 25:31–46, where His judicial proceedings are set fort. And our Savior testifies to His enemies that He would come again in Matthew 26:64: "Hereafter shall ye see the Son of man sitting at the right hand of power, coming in the clouds of heaven."

And our Savior testified by His angel to John, His beloved disciple, after His ascension into heaven that He would come again, especially in Revelation 22, where we have three promises of the same thing. Verse 7: "Behold I come quickly blessed is He that keepeth the sayings of this book." Verse 12: "Behold I come quickly, and My reward is with Me, to give every man according to His works." Verse 20: "Surely I come quickly, Amen, even so, come Lord Jesus."

If any one word in the whole book of God may be believed, this concerning Christ's second coming and appearance may be believed, of which we have such frequent and evident testimonies in the Word.

Surely as He came the first time in the flesh, according to the predictions hereof in the Old Testament, so surely will He come the second time in glory, according to the predictions of the New Testament. God can as soon cease to be God as His word concerning Christ's second coming can fail.

When the sun goes down in the evening, we believe it will return and rise at such a time in the morning and, accordingly, it comes to pass. So now, Christ the Sun of righteousness is gone into heaven; while the night of this world lasts, though we cannot know the certain time, yet we may believe that He will certainly return and come down from heaven in the morning of the resurrection. It is more possible that the sun, when it is set, should abide forever in the other part of the world, and never arise any more in our horizon, than that Christ should abide forever in heaven and not return to judge the world, when the thing is evidently revealed and frequently promised in Scripture.

2. *That the Scriptures are true is evident, because they are the Word of God, who is a God of truth and cannot lie;* who can as soon cease to be God as cease to be true. Untruth in God would argue weakness and imperfection in God, which cannot be, since to be infinitely perfect is His essential property. That God knows whether Christ shall appear to judgment, I suppose none will deny who acknowledge the Deity and, by consequence, His omniscience and prescience; especially when the futurity of things depends upon His predeterminations. And that His revelations of future things are true, I suppose, none will deny who acknowledge His being and perfection,

whence follows an impossibility of God's speaking untruths and falsehood, besides that He need not do it. But then the question will be concerning the divine authority of the Scriptures, whether they are indeed the Word of God, which if proved will evidence the certainty of Christ coming to judgment, which is there revealed and foretold.

Proof that the Scriptures are the Word of God

That the Scriptures are the Word of God will appear:

From the superscription and image of God upon them;

From the marvelous power and efficacy of them;

From the historical relations in them of prophecies fulfilled, and miracles whereby they were confirmed, and the rationally unquestionable certainty of this history as it is handed down to posterity.

From the superscription and image of God upon them. I mean in that they bear the name of the word of God; and in that they bear such evident marks and characters of divinity.

The Scriptures bear the name of the Word of God, 2 Timothy 3:16. All scripture is given by divine inspiration. We cannot rationally imagine that the all-seeing and jealous God should permit such an impious forgery and deceit to receive credit for so many generations among the most zealous worshippers of Him in the world; and by such wonderful providences preserve and maintain the Scriptures against the rage and fury of an ungodly world, who has opposed the truths therein contained, and endeavored to suppress the light which herein has shined, if so be that they had been a forgery and deceit indeed, and the fancies and inventions of men, and fathered upon Him as His Word and will, and proceeding from the inspiration of His Spirit. But it is reasonable to believe that He would have made known their falsehood unto some at least, who had the greatest love and respect unto His name and honor, and have been the most diligent inquirers after truth, and unwilling to be imposed upon with deceits, especially in such things as are of the highest concernment, which the Lord, having given no testimony against, but all along owned, and when none in the world, either worshippers of Him, or others of highest pretensions to reason, have any evidence and swaying reason to believe that the Scriptures are deceit (whatever some black mouths mutter in corners); it is not irrational for us to believe that the Scriptures are, indeed, the Word of God, which they bear the title of.

Moreover, and especially, the Scriptures appear to be of divine inspiration inasmuch as they bear such evident marks and characters of divinity beyond all other books.

The first character of divinity in the Scriptures is the clear discoveries and high praises which they give of God, and the chief design of the whole book, which is God's glory. No heathen philosopher or writer could think or speak so highly of God as the Scriptures speak. However, God has put characters upon Himself in the book of the creatures to be read of all, making known, by His works, His eternal being, His infinite power, wisdom and goodness. Yet most of the wisest men who have lived in the heathen world, and have been the greatest students of the book of the creatures, and have had no view of the book of the Scriptures, have been so gross in their conceptions of God that, as the Apostle said in Romans 1:22–23: "When they professed themselves to be wise they became fools, and changed the glory of the incorruptible God into an image made like to corruptible man, and to birds and four-footed beasts, and creeping things." They have figured to themselves, and worshipped many gods unto the dishonor of the true God. And if some of them have arrived by the light of nature unto the notion of God, yet their conceptions of Him have been low, mean, and unworthy of Him; and in no book in the world is God set forth so fully and highly in His glorious attributes and superlative excellencies as He has set forth Himself in the book of the Scriptures.

We may find in heathen writings high eulogies and panegyrics of some men and women who were famous in their time for their valor and some moral virtues, whom they deified in other ages and gave room among their feigned gods and goddesses, dedicating temples, and giving worship unto them. But in no heathen writings shall we find the praises of the true God, and rules given for the service and worship of Him alone as we shall find in the Scriptures. Large volumes some heathens have left behind them, the design of which has been their own glory, and (as much as in them lay) the eternalizing of their fame, which is an evidence that they themselves were the authors of them; because we

cannot rationally think that any motive should in-
duce others to make and put forth books in their
names that they might obtain glory for them unto
whom it does not belong. So this little volume of the
Scriptures, designing the glory of God and promot-
ing His interest in the hearts of men, and the penmen employed in the writing thereof not in the
least pretending that what they wrote was the invention of their own brain, evidences God Himself to be
the Author of this book. Wherefore, the Scriptures,
being so clear in the discoveries of the one true
God, and setting Him forth more gloriously than
any other book, and ascribing all praise and honor
to Him, and appointing all religious worship to be
given to Him only, and designing His glory
throughout the whole, gives evidence that they are
indeed the Word of God.

The second character of divinity in the Scriptures is the sublime mysteries therein revealed;
namely, concerning the Trinity of persons in one
nature and essence of God, the hypostatic union of
the two natures of God and man in one person of
Christ, the mystical union of Christ and His members, and the like. These mysteries are so sublime
and so high that no mortal man of the highest reason and most elevated understanding could possibly
invent. Inasmuch as now they are revealed, they exceed the capacity of the most enlightened to understand, especially if we further consider by whom
these mysteries were revealed. It is not by the great
scholars and subtle philosophers of the world. It is
not by those who were brought up in schools and
had conversed with books and learned men of high

parts who had polished their reason and heightened their understandings by all possible human helps. But most of the penmen of the Scripture, especially these by whom the greatest mysteries are revealed, were fishermen, publicans, and the like men of mean education—illiterate men, men of no reading, and but of mean natural abilities, as appears not only by the history, but also by the style of their writings which does not have that politeness as is to be found in many human authors, which does not run in such golden streams of eloquence, neither is it dressed with such neatness of wit, nor garnished with such flowers of rhetoric. It is not methodized by the rules of logic, nor interlarded with any peepings of human wisdom. It does not savor of high parts, and great natural ingenuity, or give the least suspicion of cunning and subtlety, which these men had above others.

But some of the highest mysteries of divinity are set forth by these penmen in a rather mean and homespun dress; yea, they are left even naked and bare of such apparel as the ingenious men of the world have clothed their matter with who have given the light of the most glorious truths and mysteries more evident discovery. Not but that some parts of the Scriptures have such a strain of divine eloquence as exceeds human writing; but the plainness of style, especially of the Apostle John in his gospel, and Matthew as well, evidences that what they delivered was not their own invention, but that they were acted upon by another Spirit in the writing of them, even by the Spirit of God, who revealed all the mysteries which they spoke of in the whole unto them.

A third character of divinity in the Scriptures is
the wisdom which appears, especially the wonderful
contrivement of God's wisdom in man's redemption
and salvation by Jesus Christ which is there made
known. No book in the world shines with such
beams of wisdom as the Word does. It teaches men
wisdom, spiritual and divine wisdom, in comparison
with which all the wisdom of the world is but fool-
ishness. It irradiates the mind with the most glorious light, and proposes to the understanding the
most noble objects. It reveals the greatest truths of
the greatest concernment; it shows the way to avoid
the most dreadful effects which sin will produce,
and to obtain the highest happiness which human
nature is capable of, which is one part of its divine
stamp. Moreover, the Scriptures set forth the infinite
wisdom of God in the wonderful contrivement of
the salvation of fallen men by His only Son the Lord
Jesus Christ, the only Savior of mankind; which wisdom, being so transcendent, evidences the contrivement thereof in the Scriptures to be from
Himself; so that as by the light of the Word we may
know what this wisdom was, even so, even by His
wisdom, we may know the Word to be the Word of
God.

To clear this argument I shall show, first, that
the way of men's salvation by Jesus Christ, which the
Scriptures reveal, must needs be the contrivement of
God's wisdom; and, second, that the revelation of
this contrivement must be from God, which I suppose will be evident demonstration of the divine authority of the Scriptures.

First, that the way of man's salvation by Jesus

Christ was the contrivement of God's wisdom will appear because it was impossible for any man of the most searching brain, and most notable invention, to have imagined it. Men being guilty of sin against the Law of God inscribed upon the hearts of all men, of which natural conscience will accuse sinners if they listen thereunto; God's justice being engaged to inflict a punishment proportionate unto the crime without a satisfaction, which right reason will say is but reasonable; and this justice of God being infinite, must in reason require an infinite satisfaction. Now what created understanding could, of itself, have contrived or conceived a way how this should be done? Everything that has a being is either God or a creature; all the creatures are finite in their beings and actions and, therefore, could not make infinite satisfaction. It is God only who is infinite, and He, being the party offended, could not make satisfaction to His own justice, especially since His justice requires punishment for satisfaction, which God as God, being impassible, is incapable of. Not to mention that anything that the same nature which committed sin should in justice suffer the punishment.

Would not reason now conclude that it was impossible for this satisfaction to be made? Surely it was none but the wisdom of God that could contrive the way of satisfaction to His justice by the incarnation of His Son, by the union of the divine nature in the second Person of the Trinity, unto the human nature in the person of Christ that, by birth of the hypostatical union, the human nature might not only be strengthened to undergo the wrath of God

which He endured before and upon the cross, but
also that, through the communication of attributes,
the sufferings of Christ might be of infinite value
because they were the sufferings of such a person as
was God, as well as man, so that they might be a full
satisfaction unto God's justice for sin, and through
God's covenant with Him, and gracious acceptance
of this satisfaction from the Surety, instead of the offenders themselves, the sins of men might be pardoned and their souls saved. Oh, the depth of the
wisdom of God! Here is the wisdom of God in a mystery! Surely they are blinded and hoodwinked by the
devil who do not acknowledge that this was the contrivement of God's wisdom.

Second, that the revelation of the contrivement
of wisdom was from God will appear in that none
could know the mind of the Lord herein unless He
Himself had discovered it. "What man," said the
Apostle, "knoweth the things of man, but the spirit
of man which is in him; even so the things of God
knoweth no man but the Spirit of God," 1 Corinthians 2:11. "And the Spirit of God searcheth all things,
even the deep things of God"; and unless the Spirit
had revealed these things, we must have remained
in our ignorance of them, since it could not have
entered into our hearts to have conceived them,
seeing that none could have discovered the deep
contrivements of God's wisdom unless God, by His
Spirit, had revealed them. And seeing these contrivements are revealed in no other book but the
book of the Scriptures, it is evident that the Scriptures must be the Word of God; which also will further appear if we consider the manner of the revela-

tion of the mystery of man's redemption and salvation by Jesus Christ, that it was revealed by pieces, and more obscurely at first, and that divers men were made use of in the discovery thereof in divers ages, who spoke hereof mostly in dark sayings; and then they spoke more clearly. Yet they themselves did not have a clear understanding of what they were moved to speak by the Holy Ghost; but searched what and what manner of time the Holy Ghost, who was in them, signified when He testified of the sufferings of Christ and the design of them; whence it is evident that they were not, neither could be, the contrivers of what they had revealed, but that the revelation was from the Spirit of God. This inspired the prophets, and was the same in all the penmen of the Holy Scriptures, whom men of insight in the Scriptures may plainly perceive to be guided and acted by the same Spirit in the revelation of the contrivement and way of man's salvation by Jesus Christ.

A fourth character of divinity in the Scriptures is the purity and holiness of them. The Scriptures are like silver and gold purified, and seven times tried in the fire, wherein no dross remains, Psalm 12:6. The Scriptures are pure and holy from the beginning of them to the end; in no history shall we find such examples of holiness as the Scriptures record. In no writings of moral philosophers shall we find such precepts of holiness as are in the Scriptures enjoined. Indeed, the light of nature has been improved by some heathens so far that they have given some excellent rules for the restraining of vice, and obtaining of moral virtues, and the ordering of their conversations in such a virtuous way that those persons who have observed these rules have been illustrious in their generations, and have shined with some kind of brightness in the dark places where they have lived. But in no book that ever issued from the brains of man shall we find such exact rules for holy living as in the book of the Scriptures. In this book, we find the moral law summarily comprehended in the Ten Commandments, which were written by God Himself on the tablets of stone when Moses was with Him on the mount; in which there are such holy precepts as no heathen author can show the like. The heathens were blind as to the duties of the first table of the law, which have a reference unto God and in observance of which man's holiness chiefly consists.

In the second table heathens had some understanding, yet they were much mistaken in some things, accounting some sin, as ambition, self-murder in some cases, and the like, to be virtues; and they did not have so deep an insight into sin. They did not apprehend the inclination of the heart, and the previous motion to the consent of the will to evil, which the Scriptures reveal to be sinful and offensive in the eyes of a pure and holy God.

Moreover, in the Scriptures, we find the holy precept of the gospel, which the heathens were strangers unto; and the way revealed not only for obtaining the pardon of sin, but also for the subduing and mortifying of sin; where means are made known not only for the restraining of a vicious nature, but also the changing of it, for the regenerating of the soul of man, and forming it after the image of the holy God in knowledge, righteousness, and true holiness; in making men partakers of the divine nature, which heathens never understood the meaning of. The Scriptures show the way of obtaining the sanctifying graces of God's Spirit, which further exceed the moral virtues of the heathens in luster than the sun exceeds the lesser stars in brightness and glory.

Marvelous are the purity and holiness of the Word, such as do not savor of anything earthly and human; yet it is such as is directly opposite to the natural bias of the hearts of all men and women in the world while they are in a state of nature. It is such as contradicts carnal affections, and against which the carnal mind has a natural enmity, and unto which all such, and none but such, have a liking and love as are regenerated by the Spirit of God. Whence it strongly follows that the Scriptures could not proceed from men, but that this holy book proceeded from the immediate inspiration of the Holy Ghost in those men who were the penmen thereof.

It will appear that the Scriptures are the Word of God from the marvelous power and efficacy of them. Such a power and spirit accompanies the preaching of the gospel which is contained in the Scriptures and evidences them to be from God alone. We read in 1 Peter 1:12 of those who preached the gospel with the Holy Ghost sent down from heaven. This has been and this is unto this day.

1. The wonderful power of the gospel in the first preaching of it evidences that it was from God, when so great a part of the world was in so short a time

subdued unto the obedience hereof; when the gospel prevailed not only among many of the Jews after Christ's ascension, and the effusion of the Holy Ghost more largely upon the apostles, so that three thousand people were converted to the faith by one sermon of the Apostle Peter, Acts 2:41, and five thousand more, Acts 4:4. But it especially prevailed among the Gentiles and heathens, and so churches of Christ were planted and brought not by carnal weapons, but by spiritual, to the subjection and obedience of the Lord Jesus.

This power will appear to have been from God if we consider:

How few men were employed in the first preaching thereof. There were not many which were read of, besides Paul and Barnabas, who preached unto the Gentiles at first. If there had been multitudes of witnesses, it might have given the more credit to the doctrine when the testimony of a few is not easily believed and received.

That these men were but of little esteem in the world; that they were Jews whom the Gentiles had an antipathy against, and so were not so ready to believe their report and entertain their messages; that their persons were contemptible in their eyes; that they were like crucified persons to the world and, therefore, unlikely to find acceptance.

That whatever human learning and wisdom any of them were endowed withal, yet they did not make use of it in their preaching; they did not come with excellency of speech and wisdom in declaring the testimony of God, but used all plainness, which was not likely of itself to produce such great effects.

That the doctrine which they preached was:

New to the world, and tended directly to pull down the old religion and superstitious worship of the heathenish gods, which they had been brought up in, and wedded unto, which could not be done by any human power.

Strange. They preached such things as were above reason and, therefore, the world might have had much show and pretense of reason to have excused themselves from yielding obedience thereunto.

Strict, severe, and contrary to natural inclination and interest. They taught the world to deny themselves, to crucify the flesh, to mortify the deeds of the body, to take up the cross, to mourn and weep for sin, to endure hardship, to forsake father and mother and wife and children, and houses and lands, if they stood in competition with Jesus Christ; to venture imprisonment, yea, to lay down their life for Christ, as many of necessity must and did, who would be Christians indeed in those days. And when the doctrine of the gospel was such, surely it was not likely of itself to receive entrance unless the power of God accompanied it.

The power of the gospel in the first preaching appears in that it met with so much opposition. The devil stirred up instruments against it; the powers of the earth were against it, as well as the powers of hell; great men opposed it; philosophers were against it; learned men opposed it; the Jews were against it and raised up persecution against the apostles; and the hearts of men naturally were against it. Surely it was none but the power of God which could cause it to prevail and conquer, and cause so many nations to bow and yield obedience thereunto.

2. The wonderful power and efficacy of the Word, where it is preached unto this day, is a strong argument that it is the Word of God.

First, note he power of the Word to search the heart and convince of sin. Hebrews 4:12: "The Word of God is quick and powerful, and sharper than a two-edged sword, piercing, even to the dividing asunder of the soul and spirit, and is a discerner of the thoughts and intents of the heart." There is a light in the Word which reveals the dark filthy corners of the heart, and convinces of secret sins; and there is a sharp edge in the Word to cut and wound. No word in the world searches and pierces like the word in the Scriptures.

And especially, the power of the Word appears in the work of conversion and regeneration which it effects. It is called the incorruptible seed by which men are born again, 1 Peter 1:23. "Of His own will He begat us by the word of truth," James 1:18. There is as great a power going along with it to break rocky hearts, to bow stubborn wills, to spiritualize carnal affections, to subdue strong lusts, to work a gracious and a thorough change in the heart of man, which exceeds the power of nature or moral persuasion, and in so much as all are not wrought upon by it which read or hear it. Yea, sometimes the more disposed subject receives no impression thereby, and the less exposed subject is effectually changed, which shows that the power proceeds from God, and that the work is effected by His Spirit and proves the divine authority of His Word.

3. The Word is powerful not only for the first working of grace, but also for the increase thereof; for the building up of believers, Acts 20:32; for the perfecting of the saints and the edifying of the body of Christ. There is milk in the Word for babes, and strong meat for strong men; wholesome words which have much spiritual nourishing virtue in them. The Word is powerful for quenching Satan's fiery darts, for repelling and drawing back the temper, for the comforting and rejoicing of distressed and disconsolate souls, when they are brought even to the brink of despair. There are no such joys in the world as those joys which Christians sometimes find in reading and applying the Word, when they mingle it with faith and have the breathing of the Spirit therewith. And there is no book in the world that can produce such powerful effects as the Scriptures do; wherefore it must follow that these Scriptures are indeed the Word of God.

The Scriptures appear to be the Word of God from the historical relations in them of prophecies fulfilled, and of miracles whereby they were confirmed, and the rationally unquestionable certainty of this history as it is handed down to posterity.

1. In the Scriptures, we have relations of prophecies and the fulfilling of them, which proves these writings to be from God alone, because He alone can certainly foretell future things. Indeed, wise men may guess, and through prudence foresee, the effects of some things and their causes, and foretell some things that are not very far off, yet not cer-

tainly, and with all their circumstances; but it is God's prerogative to foresee and to foretell such things certainly and with their circumstances, and long before the time, for which no cause in nature can be assigned, such as many of the prophecies of the Scriptures were. By this argument, God, by the prophet Isaiah, proved the heathenish gods to be no gods, because they could not foretell future events. Isaiah 41:21–23: "Produce your cause, saith the Lord, bring forth your strong reasons: let them shew us what shall happen, and declare things to come: shew the things that are to come hereafter, that we may know that ye are gods." And verse 26: "There is none that sheweth, there is none that declareth." Therefore, he concluded in verse 29: "Behold, they are all vanity, their works are nothing; their molten images are wind and confusion."

The prophecies of Scripture, as they prove the Lord, who spoke them by the prophets, to be God, so they prove the Scriptures in which they were spoken to be of divine authority. It would take up too much room in this small treatise to enumerate all the prophecies of Scripture; take two or three instances. See Genesis 15:1–14, where God foretold Abraham that his seed should be strangers in the land which was not theirs and serve them and be afflicted by them four hundred years, and that afterwards they should come forth with great substance. This prophecy is fulfilled in Exodus 12.

So also the return of the children of Israel from the Babylonian captivity, after seventy years was foretold, Jeremiah 25:12. And the same of Cyrus who should deliver them before he was born, Isaiah 45:1–

2. So also the name of Josiah, who should destroy the altar which Jeroboam had reared up, and burn the bones of the priests upon it, was foretold three hundred thirty-three years before he was born; the prophecy is in 1 Kings 13:2. The fulfilling of it is in 2 Kings 23:17. But especially the prophecies in the Scriptures concerning the Messiah are remarkable, of His birth, life, death, and the fulfilling of them in the history of the evangelists; the prophecies of the destruction of the temple and Jerusalem by Daniel, and especially by our Savior, and the fulfilling thereof, before that generation wherein our Savior lived were all in their graves.

2. In the Scriptures, we have relations of miracles whereby they were confirmed, such as the plagues of Egypt, the dividing of the sea for the Israelites to pass through, the raining of manna from heaven, the standing still and going back of the sun, the preservation of the three children in the fiery furnace, and the like in the Old Testament; especially the miracles wrought by our Savior and His disciples, which the New Testament records, such as healing the sick, the lame, blind, deaf, leprous, by a word, the feeding of many thousands with a few loaves of bread, the calming of the sea, the raising of the dead after burial, and the like; all of which exceed the power of nature. And, however wonderful things might be wrought by men in a prestidigitory way, which God may permit some to be deluded with, yet all true miracles as these were could be wrought by none without His immediate power, which He would never put forth for the confirmation of lies and deceits. Therefore we may strongly

argue from hence that the Scriptures, which have been confirmed by these miracles, are indeed the Word of God. I know the great question then will be whether ever there were such miracles wrought which the Scriptures make mention of, whether the historical relations, both of prophecies and of miracles, are not a forgery for the introduction of the worship which the Scriptures call for. Therefore:

3. I might show at large the rationally unquestionable certainty of Scripture history as handed to posterity. But, in brief, these things were so notable and remarked in their times. They were not done in corners; they were the object of sense. There were so many spectators and witnesses. There are divers records of the same things and all in the main agreeing. The way they are declared in speak so much simplicity in the relators. There were so many copies of the records dispersed into so many divers places. Enemies could not deny the truth of things recorded, only imputed them to other causes. Mention is made of these things in profane histories. We have the writings of the ancient fathers by us, who lived in all the centuries between us and the time of Christ, and with one consent acknowledge these things, who might have easily found out the deceit, had there been any; when they lived, some of them, so near to the days wherein the chief of these things were done. We cannot rationally assign an end which should move Christians to deceive themselves and posterity, since they exposed themselves to such losses, persecutions, reproaches, and afflictions, by their profession of Christianity—neither can we rationally imagine how all the Christians in

the world could meet together from so many countries, for the foregoing of things which were never done. Much less, how they should keep this secret, but their adversaries would have found it out, and made it known; some hint of it would have been given in history.

All these things being laid together, we may rationally conclude that the history of the Scriptures is certain; yea, more certain than any profane history, which we have not the least doubt of, and in the histories of prophecies fulfilled, and miracles wrought to be true. It is a strong argument that the Scriptures, which hereby are confirmed, are indeed the Word of God. These arguments for the divine authority of the Scriptures may be sufficient to stop the mouth of gainsayers, but without the testimony of the Spirit in and by them, none will be sufficient to effect a saving faith. Thus it is evident from the truth, and divine authority of the Scriptures, which so clearly reveal and foretell it, that the Lord Jesus Christ will certainly appear to judgment.

ARGUMENT 2. The second argument to prove the certainty of Christ's appearance may be drawn from the certainty of the resurrection. If all the dead shall certainly be raised at the last day, and the Lord Jesus Christ shall raise them, then the appearance of the Lord Jesus to do it is certain; but all the dead shall certainly be raised at the last day, and the Lord Jesus Christ shall raise them; therefore, the appearance of the Lord Jesus Christ is certain.

1. That all the dead which are, or shall be, brought into that state shall be raised at the last day

is a truth so clear in the Scriptures that nothing is more clear. The general resurrection of the dead is one great article of our Christian faith, one principle of the doctrine of Christ made mention of by the Apostle, Hebrews 6:1-2. The dead, small and great, shall be raised and stand before God, Revelation 20:12. We read of the resurrection of the just and unjust, Acts 24:15. I might multiply many Scriptures to prove this doctrine of the resurrection, but I shall further speak but of two places which purposely speak thereof, and being so full of argument, I shall make use of no other than there I find for the evidencing of this truth.

The first Scripture is Matthew 22:23–34:

> The same day came Sadducees to Him which say there is no resurrection, and asked Him, saying, Master, Moses said, If a man die having no children, his brother shall marry his wife, and raise up seed to his brother. Now there were with us seven brethren and the first when he had married a wife deceased, and having no issue, left his wife unto his brother; likewise the second also, and the third unto the seventh: and last of all the woman died also. Therefore, in the resurrection, whose wife shall she be of the seven? For they all had her. Jesus answered and said unto them, ye do err, not knowing the Scriptures, nor the power of God: for in the resurrection they neither marry, nor are given in marriage, but are like the angels of God in heaven. But as touching the resurrection of the dead, have ye not read that what was spoken unto you by God, saying, I am the God of Abraham, and the God of Isaac, and the God of Jacob? God is not a God of the dead, but of

the living. And when the multitude heard this,
they were astonished at His doctrine.

And in verse 34 it is said, "He put the Sadducees to silence." Here we have a disputation concerning the
doctrine of the resurrection, wherein we may take
notice of:

The opponents: they were the Sadducees who
denied the resurrection. They denied the immortality of the soul, for they said that there was no angel
nor spirit, Acts 23:8. And they denied the resurrection of the body.

The respondent: that was the Lord Jesus Christ,
the wisdom of the Father. When He was about twelve
years old, He disputed with the doctors in the temple, and filled all that heard Him with astonishment
at His understanding and answers, Luke 2:46–47.
And much more now, when He was so much increased in wisdom, He was able to deal with the
Sadducees, and answer them about this truth, of
which (He being out of the bosom of the Father,
and being acquainted with His secrets) He had so
perfect knowledge. He had answered the Herodians
before most wisely to their ensnaring question
whether it was lawful to pay tribute to Caesar; and He
was now able to give answer to the Sadducees about
the resurrection.

The objection of the Sadducees: "Master, Moses
said," etc. Their argument against the resurrection
is this: "If there were a resurrection, then there
would be a confusion in relations in so much as
seven men having been in the world married to one
woman, all of them would claim a property in her,

and to whom should she belong? Would not this breed disorder? Must not six of them with grief be deprived of her who once was their wife? And could this agree with the state of perfection and happiness in which all the just should be raised?" The Sadducees thought now they had our Savior upon the hip. They thought now it is likely that they should confound Him with this argument; that they should gravel Him, and shame Him before the people. They could not answer it themselves, and they thought that our Savior could not answer it either; and truly the objection has subtlety in it.

The answer of our Savior lies in verse 30: "In the resurrection they neither marry nor are given in marriage, but are like the angels of God in heaven." Hereby He gives them to understand that there would be no confusion in relations at the resurrection, that there would be no enjoyment or deprivation of conjugal relations there because such relations would then cease; and men and women would be like angels, who neither have such relations nor stand in need of them. The end of such relations will then cease, and the relations will cease too.

One end of the conjugal relation here is the propagation of mankind, in so much as the number is incomplete and will be incomplete till the end of the world. And the number is incomplete by generation; but in the resurrection the number of mankind will be complete. The number of the elect will be perfect and, in this regard, they will be like angels whose number was complete at the first; and, therefore, this end of marriage ceasing, the relation will cease also.

Another end of marriage is mutual help; and this end also will cease. At the resurrection, the wicked shall have no help and the righteous shall have no need of help from such relations. God will supply all and in all. God will be, instead, a Father, Mother, Husband, and Wife unto them; like angels they shall behold the face of their Father, and have no need of conjugal relations.

And in this answer to the Sadducees' objection, we may take notice of Christ's discovery of their error, and the grounds thereof; namely, their ignorance of the Scripture and the power of God, whereby our Savior suggests a strong argument to prove the doctrine of the resurrection drawn from the power of God and the Scriptures. The argument is this: if there is power in God to raise the dead, and in the Scriptures He has revealed that He will do it, then there will certainly be a resurrection of the dead; but there is power in God to raise the dead, and in the Scriptures He has revealed that He will do it.

That there is power in God to raise the dead is evident, and none which acknowledge His deity can rationally deny it. He that had power to make the world out of nothing has power to raise the dead out of their graves. He that has power to give life has power to restore it. He that has all power has this power. He who is infinite in power, who is omnipotent, unto whom nothing is difficult, can raise the dead and join soul and body together after a long separation. There is little doubt but God can raise the dead, but the great question lies in His will, whether He will or not.

Therefore, the Scriptures reveal His will herein. He that in the Scriptures has promised that He will raise the dead, being so powerful and faithful, He will certainly do it; but God has promised in the Scriptures that He will raise the dead. And though, in the Old Testament, the doctrine of the resurrection is spoken of more obscurely, yet our Savior fetches a proof of the doctrine out of the book of Moses, which the Sadducees, as it is observed, only acknowledged, Matthew 22:31–32: "As touching the resurrection of the dead, have ye not read what was said to you by God? I am the God of Abraham." God is not the God of the dead, but of the living. Our Savior proves the doctrine by strong inferences drawn from this place, which needs a little opening to perceive the argument.

It is not unlikely but our Savior cleared the thing in more words, for we have but the heads in Scripture of many things which were delivered in large discourses. Matthew made it clear that it satisfied the people, and silenced the Sadducees.

The argument formed up is this: if God is the God of Abraham, and the God of Isaac, and the God of Jacob, when they are dead, then Abraham, Isaac and Jacob will rise again from the dead, and so there shall be a resurrection from the dead; but God calls Himself the God of Abraham, and the God of Isaac, and the God of Jacob when they are dead. As they were when He spoke those words to Moses out of the bush, therefore, they shall rise from the dead. The consequence our Savior proves because He is the God of the living, and not of the dead; if that Abraham, and Isaac, and Jacob are living before

God, with regard to His purpose to raise them from the dead, because He is their God, when their bodies lie rotting in the grave, and, therefore, they may be called living when dead by Him who quickens the dead and calls these things which are not, but shall be, as though they were, Romans 4:17.

Then Abraham, Isaac, and Jacob shall be raised from the dead as certainly as if they were actually living; but they are living before God with regard to His purpose and promise to make them alive, which is evident from the nature of the covenant which He has made with them, which includes a promise of blessedness and perfect happiness which He will give unto them. If God is the God of Abraham, Isaac, and Jacob, He is their God in covenant and, by consequence, will make them perfectly happy not only with regard to their souls, but receiving them into glory when they die. But also with regard to their bodies too, by raising them from the dead at the last day, till which time their happiness is but in part and imperfect. And, therefore, from hence it may strongly be inferred that they shall be raised; and, by consequence, all in covenant shall be raised to receive the perfect happiness promised in the covenant; and by parity of reason that all out of covenant shall be raised to receive the complete punishment threatened to sinners for their sin; and by consequence that there shall be a general resurrection. Thus our Savior confirms this great doctrine of the resurrection, whereby He stops the mouths of the Sadducees. His answer made the people astonished and the Sadducees confounded. They came with their mouths open, but they went away with their mouths shut. They came with full cry, but they went away in silence. He put the Sadducees to silence.

The second Scripture to prove the resurrection is in 1 Corinthians 15. It seems that some among the Corinthians who called themselves Christians denied the resurrection. Now the scope of this chapter is to refute this dangerous error, and to prove the truth, which the Apostle does by several arguments.

1. The first argument is drawn from the resurrection of Christ. If Christ is risen from the dead, then believers, who are His members, shall be raised also. He shall not suffer His members to lie forever rotting in the grave, because His mystical body then would never be grown up into perfection, verse 20. As certainly as He was awakened out of His sleep in the grave on the third day, so certainly shall all those that die, or shall sleep in Jesus, be awakened out of their graves at the last day; but Christ is certainly risen from the dead, which the Apostle proves:

From the prediction thereof in the Scriptures; as His death was foretold, so also His resurrection was foretold in the type of Jonah's being cast out of the belly of the whale on the third day.

From the testimony of those persons to whom the Lord Jesus Christ appeared after His resurrection, namely Cephas, all the Apostles, and about five hundred brethren at once who saw Him before His ascension; and, last of all, in that He was seen by Paul himself upon the way to Damascus after His ascension, all which witnesses, with one mouth, confirmed the truth of Christ's resurrection.

From the absurdities which would follow if Christ were not risen.

The apostles would then be found false witnesses, and the Spirit of God which spoke in them would be a false spirit, which is impossible.

Then their preaching would be vain, and the whole doctrine of Christianity, which was built partly upon this foundation, would fall to the ground.

Then their faith would be in vain because, if Christ were still dead, He would not be a meet object of their faith; for then He would not be the Son of God, nor a Mediator between God and man.

Then believers would be yet in their sins. Their sins would remain unpardonable because satisfaction of God's justice would not have been complete had the bonds of death still held our Savior.

Then they which are fallen asleep in Christ would be perished, with regard to their bodies, like the beasts when they die; because, if Christ were not risen, it would be impossible that they should ever rise any more.

Then believers should have hope only in this life; because Christ was not risen and ascended into heaven to prepare room for them there. They could not have any good grounded hope of ever being received into that place; and, by consequence, it would follow that believers, the best of men upon the earth, would be the most miserable men of all others because they are exposed to so many sufferings for the sake of Jesus Christ. If they had hope only in this life, they would be most miserable with regard to sorrow, though not with regard to sin; for their

hopes of future glory support and comfort them under all their afflictions. If they should lose their
hopes, they would lose their comforts and be, of all
others, the most forlorn and sorrowful. It would
break their hearts and bring them to despair.
Certainly, then, Christ is risen and as certainly shall
the dead be raised.

2. The second argument whereby the Apostle
proves the resurrection is drawn from the parallel
between the first Adam and Christ, the second
Adam, verses 21–22. Since by man came death, by
man also shall come the resurrection; for as in
Adam all die, so in Christ shall all be made alive. By
Adam, sin came into the world, and death by sin,
and death passed upon all his posterity, because all
have sinned, at least in him. By Christ came righteousness into the world and, by righteousness, life;
and all His posterity shall be raised by Him unto
eternal life in the last day because all are partakers
of His righteousness.

3. The third argument is drawn from the reign of
Christ at the right hand of His Father until all His
enemies are put under His feet; and the last enemy
which shall be destroyed is death; and death is in no
way perfectly destroyed but by the resurrection of the
dead out of their graves, and the putting of immortality upon the body. Then, when this corruptible
shall put on incorruption, and this mortal shall put
on immortality, death shall be swallowed up in victory; therefore, since death with other enemies shall
be put under Christ's feet, it is of necessity there
should be a resurrection.

4. The fourth argument is in verse 29. Else what

shall they do who are baptized for the dead? If the dead rise not, why are they baptized for the dead? The words are difficult; of the various interpretations which are given, I like Calvin's best, if it will hold with the words. Why are they baptized? For the dead? That is, why are they that are dying, given over for dead, baptized? If the dead rise not, why will any when they are going out of the world be baptized in the name of Christ, if they do not hope for a resurrection at the last? As they are buried with Him by baptism unto death, so they should rise with Him not only unto newness of life here, but also unto everlasting life, and glory hereafter.

5. The fifth argument is drawn from the jeopardy and sufferings of Christians, which they would not undergo unless they had hopes of the resurrection.

The denial of this doctrine opens a door to licentiousness. People would eat and drink and let loose the reins to sensual delights, and commit sin with greediness if they must die and there were no hopes of a resurrection to glory and happiness, and no fears of a resurrection to torment and misery.

Besides Scripture testimony and arguments, which are the only proofs of the resurrection, I might add for illustration some emblems of the resurrection in nature.

Naturalists tell us of a Phoenix which rises out of the ashes into which she has burned herself before. But it is most certain that some birds lie in holes dead all the winter and get life again in the summer; we see plants, herbs, flowers, and the like, wither in the winter, and spring forth again when the cold weather is gone. We see the sun set at night and rise again in the morning; and we ourselves, as we have an emblem of death upon us when we are asleep, so our awaking again and rising from our bed is an emblem of our resurrection at the last day. It is certain that the dead shall be raised, which has been proved.

Second, it is certain that Christ shall raise them. "I will raise them at the last day," John 6:40. This is spoken of believers, but it is spoken also of the wicked. John 5:28–29: "The hour is coming in the which all that are in their graves shall hear His voice, and come forth: they that have done good to the resurrection of life, and they that have done evil to the resurrection of damnation."

Hence it strongly follows that, if the dead shall certainly be raised, and the Lord Jesus shall raise them, that the appearance of Christ to do it is certain.

ARGUMENT 3. The third argument to prove the certainty of Christ's second appearance may be drawn from the certainty of the last general judgment. If there will certainly be a day of general judgment, and the Lord Jesus Christ will be the Judge, then the second appearance of Christ is certain; but there will certainly be a day of judgment; and the Lord Jesus Christ will be the Judge, therefore Christ's appearance is certain.

The certainty of the last judgment is evident from Scripture, Hebrews 6:2; 2 Peter 2:9; Romans 2:5–7. And elsewhere frequently, and I shall further prove it by Scripture argument.

It appears there will be a day of judgment:

1. From God's appointment. Acts 17:31: "He hath appointed a day wherein He will judge the world in righteousness." God appointed the creation of the world which accordingly He effected; He appointed the reconciliation of the world to Himself which He brought to pass; and having appointed the judgment of the world, it shall as certainly be brought to pass in its day. Nothing can frustrate God's appointment; God, being so infinite in wisdom, does not appoint anything about which there shall be any reason to alter His determination; and God being so infinite in power, nothing can hinder the effecting of what He has determined shall be done.

2. From God's supreme and universal sovereignty. He is the blessed and great Potentate who rules over all the kingdoms of the earth. He is the King of kings and the Lord of lords, 1 Timothy 6:15. All the children of men are not only His creatures, but also His subjects. As it is the work of earthly kings to judge their subjects, and to dispense rewards and punishments; so God, being the supreme Sovereign, will judge all His subjects. Kings are but God's vice-regents; they rule under Him, and they must give an account unto Him. God will judge the judges of the earth. Men often judge unrighteously, sometimes through their own wickedness and partiality, sometimes through ignorance and false information. The righteous are condemned by some and notorious offenders are acquitted; and those who judge most righteously cannot find out all that should fall under the lash of the law; and the strictest laws of men do not reach all offenses against God. Therefore, there is need that the

sovereign Lord and King should call the whole world to another judgment which will be at the last day.

3. From God's most excellent wisdom in the management of His government over the children of men. The wisdom of God now is much out of sight and little taken notice of in the world. There seems now to be great disorder and confusion in the government of man; the most faithful subjects of the King of heaven, in most places, are trodden under foot and have many bitter cups put into their hands. And the most vile rebels and traitors against the highest Majesty are lifted up into the seat of honor and spend much of their days in mirth and jollity. We read in Scripture of the various and great afflictions of God's people, Hebrews 11:36–37. Some there were mocked, scourged, tortured, and were sawn asunder; they were slain with the sword; they wandered about in sheepskins and goatskins, being destitute, afflicted, and tormented; and yet they were such as the world was not worthy of. Whereas it is said of the wicked, Psalm 73:5, 7, 10: "Their eyes stand out with fatness, they have more than heart could wish, and waters of a full cup are wrung out unto them, and they are not in trouble like other men, neither are they plagued like other men." See also Psalm 17:14.

So that, if there were not another judgment, God would seem to have been an ill contriver of government for the welfare of His people, and to have ill consulted His own glory in the world; yea, His enemies would seem to have outwitted Him. Therefore, it is needful that there should be a day of judgment when all things should be set right and plainly appear in the view of all, and His glory be made manifest; when His people shall be exalted and His enemies debased.

4. From the infinite holiness of God. Now the holiness of God is trampled under foot by ungodly sinners; they scorn and deride it wherever they see any image or appearance thereof. They scoff at the name of a saint; they hate holiness, and many do their uttermost to banish it from the world, which is a high affront which some persons offer to the highest Majesty in His highest attribute. It is, therefore, necessary that there should be a day of judgment, that God may redeem the honor of His holiness which now lies under their contempt. Then He will make His holiness shine with an amazing excellency in the eyes of all those that despised it.

5. From God's justice and righteousness. God has given unto men a most just and righteous law, and has annexed threatenings of everlasting punishment which He will inflict upon the breakers thereof. God's justice cannot be satisfied without execution of His vengeance in the punishment of all transgressors unless it is of such who have an interest in the satisfaction which was made by the Lord Jesus Christ; and all the children of Adam are transgressors, and very few of them have an interest in Christ and His merits, and none receive condign punishment for their sins in this life. Therefore, there will be a day of the revelation of the just and righteous judgment of God, Romans 2:5. The righteousness of God engages Him not only to punish the wicked for their sins, but also to give His people

that reward which the Lord Jesus Christ has purchased and prepared for them; therefore, there must be a day for Him to do it in.

Thus it appears that there will be a day of general judgment.

That Christ will be the Judge is also evident from Scripture. Acts 17:31: "He hath appointed a day wherein He will judge the world in righteousness, by the man whom He hath ordained, whereof He hath given assurance unto all men, in that He hath raised Him from the dead." Romans 14:10: "We shall all stand before the judgment seat of Christ." And 2 Corinthians 5:10: "For we must all appear before the judgment seat of Christ, that every one may receive the things done in his body, according to that he hath done, whether it be good or bad."

And Christ's judicial proceedings are set forth at large, Matthew 25. Hence then it follows that the Lord Jesus shall certainly appear to judgment. I might add other arguments drawn from the faith, hope, and expectation of the righteous, and Christ's faithfulness, love, and the engagement of His honor to appear again; but so much concerning the certainty of Christ's second appearance.

Chapter 11

Jesus Christ Will Appear Quickly

The third thing I promised is to show that the Lord Jesus Christ will quickly appear; that is:

He will come within a short time.

He will come suddenly and unexpectedly when He does appear.

Christ will come quickly, that is, within a short time, Hebrews 10:37: "Yet a little while, and He that shall come, will come, and will not tarry." He that shall come will come; there is the certainty of His coming, and yet a little while He will come and will not tarry; there is the speediness of His coming. The Lord is at hand, Philippians 4:5. The coming of the Lord draws nigh, James 5:8. The Judge stands at the door, verse 9. The end of all things is at hand, 1 Peter 4:7. Therefore, our days are called "the last days," 2 Timothy 3:1. And upon us the ends of the world are come, 1 Corinthians 10:11. We live in the end of the world, in the last days, in the old age thereof. The world has, as it were, three ages: the youth, the middle age, and the old age. The youth of the world was from the creation to the flood; the middle age from the flood to the coming of Christ; the old age from the first coming of Christ to the second coming; the old age and last days of the world began in the Apostles' time. Now, many of

them are spent, and we are come not only to the de-
clining years, but also the decrepit age of the world;
and if the Lord Jesus Christ were to come shortly in
the days of the Apostles, much more shortly will He
come now when so many years are past since the
Scripture was written and these things foretold.

If any should doubt the certainty of Christ's appearance, because the Scripture speaks of the speediness thereof, as if Christ had been in those days
presently to come, and yet above seventeen hundred
years are past since the promise was made, I answer
that the Apostle Paul, in his first epistle to the
Thessalonians, speaks of Christ's coming as if it
might be in his time, 1 Thessalonians 4:16–17: "The
Lord Himself will descend from heaven with a
shout. And the dead in Christ shall rise first; then
we which are alive and remain shall be caught up in
the clouds." The same Apostle tells the Thessalonians in his second epistle, chapter 2:3, that the day of
the Lord should not come till there was a falling
away, and the man of sin should be revealed. And,
verse 7, that there was then a stop to the revelation
of the man of sin which was the heathenish Roman
empire, which it was not likely in haste, neither was
removed till some hundreds of years after; and,
therefore, it is evident from that place that the coming of the Lord was not to be until several ages after
the writing of the Scriptures. This may be sufficient
to give satisfaction concerning the length of time,
since the Scriptures tell us that the Lord Jesus Christ
would quickly appear.

If any profane mocker shall scoff at this answer
and say, "Where is the promise of His coming? Do

not all things remain as they were since the creation? Do not the sun and moon and stars keep their constant course? And what likelihood of the darkening of the sun, and the falling of the stars, and the passing away of the heaven with a great noise? Is not the earth established upon sure foundations, and what likelihood of moving it, and burning it with the works which are upon it? And if Christ would have come so quickly, would not He have been here before now?" I answer:

1. The Apostle Peter foretells that in the last days such scoffers should arise, 2 Peter 3:3–4.

2. All things are *not* as they were from the creation, for the world in the time of Noah was drowned with the flood, Noah only excepted, and those which were with him in the ark; surely there was a great transformation of things in that age, verse 5–6.

3. That by the same word of command whereby the old world was drowned with water, by the same word the world that now is shall be burned with fire at the day of judgment and perdition of the ungodly, verse 7.

4. Though many hundred years are past since the promise that the Lord would come quickly, yet there is not a failure with regard to God; for though the time is long in our account who are of so short continuance, and time seems tedious to us because of the miseries of our short life; yet, with regard to the eternal God, the time is but short for in His sight a thousand years are as but one day, and by that account there are not yet two days past since the promise, verse 8.

5. The reason for God's protracting this appearance of Jesus Christ to judgment is for our sakes; it is from His long-suffering toward us that hereby He might lead us unto repentance, verse 9. The Lord has a number to be called, some of which might be unborn, others not yet newborn, but scattered amongst the wicked. But when the elect are all called and persuaded to repent and believe, and are gathered unto God's family, I doubt not but the Lord Jesus Christ will be here immediately. The Lord Jesus surely now will come within a short time; the certain time of His appearance is unknown, Matthew 24:36, "But of that day and hour knoweth no man, no, not the angels, but the Father only." This is a secret which God has locked up in His own breast; it is written in the book of His decrees and, however other things are revealed and unfolded, it is sealed so that none can read it. Yet surely it cannot be long before the mystery is finished and Christ is revealed from heaven. Yet a little while and He will be here; He stands at the door, and the door will quickly be opened, and then He will make His appearance.

The Lord Jesus Christ will come quickly, that is, suddenly and unexpectedly, especially with regard to the ungodly world. "The day of the Lord will come as a snare upon all them that dwell on the face of the whole earth," Luke 21:34–35. "And sudden destruction will come upon the wicked, as pains on a woman with child," 1 Thessalonians 5:3. "The Lord will come in a moment, a twinkling of an eye," 1 Corinthians 15:52. "As lightning cometh forth from the east, and shineth unto the west, so shall the coming of the Son of man be," Matthew 24:27.

The coming of the Lord is set forth by four things

Further, this coming of the Lord Jesus is set forth in the Scripture:

1. By the coming of a thief in the night. Revelation 16:15: "Behold I come as a thief." 1 Thessalonians 5:2: "For yourselves know perfectly that the day of the Lord so cometh as a thief in the night." 2 Peter 3:10: "The day of the Lord cometh as a thief in the night, in which the heavens shall pass away with a great noise." The Lord will not come like a thief with regard to any wicked purpose and design, but He will come like a thief with regard to the suddenness and unexpectedness of His coming. Men do not think of, they do not know of, they are not aware of, they do not desire the coming of thieves. So the Lord will come at a time which men do not know of, when they do not think of it, when they are not aware of it; and He will be more unwelcome at His second appearance to the greatest part of the world than a thief who comes suddenly in the night and breaks in upon their houses to steal their goods and take away their lives. When the Lord Jesus shall suddenly unfold the doors of heaven, come down in His glory, and summon the wicked to judgment, how will they start and be affrighted out of their deep sleep of security, and be filled with horror and amazement!

2. Christ's coming is set forth by the coming of a bridegroom at midnight in the parable of the ten

virgins. Matthew 25:6: "At midnight there was a cry made, Behold the bridegroom cometh, go ye forth to meet him." The virgins were all asleep, the wise as well as the foolish; they did not expect the bridegroom at that time. The coming of Christ will be sudden and unexpected as to the particular time unto His own disciples; yet they will quickly arise and trim their lamps and receive Him with joy when the lamps of the foolish virgins, for want of oil, will go out; and they shall be shut out of the bride's chamber of heaven for ever.

3. Christ's coming is set forth by the coming of the flood upon the old world, and Noah's entering into the ark. Luke 17:26–27: "And as it was in the days of Noah, so shall it be in the days of the Son of man. They did eat, they drank, they married wives, and were given in marriage, until the day that Noah entered into the ark, and the flood came and destroyed them all." The old world was very licentious and secure in the days of Noah. Though universal ruin and destruction was so near, yet, it being a thing that was unseen, they did not expect it nor take any care to prevent it. It is said of Noah, Hebrews 11:7, that by faith, being warned of God of things not seen as yet, moved with fear, he prepared an ark to the saving of his household; by faith, he knew that the flood would come when there was no appearance of it, nor possibility, with regard to the ordinary way of the working of the second causes; he believed it because God, who could effect it and who cannot lie, had foretold it; and, therefore, he prepared, according to God's direction, this great vessel to defend himself and his family, and some living

creatures of every kind, against the waters which he foresaw were coming upon the earth. But the ungodly world, having no eyes of faith, could not discern this unseen thing.

It is most likely they heard often of it by Noah, who was a preacher of righteousness, but they did not believe; therefore they did not expect it, nor fear it, nor prepare for it. They ate and they drank; they slept and sinned as if no such thing had been coming upon them. It is likely, when they saw Noah build the ark, such a large capacious vessel on the dry land, that they scoffed at him and accounted him no better than a madman, as we should do to a man that should build a ship on the top of a mountain and expect that waters should come up hither and wash it away.

But when the days of a hundred and twenty years, which the Lord had appointed the old world to continue after His threatening of the destruction, were expired, when the decree had brought forth, and the year of God's recompense was come, and the day of His fierce anger, wherein He sent the flood upon the earth, oh, the terror and amazement which surprised the secure sinners of the world at that time! When the windows of heaven were opened from above, out of which God looked forth upon sinners with such a furious countenance, and poured forth His anger in such streams of water, and the fountains of the great depth were opened from beneath, and the flood began to arise, and lift up the head, and swell about them; when the valleys were filled with running waters and the plains were covered as if they had been a sea; when this enemy combined so many forces together (having a commission from God to destroy) and strengthened itself on every side, and environed these rebellious sinners round about and assailed them on every quarter; when not only smaller cottages were overturned, but also the streams broke in with irresistible force upon the strongest and greatest edifices; when great doors were lifted off their hinges, or broken to pieces, and the water (like a thief) climbed in at the windows and, roaring all about with a hideous noise, pursued these that fled from it, following them up stairs even to the highest room until it had overtaken them and destroyed them without mercy; think what a hurry and affright the world was in at that time! How everyone shifted for himself, if possible, to preserve himself from the fury of this conqueror! How they forsook the lower grounds and flocked together to the hill countries in great haste, leaving their substance behind them with a sad heart! How they were drenched with the rain from heaven, and wet to the skin, as they went along, and scarcely were able to take breath, the storms were so impetuous about them; when they perceived the flood to beset the highest mountains (whither some of them were fled) and upon the top of which some of them had climbed, hoping (it may be) that they had got into an inaccessible place, and that the billows were mounting towards them.

And now, the whole world sees their death and ruin to be inevitable, that there was not contending with, nor resisting, nor flying from these armed waters which God had sent to execute vengeance upon them for their sins. We may imagine something of the horrible perplexity of their minds. Oh, how they looked upon one another when such a judgment as this was come upon them, which they never looked for! How they spoke! How they wept! How they cried and shrieked! What distress was there then upon all nations! And how did their hearts fail them, and sink within them for fear, when they looked upon the flood that was come upon the earth; when they heard the winds blowing and waves roaring and saw no way of escaping!

Then they who had heard God foretell and threaten them with His judgment too late believed the truth of His words which before they did not regard. Then they who had seen Noah build the ark, and had counted him no better than mad, were convinced of their own folly and madness that they did not with him take some course for the defense of themselves at this time, when they were persuaded of Noah's wisdom above all others in the earth, and could have wished that they had imitated his wisdom in building for themselves such another ark, or that they were with him in his. And possibly some, when the waters had come and Noah was shut in by God in the ark, ran to the place and endeavored to clamber into it, only to be washed off with the stream.

Thus it will be at the second coming of the Lord Jesus Christ to judgment. His coming will be sudden and unexpected; the wicked of the earth will be eating, drinking, marrying and giving in marriage. They will be as sensual, sinful, and as secure as they are at this day. They are told frequently by the preaching of the Word that the day of judgment is appointed, and that it hastens greatly; and the Lord Jesus Christ will come, and that He will come quickly; but they want faith to believe it and, therefore, they do not expect it, nor fear it, nor prepare for it. It is said in Luke 18:8: "when the Son of man cometh, shall He find faith on the earth?"

Some interpret this place as not spoken of Christ's second personal coming to judgment, but of His coming in a way of eminent deliverance of His people from the cruelty and oppression of their enemies, which will be so strange and unexpected, because they shall be brought so low, insomuch that there will hardly be faith in any to believe a deliverance. Others interpret this place as speaking of Christ's last appearance to judgment; that the earth will then be generally secure, and that wicked men, unbelievers, and oppressors of God's people will abound, and that true believers will be rare and very hard to be found. I shall not determine which is the true sense of the place; but sure I am that the wicked will be many and very secure at the day of Christ's appearance. Though the wicked are forewarned of this day, yet they do not believe this thing than which nothing is more certain. The wicked which are mingled among God's people think it strange that they do not run with them into the same excess of riot; they look upon them as no better than fools, and people beside themselves, when they see them deny themselves, slight the pleasures, profits, and vanities of the world, and are so solicitous above all other things to prepare an ark for the saving of their souls, to get an interest in Jesus Christ, typified by the ark, that under His shelter they may be defended from the storm of God's wrath, which shall bear upon the head of the wicked at the last day. The wicked expect Christ's coming no more than the old world did the flood in the days of Noah.

But when the time which the Lord has appointed the world to continue is expired, and the angel has lifted up his hand to heaven and sworn by Him that lives forever and ever, then time shall be no longer. When the mystery of God is finished, and all the things to be done in the world are accomplished, and the day of judgment of old ordained is now come, and Christ has received His commission from His Father to summon all to His judgmentseat, oh, the dread that will, on that day, fall upon the wicked tribes of the earth! When they shall see the heaven opened above, and such a glorious Majesty with such a glorious train appear in the air; and when the earth and the grave shall be opened beneath, and all the dead bodies of all generations shall be raised and come forth, and some of them shall be caught up to meet the Lord in the clouds, and themselves with the most to be left behind; and when they feel the wrath of God begin to assail them like a flood, and to be poured into their souls like water; when they see Christ coming in flaming fire to take vengeance upon them for their sins; oh, this will be an unexpected and terrible appearance, and so much the more terrible, by how much the less expected!

Then they will not endeavor to climb up mountains, but to creep under them, to hide them from the wrath of the Lamb, but all to no purpose. No mountain will receive them, for all the mountains and the earth itself, with the heavens, will fly away from the face of the Lord Jesus Christ when His throne is set for judgment, Revelation 20:11. They will then look about them, and perceive all refuge to fail them, and no way of escaping for them; they will, with grief, remember the warning which they had of these things, and be vexed at the very heart that they did not take warning. Then they will wish for an ark, and oh, that they had an interest in Jesus Christ! And they will account believers, whom once they esteemed as fools and mad men, to have been the wisest people upon the earth. And oh, that they were in their condition! Possibly some may endeavor to clamber up into the air with them, when they are ascending to the Lord, but they will have weight sufficient to keep them down. The dread of sinners at the last day, when Christ comes so suddenly and unexpectedly, will be far greater than the dread of the old world in the days of the flood.

4. And lastly, to name no more, the suddenness and unexpectedness of Christ's coming is set forth by the raining of fire and brimstone from heaven upon Sodom, and Lot's going out of that wicked place. Luke 17:28–30: "Likewise as it was in the days of Lot, they did eat, they drank, they bought, they sold, they planted, they built. But the same day that Lot went out of Sodom, it rained fire and brimstone from heaven, and destroyed them all. Even thus shall it be in the day when the Son of man shall be revealed." The Sodomites were notoriously wicked; they were worse than beasts. They would have offered violence and assaulted the very angels which were sent to Lot; they were generally wicked; they

were not so many as ten righteous persons in the place, though righteous Lot dwelt among them. It is likely that there was not one righteous person besides what was in Lot's family; and, though they were so wicked, and the cry of their sins was gone up to heaven, and the Lord was provoked to so great displeasure by them, yet they were jovial and secure. They did not think, in the midst of their peace, that sudden destruction was so near. Abraham with his servants had not long before delivered them out of the hand of Chedorlaomer (against whom they had rebelled) and Amraphel, and the other kings which had conquered them and sacked the place. They did not think of a more furious enemy who was arming himself against them, even the King of heaven, against whom they had worse rebelled, and out of whose hand none could deliver them. They ate and they drank; they did not think that their flesh and all their provisions thereof should so soon be devoured by flames. They bought and they sold; they did little expect that both money and merchandise should be consumed so suddenly. They planted and they built; they did not in the least imagine that instead of showers of rain from heaven to water their plants to make them grow, they should have showers of fire and brimstone to burn up their plants, and burn down their houses to the ground. The Sodomites did not in the least look for such a judgment as this.

It is said in Genesis 19:14 that "Lot went out, and spake to his sons-in-law, which had married his daughters, and said, Up, get you out of this place, for the Lord will destroy this city; but he seemed as one that mocked unto his sons-in-law." His words were unto them like idle tales which they did not believe; otherwise they would not have remained in the place until they had been consumed; and, if Lot's sons-in-law, who in all likelihood were some residents of the place, did not believe nor expect the judgment, though they were forewarned by their father, much less did the rest of the Sodomites expect it, that had not before heard of it. The fire from heaven was altogether unexpected in Sodom.

"But the same day that Lot went out of Sodom, it rained fire and brimstone upon them and destroyed them all." The morning was clear when Lot went forth, and the sun shone with a glorious brightness when he got into Zoar; but then we may imagine that a strange darkness quickly filled the heavens, when the Lord came down clothed with vengeance as with a garment, and wrapped in thick clouds of the sky; when the Lord thundered in the heavens, and the Highest gave His voice, hailstones, and coals of fire; when the Lord rained fire and brimstone upon the place. Who can utter the horrible perplexity of the Sodomites on that day, under this unthought-of, unexpected, sudden, and so dreadful, unheard-of judgment? When they opened their windows and the doors of their houses in the morning, and perceived the fashion of the heavens to be altered, and the tempest of fire and brimstone to beat in upon them so sorely and suddenly; when the air was strangely converted into fire, and such scalding sulphurous matter enkindled by the breath of God fell upon them; when the whole place was put into flames together and every house was set on fire by this fire from heaven; when they saw if they went out of doors they should be burnt by the fire of heaven, if they stayed within they should be burned by the fire of their house; when there was such a dreadful burning heat by the fire, accompanied with such a stinking, noisome, suffocating smoke by the brimstone; when there was a little kind of hell in that place, both for torment and sin; oh, the dread of the Sodomites at that time! Then those beasts which would have forced themselves into Lot's doors to commit lewdness, and were struck by the angels with blindness, when they began to feel the violence of this fire, and their pampered flesh began to be roasted by these flames, how did they howl like dogs! How did they roar and yell with anguish and horror! Then all the sinners of the place, whose sins before went up with a loud cry into the ears of God, what a loud cry did they send forth out of every house, under the sense of their torments! Then the sons-in-law of Lot who were warned, I believe, were above others perplexed and filled with unspeakable vexation, that they did not hearken to the voice of their father and remove with him from that place before the fire came; then they knew he did not mock them, but was in good earnest, and that his words were not idle tales, but the truth of God's intention, which he was sent to give them notice of. Sodom is now made a fiery furnace, and all the wicked of the place are consumed together, suddenly and unexpectedly.

Even thus will it be in the day when the Son of man shall be revealed, when the Lord Jesus Christ shall come to judgment. The world is very wicked and, the longer it continues, the worse it grows; the sins of the wicked world, like the sins of Sodom, have gone up with a loud cry to God; and the Lord has exercised His patience a long time to lead them to repentance; and if there had not been some righteous persons on the earth, the day of judgment would have been long ago. If there had not been some Lots in Sodom, I mean some elect persons in their sins that are not yet called, and some as yet unborn that must be gathered, the world would ere this have been consumed for the wickedness thereof. There is a measure appointed for the world's sins which will be filled up; and there is a number appointed of chosen people which ere long will be brought in, and as soon as Lot had gone unto Zoar, God rained fire and brimstone upon Sodom. I conceive that as soon as the elect persons are gotten into Christ, then Christ will appear unto judgment. As it was in the days of Lot, so will it be in the day of Christ's appearance; the wicked of the world will be secure, eating and drinking, buying and selling, planting and building.

The day before Christ's coming will be a merry day with some ungodly sinners; they will be eating, drinking, feasting, carousing, singing, rejoicing, and putting the evil day far from them, even when it is so very near; but how will their cheer be changed the next morning! How will their singing be turned into howling! And their joy into heaviness and dreadful terror!

The day before will be a gainful day, it may be, with many in their buying and selling; possibly they may have gotten a good bargain in their buying, and gotten good profit in their selling; and it may be a busy day with others in their planting and building, which may fill their time and thoughts with worldly cares and contrivements for many years to come, little thinking that the world is not of a year, or two days standing longer. But oh, what terror will seize upon these worldlings the next morning when Christ appears to judge them! And they find that, while they have gained something in the world, which they cannot now keep, and will yield no profit in this day of wrath, they have lost their souls and happiness forever, which they cannot regain; that, while they have been busy about trifles, they have neglected the one thing necessary. Then they will wish that, instead of planting trees in their ground, they had spent their time in getting grace planted in their hearts; that, instead of building houses for their bodies, they had laid a good foundation for this time and gotten a title to the building of God, the house not made with hands, which is durable and eternal.

The day before Christ's coming will be a sinning day with all the wicked, and a day of general security. Some will be swearing and cursing; others will be oppressing and grinding the face of the poor; others will be reproaching and persecuting God's people; and the very night before, it may be, many wicked persons may get together carding, dicing, and drinking all night unto drunkenness; and others lie in their wickedness, and all will be sleeping in sin and security. But the sound of the last trumpet will startle and awaken them all.

When sinners open their eyes upon this morn-

ing and see the heavens open before them, and the
Lord Jesus Christ descend in such glory as has been
described, none can utter what their perplexity will
be at that day, and the suddenness of Christ's coming will make their horror the greater; some of
them were told of this day of fire, when the heavens
should pass away with a great noise, the elements
should melt with fervent heat, and the earth with
the works thereof should be burned up, and what
course they should take to escape the vengeance of
this day. They were persuaded to leave their sins, to
fly from the wrath to come, to hasten out of Sodom,
if they would not be consumed in its flames; to get
away and not to look back; to flee presently into
Zoar, where only they could be hid; to get into the
city of refuge, if they would escape the vengeance
which pursued them, which had them upon the
chase. They were invited into God's family, and into
the arms of His mercy; they were invited into Christ,
and to partake of grace freely. They were told again
and again that, if they went on in the way of sin, iniquity would be their ruin; that, as long as they
abided in a state of impenitence and unbelief, the
wrath of God abided on them. They were told how
sweet a Savior the Lord Jesus Christ was, and how
ready He would be to receive them, if they had ap-
plied themselves by faith, with repentance for sin,
unto Him. And they were told how furious and inexorable a Judge He would be, and what vengeance He
would take upon them at the last day, if they did not
take warning in the day of grace which was allowed
them. They were told that hellfire was very hot and
intolerable, and that heaven's pleasures were very

sweet, and most desirable, and they were earnestly entreated to flee from the former and accept the latter upon the most reasonable terms on which they were offered; but they were like Lot's sons-in-law. They did not believe.

Ministers who warned them seemed, in their eyes, as if they had mocked them; their words seemed like idle tales. Whatever haste the Lots made out of Sodom, they would not stir. They did not look after Zoar to fly unto; they hugged their sins and would not leave them. They heard of Christ, but they neglected, slighted, and refused Him. They did not apprehend such need which they had of a Savior; they were fearless of future wrath and careless of the salvation and happiness of their souls. But when Christ comes down so suddenly and unexpectedly to judge and condemn them, and shall cast them into the lake which burns with fire and brimstone, then they will remember these things with vexations far greater than those of Lot's sons-in-law (when fire and brimstone rained from heaven upon them), who would not hearken to the counsel of their father to escape it.

Chapter 12

The Application

The Lord Jesus will certainly and quickly appear.

The day is appointed by the eternal and unalterable decree of God, and He has revealed the thing, though not the time, in His Word of truth. The day approaches; it cannot be far off; time is flying away upon swift wings; the day of the world is almost spent; the shadow of its evening is stretched forth to a great length. Yet a little while and Christ will be here, He will appear in His glory; never did eye of man behold such glory and majesty in the greatest earthly potentate as will be seen in the Lord Jesus Christ on this day. All the stores, pomp, splendor, and glittering glory which some princes have been decked with in their triumphant shows are no more to be compared with the pomp and splendor of the Lord Jesus Christ in His appearance than the shining of a candle or glowworm, or a rotten stick in the night is to be compared with the shining of the sun in its noonday glory. Ere long, the great gates of heaven will lift up their heads and those everlasting doors (within which Christ, for the present, remains) will be opened; and then this King of glory will come forth and come down with marvelous splendor and brightness of majesty.

It is said in Psalm 47:5: "God is gone up with a shout, the Lord with the sound of a trumpet." Then

God "will come down with a shout, the Lord with the sound of a trumpet," 1 Thessalonians 4:16. "The chariots of the Lord are twenty thousand, even thousands of angels," Psalm 68:17. All the holy angels shall attend upon Him, and blow the trumpet before Him at His last assize, to awaken and summon the world to judgment. Then the sun in the firmament will be darkened when this most glorious Son appears; when the whole frame of heaven will shake, and the foundation of the earth will be moved, the everlasting mountains will bow, and the perpetual hills will shrink. Yea, the heavens will pass away with the great noise and, like a scroll, be rolled together, the elements will melt with fervent heat, the earth will be on fire, and every mountain and island shall flee away from before His face. Then the sea will roar and all living creatures likely will be in a strange consternation; then the wicked tribes of the earth will mourn, and the saints will rejoice at the glorious appearance of the great God and their Savior.

But who will be alive on this glorious day? Who will be the spectators of these great things? Whose eyes shall behold this blessed sight? Who shall see the Lord Jesus come in such glory? Many kings, prophets, and righteous men desired to see Christ come in the flesh and did not see Him; they desired to hear the things which He taught, but they did not obtain their desire; many generations were asleep in their graves before Christ's first appearance; the righteous saw Him afar off, and darkly in types and figures; few lived in the days when our Savior's abode was upon the earth. He had not many disciples whom He made happy with His personal acquaintance and abode with them. A great access there has been, since Christ's departure, into the church who, though they have loved Him and believed in Him, yet they never saw Him with bodily eyes.

Three things one desired to see: Christ in the flesh, Paul in the pulpit, and Rome in its glory. But past things are fled out of sight, and the wishes of such things are to no purpose. Death has closed the eyes of many millions of Christ's disciples who have heard the report of Him but never saw Him. And is not their hope of seeing Christ perished in the grave with their bodies, which are turned into rottenness and putrefaction? And are not all hastening towards these dark chambers where no beam of light shines and nothing is to be seen? The righteous indeed which remain when Christ comes down will be happy when they see the Lord in the air; but, if we die before the time, what shall we be the better?

Beloved, let me tell you, or rather believe the Word of God which tells you, that all of you will be spectators of the great things which shall come to pass at the last day. All generations of men and women that ever lived upon the face of the earth, and are sleeping in the dust, shall then be awakened and raised, and be alive together, and you shall be found alive among them. That which our Savior spoke to the chief priests and elders of the Jews, before whom He was accused and stood as a prisoner, "Hereafter shall ye see the Son of man sitting at the right hand of power, and coming in the clouds of

heaven," Matthew 26:64—the same may I say unto all
you who hear me this day. Hereafter shall you see
the Son of man coming in the clouds of heaven.
Revelation 1:7: "Behold, He cometh in the clouds,
and every eye shall see Him." These very eyes with
which you look upon me, or upon one another,
shall see the Lord Jesus Christ come in the air; these
very ears with which you hear me preach this doctrine unto you shall hear the sound of the last trumpet, and the great sound with which Christ will descend out of His Father's palace into this inferior
world. These very bodies which are standing or sitting in this place must stand before Christ's tribunal seat at the last day.

Death had a commission from God to pull you
out of your habitation and drag your bodies into its
prison; and this enemy is upon the way, and has you
all in pursuit. And how near He is come to your door
you do not know. His arrows are flying about your
ears, and you will be smitten sooner or later, either
when you are younger or older. None can escape the
stroke; your time is wasting, your glass is running
and, ere long, you will be expiring your last breath;
and these bodies which you are clothing, feeding,
and providing for every day will lie a-dying, and will
be carried by your mourning friends to your graves.
And as certain as death, so certain will your resurrection be at Christ's coming.

Christ has received a commission from God to
judge the world, and He will come down from
heaven with the keys of death and hell and open the
doors where you shall have your lodging, and bring
you forth to judgment. I must awake on that day if I

fall asleep into my grave before, and arise, and give an account of myself, and the souls committed to my charge, unto my Lord and Master; and you must awake also and give an account of yourselves and your actions unto this glorious Judge. Your lives then will be reviewed and your actions will be examined; and it will be known then what you have been doing ever since you came into the world; how you have spent your time; how you have improved the seasons and means of grace. Then it will appear who are Christ's sheep and who the goats, however they now flock together, sometimes in our company; who are wise and who are foolish virgins, however now all have lamps shining.

Then it will be known who have been wise unto salvation; who have made their peace with God in the way; who have furnished their hearts with grace, laid up their treasures in heaven, and improved their talents for their Master's use upon earth; and who have foolishly slept and sinned away the harvest and day of grace, neglecting Christ, and the things which belonged to their peace and happiness until they were hid from their eyes; who have been hypocrites and unbelievers, and served divers lusts instead of serving the Lord of life and glory. And all ungodly sinners will be found out and punished. Then all of you, yea, the whole world will believe the doctrine which we now preach concerning the vanity of the creatures, the evil of sin, the necessity of Christ, the excellency of grace, and the happiness of God's children. And oh, what will the pardon of sin, the favor of God, the least measure of grace be worth then! Our doctrine concerning these things is as true now, and the worth of Christ, grace, and salvation as great, though then men's valuation will be greater, because the worth will be more apparent.

But give me leave to apply this doctrine concerning the certainty and speediness of the coming of Christ to judgment. I shall speak to sinners, to believers, and to both.

1. To sinners: to discover them, to awaken them, and to exhort them.

For the discovery of sinners. Will the Lord Jesus Christ certainly and quickly appear to judgment? And must the whole world be summoned unto this bar? Surely then, above all things, it concerns all of you to sit down and consider how you are provided for this day. All of you will be spectators of Christ and His glory on that day; but you will not be idle spectators, as sometimes you have been of great shows in that city while it was yet standing, which have passed away; and you have gone away without much regard of the things you have seen. No, you will all be most highly concerned in this appearance of Christ, more than persons who are to be tried for their lives are concerned at the appearance of the judge who comes to pass sentence upon them. You will be tried upon that day, and your everlasting well or woe depends upon the account you shall give and the sentence which shall be pronounced upon you by the great Judge.

Therefore, let me beseech you all to examine yourselves whether you are prepared for this day of judgment. It will be a woeful day for such sinners whom the Lord Jesus will condemn into everlasting torments! And are there no such persons among you? Are there no ungodly ones gathered together into this place? Are all of you saints and children of God? If you are not such, you will wish you had been such at that time. But are you all such now? The worst of you may be such if you seriously, diligently, and timely seek such a privilege. But are you such yet? Are there not many here whom the Lord Jesus Christ will come in flaming fire to take vengeance upon? It would take up too much room to speak of all those sinners whom Christ will condemn, especially having already spoken particularly of them. But briefly, and more summarily, for the discovery of such persons, that you may examine yourselves whether you are in their number, the sinners whom Christ will condemn at His appearance may be known by certain characteristics. They are carnal, sensual, earthly, and devilish.

Christ will condemn such as are carnal. By that I mean such as are in the flesh; such as are in a state of nature, such as never were regenerated, or born again by the Word and Spirit, as never have had experience of a work of grace upon their hearts; such as are blind, and never had their eyes open to see their sin and their Savior, who are muffled up in darkness and hoodwinked with the veil of ignorance and unbelief, and upon whose eyes there are such thick scales that the glorious light of the gospel has never been discerned by them in a spiritual and saving way; such who are asleep and never had their consciences awakened out of their carnal security, whose consciences are seared as with a hot iron and permit them to sin with little check or control; such who are dead in sin, and never were quickened by the Spirit of life; such as are slaves to their lusts, and under the reigning power of sin, and never were delivered from this worse than Turkish bondage. They never were humbled and emptied of themselves, never truly repented and mourned for sin, never were powerfully drawn unto, and savingly closed with Christ Jesus. They never were renewed in their minds and hearts, transformed after the image of God, transplanted into the garden of the Lord, and engrafted into the new stock; such in whom all old things remain and are wholly carnal, in the same state in which they were first born; their persons will be condemned by the Judge, John 3:3; Matthew 13:30; Romans 8:13; 2 Corinthians 5:17; Ephesians 4:22–24; 1 Corinthians 15:50; Matthew 5:8; Hebrews 12:25; Luke 13:3; Revelation 21:27.

Christ will condemn the sensual. By that I mean all such as are so far from denying themselves, crucifying the flesh, mortifying the deeds of the body, taking up the cross, walking in the narrow way of strict obedience, striving to enter in at the strait gate, which alone can bring into eternal life and happiness, and subjugating their thoughts, will, and affections unto the government of Christ, and so living as if they were His servants indeed, whose name they bear that they labor either to imprison, banish, or hide themselves from the light of those truths which would teach them these things; to bribe or muzzle conscience, which would urge them; yea, to shake off the government of reason itself which would put a curb upon them, and to give up themselves to licentiousness, making provision for the flesh to fulfill the lusts thereof with all greediness;

such who are so far degenerated, and fallen from that primitive holiness which nature was endowed with at the first creation, that blotted out the characters of His Law engraved upon the hearts of all men, and have made themselves like beasts, yea, more vile than the beasts that perish. Such are they that are sensual and luxurious, and seek for their chief happiness in pleasing their sensual appetites, such as drunkards, and gluttons, and adulterers, who wallow in the mire of such sins, who spend their days in such pleasures, and gather as much of them as they can find without any regard to God's law which forbids them, or to those higher, sweeter pleasures which they are capable of, and might obtain, if they sought after them in the way which God had appointed; all those which fulfill the desires of the flesh are children of wrath, Ephesians 2:3. And they which please themselves, and live deliciously here, will have torment and sorrow given them by Christ at His appearance, Revelation 18:7; Luke 6:25.

Christ will condemn the earthly. They are those who lay up for themselves treasures on earth and neglect the heavenly treasure, Matthew 6:19–20; who love the world and the things in the world, and have no true love for the Father who is the God of love and the chief good of mankind, 1 John 2:15. All covetous worldlings will be condemned by Jesus Christ for their heart idolatry, Ephesians 5:5–6; especially unjust and unrighteous persons, oppressors and extortioners. Earth will be all the portion of such who make choice of it, and no room will be found for them in the kingdom of heaven, 1 Corinthians 6:9–10.

Christ will condemn the devilish. These are all such as are children of the devil, as bear his image and do his work, that yield themselves to be his slaves and servants, and endeavor to promote the interest of his kingdom; all such as are under the power of devilish pride, devilish envy, and devilish malice, who are devilish liars, devilish slanderers, and devilish persecutors of God's people. In a word, all such persons as live in a course of sin, and never break off the trade thereof by repentance, and obtain a pardon of sin through faith, and yield up themselves to the obedience of the gospel, will be condemned by Christ at His appearance.

Beloved, examine yourselves seriously hereby, and what has been before said, Are you in the number of those persons? Are any of you carnal and in a state of nature? Are any of you sensual or earthly? Are any of you are children of the devil? Are any of you are drunkards, adulterers, liars, slanderers, unjust, unrighteous and, withal, impenitent persons, unbelievers, and children of disobedience, against whom the wrath of God will be revealed when the Lord Jesus Christ shall be revealed from heaven to judgment?

For the awakening of sinners. Will the Lord Jesus Christ certainly and quickly appear to judgment? I think this doctrine should awake sleepy sinners and rouse them out of their carnal security. Does conscience accuse you and secretly tell any of you that you are in the number of those persons whom the Lord will condemn at the last day, and sentence unto hell? I think it should make you startle, and look about you; I think it should make your hair stand on end and every joint tremble; I think it should fill you with fear, and imprint such trouble upon your spirits as would dampen all your earthly comforts and delights to consider the danger which you are in by reason of sin, the guilt of which still lies upon you. Every word of this doctrine is awakening.

Awake, sinners, awake! Christ will appear to judgment; Christ will appear whom you have read of, heard of, and have had several offers of, but could never be prevailed to accept of. Christ will appear in glory, in whom you could see no beauty or desirableness; Christ will appear as a Judge whom you might have had as a Savior. Sinner, the Judge of the whole world will appear, and can you sleep under the guilt of sin? He will be a most glorious, powerful, wise, holy, righteous, strict, furious, inexorable Judge, as has been shown. And yet are you secure and fearless? You have heard God's terrible voice in the city, and that has not awakened you; and will not Christ's appearance to judgment awaken you either? You have been asleep under the sound of temporal judgment. And can you sleep under the thoughts of the last judgment, when the punishment which will then be inflicted will be eternal?

Awake, sinners, awake! Christ will certainly appear to judgment. If there were only a possibility of Christ's coming to judgment, I think it should awaken the guilty; but when there is a certainty of it, how should it awaken you! As certainly as God is true, as certainly as the Scriptures are His Word, as certainly as you are creatures and sinners, so certainly will the Lord Jesus Christ appear to judge the ungodly world for sin at the last day.

England has, of late, been under the stroke of several temporal judgments. England is in danger of further and greater calamities. God may put a more bitter cup into our hands to drink than yet we have tasted of, the danger of which should awaken secure sinners, because they cannot promise to themselves any shelter at such a time. Yet, there is a possibility that the Lord may be entreated to spare, to put up His sword and prevent our ruin which we have deserved; but the day of judgment is most certain. God, who cannot change, has decreed it; God, who cannot lie, has revealed it. The iniquities of the world, which are great, call for it; therefore, it must be that the day will certainly come; and yet can you sleep in sin? If a thief knew that, after he had robbed his neighbor, he should certainly be taken, judged, condemned, and punished, it would frighten him. You may know that Christ will certainly come to judgment, and that all guilty sinners shall be brought forth and condemned; and should not this awaken you, especially since, if you sleep on, your damnation and eternal punishment will be certain.

Awake, sinners, awake! Christ will quickly appear to judgment; the coming of the Lord draws nigh; the Judge stands at the door; the Lord will suddenly come down; when you least expect it, the Lord may be here. And can you sleep when the appearance of Christ is so sure, and so near too? Can you slumber when your judgment does not linger and your damnation does not slumber? If the day of general judgment should be protracted for some time longer until all the elect be gathered, and the things foretold in the word be fulfilled, yet your time for preparation may be almost spent; you may suddenly go down into your graves where there is no operation. And can you sleep in sin when you are liable every day to the stroke of death which will cut you off from all opportunities of making your peace with God forever, and deliver you up at the last day into the hands of the Judge under the same guilt as it found you when it first laid its arrest upon you?

Awake, sinners, awake! When Christ appears, you shall also appear; when Christ is descended from heaven, you shall be raised from the earth. You shall be awakened out of the sleep of death, and will not you be awakened out of this sleep of sin? If there were any hopes that, by getting into your graves before this day, you could hide yourselves and lie buried there forever, you might be the more secure. But when your death is not more certain than your resurrection will be, when the appearing of Christ to judgment is not more certain than your appearance on that day to be judged, you have reason to shake off sleep and think to yourselves how you are provided. Death will be terrible to you if it comes with the sting of sin in its mouth; if it shoots its poisoned arrows into you. But your resurrection will be a thousandfold more dreadful if you awake at the last day with the guilt of sin in your consciences. Sinners, think what terror will invade you when you are raised out of your graves; when you first lift up your heads and eyes to heaven and see the Lord Jesus Christ, the glorious Judge of the world, come down with millions of mighty angels clothed with vengeance like flames of fire, and look down with a furious countenance upon you; when in your rising you hear the sound of the trumpet, and such a shout given in the air as will make a louder noise than if twenty thousand great pieces of cannon were shot off together just before you; when you have a summon given you, and you are dragged with the rest of that damned crew which have lived in all the ages of the world to the tribunal seat of Christ. Oh, how will you quiver and tremble and be filled with confusion then! And yet can you sleep securely now, as if you were not at all concerned?

Awake, sinners, awake! When Christ appears, you shall be judged by Him. When the books will be opened where all your actions are recorded, then your sins (now it may be forgotten and slighted) will be called to remembrance, and your secret sins which now you are ashamed of will then be made manifest before the whole world. Your old sins will be reviewed, your old uncleanness, your old drunkenness, your old unrighteousness, and you will be made to hear all your sins, past and gone many years before, in such a manner as shall make your ears to tingle, your hearts to quake and tremble. And God's justice shall arraign you and the devil accuse you, and your conscience shall bear witness against you and the Lord Jesus Christ shall pronounce the sentence upon you: "Depart from Me, ye cursed, into everlasting fire, prepared for the devil and his angels"; and the saints (it may be) accompany Him with a loud shout: "Even so, Amen!" Or they may say with one voice, "Go, ye cursed, into everlasting fire," and so pass from you into heaven and leave the devil and

his angels to drag you into torments. And when you
see there is no remedy, no revision of your condemnation, and the devils seize upon you, tear you, and
haul you away, oh, how terrible will the judgment be
unto you! Oh, how will the terrors of the Almighty
flow in upon you! How will your consciences gnaw
and sting and torment you! How will your spirits fail
and sink within you, and your hearts melt like drops
of water! How will you weep and wail and gnash your
teeth, and cry out in the fearfulness of horror of
your spirits, "Woe, woe, woe be unto us that ever we
were born! Woe, woe, woe unto us that ever we have
sinned!"

Awake, sinners, awake! The execution of the sentence which Christ will pronounce upon you for
your sins at the last day will be in hell. And do you
know what hell is? What tongue can express the future torments which the damned shall endure!
What heart can conceive the miseries which God
has prepared for sinners in hell! Yet look into the
perspective glass of the Word and you may perceive
something of the dreadfulness of the punishment
which will be inflicted upon you if you are found in
your sins at Christ's second appearance.

Sinner, consider the greatness of the punishment. You must dwell with devouring fire and inhabit most horrible burnings; and think with yourselves how you will be able to endure to have those
bodies (unto whom the prick of a pin is so irksome,
and a little scorch of a culinary fire is so painful)
cast into the great furnace of fire which God will
kindle with His breath, which will turn them (it may
be) into a burning coal, that shall not waste neither

ever be consumed. Be sure it will torment them with a thousandfold more acute sense of pain than the body is capable now of feeling under the most exquisite torment. Think what the overwhelming grief, what the horrible anxiety, what the despairing agonies, what the hideous terror and inexpressible anguish of your souls will be under the immediate sense of God's wrath and indignation, and the thoughts of that glory and happiness of heaven, once offered unto you, but refused by you, which you will then perceive yourselves shut out of forever.

Awake, sinners, awake! Will you sleep in sin until you are awakened in the midst of flames? Will you not leave off sinning until you have sinned yourselves into hell? Must you run into those burnings? Awake! Open your eyes a little and look down, and see how deep the pit is into which you are leaping; it is a bottomless pit from whence there will be no returning. Consider how hot the fire of hell will be unto which you are hastening; it will be an inconceivably hot fire which there will be no avoiding, if you go on in that broad way of sin which is leading thereunto. Awake and look up, sinners; there is a door open. The door of mercy is open and the door of heaven is open. And will you shut your eyes and turn your backs upon God, and refuse the offers of grace which are made to you? Will you trample crowns under your feet, and slight future glory and happiness, which now is possible for you to obtain? Will not this tear your heart in hell, to remember that you have been the cause of your own ruin and brought misery upon yourselves; that you suffered yourselves to be cheated by the devil, and your own deceitful lusts, of the unspeakable joys and glory of heaven, which God once made tenders of unto you?

Sinners, consider the sureness of the punishment of hell. It is most certain that God has prepared such a punishment, and it is certain that you shall endure this punishment if you abide under the guilt, and persevere in the way of sin which you are now walking in. God has threatened this punishment, and His justice requires it, and His truth engages Him to execute His threatened wrath and inflict this deserved punishment upon you. And can you then have the least hopes to escape it? Will God, can God, prove a liar to save you from the torments of hell? Is it not equal that you should reap that which you have sown? That you should gather and taste the bitter fruits of your own evil ways? If you sow to the flesh, will not torment be the fruit thereof? If you sow sin, will not you reap hell?

Awake, sinners, awake! Are not all your hopes of happiness in the uncertain and empty cisterns of the creature mere dreams, when such dreadful miseries are so surely prepared for you? What senseless dreams then are your hopes of heaven and salvation, while you are going on in the way of sin to hell and destruction? Is there any mercy for the impenitent? Is there any pardon for unbelievers? Does God love those who are haters of Him? Shall those live with Him who have no likeness to Him? Shall they join these things together which God has never joined? This is like the senseless fancies in the sleep of strange monsters which nature never produced.

Awake, sinner! It is but an idle fancy to join heaven to the end of sinful courses. No, the footsteps of sin will certainly take hold of hell; and, without holiness, none shall see God. And, as one says, "Sooner may angels turn devils, men beasts, and beasts stones, and all the world just nothing, than that an unholy person should have entrance into heaven; yea, and it is as possible that God should cease to be God as that any man, not made after the image of God, should be received into the blessed vision, possession and fruition of Him in glory." Sinners, if there is no room for you in heaven, and your entrance there is impossible while you are in a state of nature, then your punishment in hell is sure, which I think should awaken you.

Sinners, consider the nearness of the punishment of hell; I mean, the soul punishment, which will be the greatest part of the punishment, the perfect and full punishment of body and soul, cannot be far off; but the punishment of your soul will begin as soon as your lives come to an end. No sooner will your souls be separated from your bodies but they will appear before God to receive their particular judgment; and they will be banished from His gracious and comfortable presence, filled with horror, through the impressions of God's wrath.

Awake, sinners, awake! You lie upon the brink of the pit; you are sleeping over the burning lake; you are like sailors who drop asleep upon the top of a mast, whom a great wind would blow into the sea. See the wind of death which may suddenly beat upon you; will blow you into hell, into the ocean of God's wrath. And can you secure yourselves a moment from the stroke of death? When you are most secure, may not death be most near? When you think you shall live many years to eat, drink, and take your pleasure, like the rich fool in the gospel, may not death knock at your door that night, break in upon you, fetch away your bodies to the grave, and devils drag your souls to hell?

Awake, then, before you sleep the sleep of death; awake out of your sleep in sin; think to yourselves, "This night we may be in hell and free, or rather bound in chains of darkness and horror among the damned; or tomorrow we may be in torments with Cain and Judas, with the devil and his angels." And, therefore, do not give sleep to your eyes, nor slumber to your eyelids, until you have redeemed yourselves out of the snare of the fowler, like a roe out of the hand of the hunter.

Sinners, consider the everlastingness of your punishment in hell. When your souls are once in, they shall never come forth until they are brought forth unto the last judgment at Christ's appearance; and, when soul and body are joined and sentenced to this place of torment, and thrust into it, the door will be shut upon you, and you will be locked in so that it will be impossible for you to get forth forever. Your bodies as well as your souls will be immortal and the fire of hell will be everlasting; those flames will never be quenched and your torments will never be ended. When you have been ten thousand times ten thousand millions of years in hell, it will not bear the proportion of a moment of time to the immeasurable space of eternity, in which you must be tormented for sin. Your punishment will be always in the beginning of it; never, never will it come to a conclusion, nor you to any hopes of it. As long as God lives and heaven continues, which will be forevermore, so long will hell continue and you abide in extremity of torments, without any possibility of release or deliverance.

Awake, sinners, awake! Think how horrible the thoughts of eternity in hell will be; extremity and eternity will be the great aggravation of your misery. I think the danger of such torment should fill you with such fear and terror that nothing should be able to remove until you had secured yourselves by an interest in Him who alone can deliver from the wrath to come; yet can you be secure when you are in the greatest danger?

Awake! Think whether the pleasures of sin for a season are to be compared with the eternal torments of hell, or the uncertain treasures of earth with the eternal stores of God's wrath, or the empty, vanishing, worldly honor with the exceeding and everlasting weight of misery which the damned shall sink under in hell? If any sleepy sinner begins to startle with such thunderclaps of judgment, and, being unwilling to part with their sins, they feel their hearts rise within them against the message and messengers for thrusting such harsh things into their ears, for molesting their spirits, and disturbing the peace which they have hitherto had in their sinful way, then they will say, "Cannot ministers let us alone? Will they be called to an account for us? Will they suffer for us? Why do they frighten us with peals of judgment?"

Beloved, we ministers are set as watchmen to sound the trumpet and warn you of judgment which, if we should neglect to do, your blood would be required at our hands, Ezekiel 33:1–11. And we shall be called to an account for the souls committed to our charge, Hebrews 13:17. Therefore, having notice given us by God in His Word of the coming of Christ to judge and punish the ungodly world at the last day, and knowing the terror of the Lord, how terrible the day of judgment will be unto you if you are found among the ungodly! How terrible the day will be unto us if we are found unfaithful to your souls! We warn and persuade you to flee from the wrath to come, and can you blame us then for using harsh language when we cannot omit it without danger to ourselves and your souls, when otherwise we cannot be faithful to you, nor to our Master who has sent us to declare these things?

We might indeed, like some, flatter and soothe you in a way of sin; we might speak smooth things unto you and prophesy deceits; but what advantage would it be to you to be deceived? If you were pleased with us, and commended us here, I am sure you would curse us for our unfaithfulness hereafter. Sinners, it is no cruelty, but pity and mercy to shoot the sharp arrows of God's threatenings into your consciences. It is not out of hatred, but tender love for your souls, that we endeavor to thrust the sword of the Spirit into your bosoms; that, if possible, we might wound sin to the heart and fetch forth the blood thereof, as it were, which, if it still lives in you, will be your ruin. Christ will certainly and quickly be here; and, when He appears, we shall appear to be judged. And is it not good you might know it beforehand so that you might be prepared?

Counsel and Exhortation

If any are so awakened by this doctrine concerning Christ's coming to judgment that they begin to feel a sting and wound in their spirits, and are so perplexed with fear of being condemned for their sins which their consciences accuses them of that they know not what to do, yet are willing to take any course to prevent their ruin and those dreadful miseries that they are in danger of at that day, I shall speak unto such by way of counsel and exhortation.

First, for the exhortation of sinners. Will the Lord Jesus Christ certainly and quickly appear to judgment? There are two things I would exhort sinners unto, that they may escape the wrath of God which, on that day, will be revealed and inflicted upon all the wicked of the earth. First, flee from sin. Second, flee unto Christ. Or, if you would flee from wrath and hell, repent for sin and then get an interest in Christ.

Then you may be able to stand with confidence before the Son of man at His appearance; yea, whatever your sins are now, do these things effectually, and when Christ appears, you also shall appear with Him in glory.

Sinners, repent of sin, Acts 17:30–31. God commands all men everywhere to repent; this is a duty which God required of all because He has appointed a day in which He will judge the world in righteousness. This is the argument to enforce this duty. It is your duty to repent, because you have sinned and God commands you to do it. And it is your interest and concern to repent, because God will judge the world by Jesus Christ for sin and condemn you if you are found to be impenitent sinners. You have tasted the sweetness of sin in the commission of it. Oh, labor to taste the bitterness of sin in your repentance for it. Your sins have been displeasing to a holy and jealous God, let them be displeasing to your souls; your sins have wounded the Lord Jesus Christ, let them pierce your hearts; the Spirit of God has been grieved and quenched by them, you be grieved and troubled for them. Grieve for sin not only because of its consequential evil, but also because of its intrinsic evil; not only because it is likely to damn you, but also because it has so greatly defiled you; not only because it is likely to sink you to hell among devils, but also because it has debased you and made you more vile than the beasts that perish.

Sinners, mourn for sin. "Be afflicted, mourn and weep; let your laughter be turned into mourning, and your joy into heaviness," James 4:9. Let your proud hearts be humbled and your hard hearts broken for those sins whereby you have broken God's law. Get your hearts broken *for* sin and your hearts broken *from* sin; break off your sins by repentance; cast away all your transgressions like menstruous clothes, saying, "Get you hence," Isaiah 30:22. "Let the wicked forsake his way, and the unrighteous man his thoughts, and turn unto the Lord," Isaiah 55:7. Thrust these inhabitants out of doors who have so long had possession; suffer them not to lodge any longer within you; remember that they are vipers which poison you, that they are enemies which will wound and kill you. Do not harbor sin any longer; do not entertain it with smiles and a pleasing countenance, but with tears and frowns. Get your heart set against sin; labor for a deep-rooted hatred of it and behave yourselves accordingly towards it. Get the strongholds of sin demolished in your heart, the rooms in which your lusts have scattered defilements washed with the tears of repentance and the blood of Jesus Christ. Let Christ have His throne where sin has reigned; let your thoughts and affections be brought into captivity and obedience unto Jesus Christ. Keep the door of your hearts with all diligence lest your old enemy enter again upon you; flee from sin as from a cockatrice; and, if you are pursued, manfully resist; resist even unto blood, striving against sin. Never parley with sin; hearken not to any terms of composition; be not enticed unto sin by pleasing baits, neither be affrighted to sin by frowns and threatenings. Fight the good fight of faith; then, by repentance, for sin, break off the course of sin and walk not in the ways thereof and turn by repentance unto the Lord. Let the bias of your hearts be turned unto Him; deliver up yourselves unto God, Romans 6. This is repentance.

Things To Help You Repent Of Sin

And that you may repent of sin:

1. Examine yourselves. Christ will examine you at the last day, and you must give an account unto Him. Examine yourselves, and call yourselves to an account, that you may repent and prevent the future misery which will be the consequence of sin; find out your sins that you may mourn and turn. That which the eye sees not, the heart will not, cannot, be

affected with; consult the register of your conscience; turn over the leaves and read what is recorded in that book. Open your hearts to the beams of the light of the Word and be ready to receive the convictions of the Spirit. Find out your sins, your original sin, the defilement of your natures, your actual sin, your great conscience-wounding sins; find out your bosom-sins which your hearts are most nearly joined unto, and are most loath to part with; find out your constitutional, your calling sins, the sins that bear the greatest sway, and are most supported by the interest of the flesh, and your hearts are ready to cloak and cover under the veil of excuses and plausible pleas. Think how you will be able to answer for them at the great day to the heart-searching Judge.

Sinners, find out your sins; otherwise, your sins will find you out, and Christ will find you out, and wrath will find you out, and then woe unto you.

2. Judge and condemn yourselves for your sins. This is the way to escape the judgment of God, 1 Corinthians 11:31. If you judge others, you shall be judged, Matthew 7:1. But, if you judge yourselves, you shall escape; and therefore:

3. Make confession of sin. Spread the black catalogue of your sins before the Lord. Come with ropes about your neck, tears in your eyes, and sorrow in your hearts unto the throne of grace; fill your mouths with humble acknowledgments of your sins; rip up your hearts before the Lord; open before Him your sores; stand not in your own defense and justification, but fall down prostrate at God's feet and confess what sinful natures you have. What vile

hearts, what wicked lives you have led! Confess how you have broken His laws and disobeyed His gospel; charge upon yourselves the guilt of your particular and most heinous sins, and do not extenuate, but aggravate them with all the circumstances you can think of; look upon yourselves as cursed wretches while under the guilt of sin; as miserable, lost, forlorn creatures while God is your enemy and His wrath abides on you. Acknowledge your sins, and the demerit of your sins, that you have not only deserved temporal plagues, but also eternal torments; that you forfeited all outward mercy, and are unworthy of the least grace and favor, much more unworthy of eternal life. Lie very low before God; lick the dust; look upon yourselves as worms, as toads; yea, as more vile and more full of poison.

4. If, under the view of sin and confession thereof, you find your hearts hard and senseless like rocks, or adamant-stones within your hearts, yet be not discouraged. The sense of hardness is some beginning of softness, but do not rest in beginnings; take pains with them to get them melted thoroughly, to get them broken to pieces. Read, consider, apply, and urge at the throne of grace the gracious promise of Ezekiel 36:26: "I will take away the stony heart out of your flesh, and will give you a heart of flesh." Be sensible of your own inability to repent of sin, and be persuaded that it is God's grace. Remember that it is free, but that it is promised; beg the influence of His Spirit upon your hearts to melt them; beg the application of the blood of Christ to mollify them. The blood of the goat only can crack an adamant-stone, and it is the

blood of Christ, the scapegoat, which alone can break the hard heart of sinners.

To Help With Discouragement In Repenting

If any are discouraged with the difficulty of repentance, that it is hard to obtain and a very grievous thing to endure, let them:

1. Consider that repentance is necessary. It is necessary by virtue of God's precept. It is a necessary duty, Acts 17:30. God commands not only some men, but all men; not only in some place, but everywhere, to repent. And it is necessary, *virtute medii*, as it is a means to avoid misery and obtain happiness. You must sow in tears if you would reap in joy; and you must go forth weeping, bearing precious seed, if you would return again rejoicing, bearing your sheaves with you, Psalm 126:5–6. The showers of tears make way for the sunshine of comfort here and the harvest of everlasting glory and joy. And, if repentance is difficult, yet, since it is absolutely necessary, this should be so far from discouraging you that it should quicken you unto more diligent endeavors after it.

2. Consider that repentance is attainable. The vilest sinners may be enabled, through God's grace, to repent as well as the most holy saint at their first turning unto God. It is difficult for you, yea, impossible for you to repent of yourselves, because there are not seeds of this grace in nature; but it is easy with God to work you to it, and He can carry you through the difficulty. Pray to God for this grace and endeavor to repent; and, in your endeavors, God may

assist. God is easy to be entreated, and is ready to give His grace unto them that desire it; but some are discouraged by Hebrews 12:17, where it is said that "Esau was rejected, and found no place for repentance, though he sought it carefully with tears." Hence they conclude that, though they seek repentance carefully with tears, they may be rejected and find no place for repentance.

I answer, first, that this place which speaks of Esau's rejections does not have a reference to this rejection by God (though that may be included in it), but his rejection by his father Isaac in reference to the blessing which his younger brother Jacob had by a wile got before him. Second, that Esau there did not seek God for repentance, but he sought his father for his blessing. Third, that he did not seek repentance for himself, but he besought his father with tears that he would repent his giving the blessing to Jacob, and give it unto him. Such as with tears seek repentance of God, it is a sign they have some measure of this grace.

3. Consider the worth and excellency of this grace; though it is difficult, yet it is excellent. The best things are not obtained without difficulty; had you this grace, you would not be without it for a world; you would not change your tears and sorrow for sin for all the sweetness and pleasure that others find in the commission of it. If you truly repented, you would not think it so grievous a thing to be borne; but, the more you had of it, the more you would desire, and be best pleased when you could act upon this grace most strongly.

4. Consider that the greatest difficulty is at first.

Flesh may contradict and violently oppose the beginning of repentance, and manifestly seek its ruin and destruction; but, after you are accustomed to the yoke, you will find it more easy. After you have gotten mastery over your flesh, and have attained some degrees of mortification, you will find it suitable to the new man to live in the exercise of repentance and reap much sweetness from it.

5. Consider that you must repent and mourn for sin here or you will be damned and burned for sin forever. You cannot avoid grief for sin; if you have it not in this world, you will be sure to have it in the other world. And is it not a thousandfold more eligible to grieve for sin here? Especially considering:

If you repent of sin now, your grief will not be in extremity; it will have some allay, some alleviation, some mixture of secret comfort; at least something will be given to support you when you are even ready to be overwhelmed. When the heart is most broken and contrite under the sense of sin and apprehensions of God's wrath, God will not suffer the spirit to fail before Him, Isaiah 57:15–16. The Lord will keep the soul from sinking, and I am confident that such persons as are most heavy laden with grief for sin would not change their condition, when at the lowest ebb, with the most prosperous worldlings; but if you repent not till hereafter your grief will be extreme, without the least mixture of comfort or support. In hell you will have nothing but weeping, wailing, and gnashing of teeth. You will be utterly consumed with terrors, overwhelmed with sorrows, and always sinking in the bottomless pit under the weight of grief which will be insupportable.

Your repentance of sin now will be pleasing unto God. We read in Luke 15 how well-pleased the father was when his prodigal son was returned home and, with grief, acknowledged that he had sinned against heaven and against him, and was not worthy to be called his son. The father met him in the way, kissed him, clothed him with the best robe, killed the fatted calf for him, and made merry with him. So, though you have been prodigals hitherto, have gone astray from God, and wasted your time and talents in the service of the devil and your own lusts, yet if at length you come to yourselves and with repentance and humble confession of your sins return unto the Lord, He will pity you. His compassion will yearn towards you while you are yet upon the way; and He will meet you, embrace you, clothe you with the robes of His Son's righteousness, and be pleased with you, and rejoice over you.

Yea, and the angels also will rejoice in your conversion. There will be joy in heaven at your repentance among the angels, and joy on earth among the saints. Ministers will be pleased and rejoice; they will pity you and pray for you; and saints will be pleased and be ready to help and advise you. But God's pity is beyond all. See how God is taken with repenting Ephraim in Jeremiah 31:18–20: "I have surely heard Ephraim bemoaning himself: 'Surely after I was turned, I repented. And after I was instructed, I smote upon my thigh. I was ashamed, yea, even confounded, because I did bear the reproach of my youth.' " Here you have described Ephraim's repentance, and the sweet words of tender love which the Lord expresses Himself in towards

Ephraim under his repentings! "Is Ephraim My dear son? Is he a pleasant child? For since I spake against him, I do earnestly remember him still: therefore My bowels are troubled for him. I will surely have mercy upon him, saith the Lord."

But if you do not repent till hereafter, your grief will not only be extreme, but also you will have none to pity you. God will not pity you in the least, but will laugh at your calamity; His compassion will be shut against you; your grief will not then be pleasing in the least, and your cries and complaints of sin then will be like the howling of a dog in His ears. He will then, instead of meeting you to embrace you, meet you to destroy you; instead of speaking kindly to you, He will speak to you in His wrath, and vex you in His hot displeasure. Angels and saints will then turn away from you and devils will draw you with them into torments.

If you repent of sin now, you may obtain the pardon of sin. "I will surely have mercy upon him, saith the Lord," concerning repenting Ephraim, Jeremiah 31:20. He that confesses his sins, that is, with repentance, so as not only to grieve for them, but also to leave and forsake them, shall find mercy, Proverbs 28:13. Yea, God has promised abundantly to pardon such as forsake their evil ways and, by repentance, turn to Him, Isaiah 55:7. And if sinners cease to do evil and learn to do well, and their sins be as scarlet, they shall be as white as snow; though they are red like crimson, they shall be as wool, Isaiah 1:16–18. And not only His mercy, but also His justice and faithfulness are engaged to pardon such as acknowledge their sins with repentance, and apply themselves to Him by faith. 1 John 1:9: "If we confess our sins, He is faithful and just to forgive us our sins, and to cleanse us from all unrighteousness."

The door of mercy is now open to all true penitents, and the golden scepter of grace and reconciliation is held forth unto them. The Lord Jesus Christ is now interceding at the right hand of God, ready to make their peace with God; but, if you do not repent until hereafter, a pardon will be unattainable; there will remain no sacrifice for sin. Then the day of grace will be quite spent and the door of mercy will be fast shut. Then Jesus Christ will have finished His interceding work, and then it will be impossible to obtain remission.

If you repent of sin now, you may get strength against sin; you shall be delivered from the reigning power of sin presently; you shall be freed from the rage and tyranny of sin by degrees, and at the last you shall obtain a perfect freedom from the being of sin and be wholly delivered from the bondage of corruption. But if you do not repent until hereafter, you will forever abide under the power of sin; you will not only be tormented in hell, but also be forever sinning in hell.

If you repent of sin now, you will escape the punishment of sin. I do not speak of some temporal calamities which God may exercise His people withal in this world; but you shall assuredly be kept from the eternal punishment of hell, which shall be inflicted upon the ungodly world. But, if you do not repent of sin until hereafter, your punishment will be unavoidable; no cries nor tears will then save you from the torments of hell, which you will be con-

demned unto. Now you are condemned for sin while
unbelievers, but in this world the sentence is re-
versible; you may flee from the bar of justice to the
throne of grace and if, with repentance and faith,
you apply yourselves to Jesus Christ, He will deliver
you from the wrath to come, and free you from condemnation. But hereafter, when the Lord Jesus
Christ shall appear unto judgment, and summon
you, examine you, find you guilty, and pass sentence
upon you to depart into everlasting fire, this sentence will be irreversible, and your repentance will
be too late to procure freedom from, or the least
mitigation of your punishment.

If you repent of sin now, your grief will be but for
a time, for a season, a short time, a few days, a night,
a moment, a short moment, 1 Peter 1:6; Revelation
2:10; Psalm 30:5; Isaiah 54:6–7. Weeping may endure
for a night, but joy comes in the morning. God will
not permit you to weep and grieve for sin long. It is
not a life of grief which He calls you unto, but a life
of faith and love; it is not grief for itself which He
requires, but in order to comfort; and, therefore, it
shall not be of long continuance. Your grief for sin
makes way for spiritual comfort, for the joys of the
Holy Ghost which, after sorrowing times, the Lord
often gives abundantly unto His children in this
world, in which they find incomparably more sweetness than ever they could find sweetness in sin or
bitterness in sorrow. They have pleasures of a higher
and more transcendent nature. Be sure, your grief
for sin will make way for your everlasting joy in
heaven, where all tears shall be wiped away from
your eyes, all sorrow and sighing shall be removed

from your hearts, and you shall obtain gladness unspeakable and everlasting. But, if you do not repent
until hereafter, as the pleasures which you found in
sin will be but for a season, and your triumphing
will be but short, death, be sure, will put a conclusion unto all. So your grief for sin then will be long;
the days of darkness and sorrow will be many; yea,
your grief will be eternal.

Repent then, sinners, repent. Christ will come
certainly to judgment; therefore, repent truly. Christ
will come quickly to judgment; therefore, repent
speedily. Protract not the time; endeavor presently
without any further delay, considering:

Your particular judgment may be sudden, and
the time of your preparation may be spent quickly.
You may be within a few months, weeks, or days, yea,
it may be, within a few hours, smitten by death's arrows and there will be no place for repentance and
preparation in the other world.

If you defer your repentance, it is a thousand to
one that you will never repent as long as you live, if
your life should continue many years; because not
one in a thousand that defer their repentance afterwards repent. There are millions in hell who lived
under the light of the gospel, who intended to repent, but were prevented by death before they were
aware. And it is a thousand to one, if you defer it any
longer, ere long you will be received into their
number. Have not you deferred your repentance before this till such and such a time? And yet, when
such times have come again and again, have not you
deferred it still? And will not your deceitful hearts
still find as plausible excuses till it is too late?

Remember this, sinners, that it is a thousand to one but you will be damned if you any longer defer your repentance.

The longer you defer your repentance, the more difficult you will find the work to be, because you will be the faster bound in Satan's chains, and not so easily loosed; because you will be the faster asleep in sin and not so easily awakened; because your hearts will grow the harder by the longer practice of sin and not so easily broken; because your sins will be the more increased which you must repent of; because your time will be the more decreased which you are to repent in; so that, if it should come to pass (which is a thousand to one) that you should repent after procrastination or deferring repentance, yet you will find the work to be very difficult.

Think what glory you may bring to God, what service you may do, if you repent and reform presently; all which time, while you defer repentance, is spent in the service of the devil and your own lusts unto the dishonor of God.

Think what measures of grace and comfort you may attain here, and what degrees of glory you may attain hereafter, if you repent without delay which, by deferring the work, you are likely to lose.

If you defer repentance, it is a question whether your late repentance will be true; and, if it should be true, it is a question whether ever you shall obtain the evidence of the truth thereof.

And lastly, if you defer your repentance, God may never call you to repentance; yea, He may give you up to judiciary hardness and seal you up unto condemnation, swearing in His wrath that you shall never enter into His rest.

Thus much for the exhortation of sinners to repentance.

Sinners, will the Lord Jesus Christ certainly and quickly appear to judgment? Be persuaded, then, to flee to Him, and get an interest in Him before His appearance. I am sure there are none of you but would be glad of an interest in Christ when He comes in His glory to judge the world. The vilest persons upon the earth, those who despise and reject Christ now, those who hate and scorn the ways of godliness as being too mean a way for their high spirits, would give ten thousand worlds, if they had them, for the room of the meanest believers who have an interest in Christ at that day. But let me tell you, sinners, that this world is the only place, and this time, while the day of grace lasts, is the only time for obtaining such a privilege as this is. If you do not have an interest in Christ while you live, it will be impossible to obtain it after death or at the resurrection; if you are none of Christ's now, He will not know you, nor own you, at the day of His glorious appearance.

Get an interest in Christ as your high Priest and Advocate; be sensible of your sins; be assured of His death for sin and satisfaction to God's justice; be persuaded of His intercession at the right hand of God, and that He is able and willing to save you. Apply yourselves to Him that, through Him, you may obtain remission of sins and an inheritance among the saints; and if, through the mediation of Christ now, you obtain a pardon of all your sins here, how welcome will your Redeemer be unto you, and with what joy will you lift your heads out of your graves when the day of your redemption and perfect salvation is come, and your Savior appears to take vengeance upon unpardoned sinners, but shall own and acquit you before the whole world!

Get Christ to be your Master. Enter yourselves among His servants and disciples; submit to His teaching; learn His lessons; believe and obey His commands; follow His example; promote His honor and interest in the world; be ready to do or suffer anything for Him; and, when our Lord and Master comes in His glory, you will find that it was not in vain to serve Him, though in ways harsh and grating to flesh and blood. Oh, what a reward will He give then to His servants! What a crown of glory will He put upon their heads! It is a sweet, encouraging promise which Christ has made now, and will make good to all His faithful servants at that day. John 12:26: "If any man serve Me, let him follow Me; and where I am, there shall also My servant be: if any man serve Me, him will My Father honor."

Get Christ to be your Husband. Sinners, we ministers are sent to invite and woo you to enter into this most near and sweet relation unto Jesus Christ. We are to tell you of the beauty and excellency of His person, of His love and tender affection to poor sinners, of His willingness to be yours, and to make you sharers in His riches. Oh, accept Christ to be your Husband; lay off your filthy garments and put on the white robes of His righteousness; join your hearts to Him; divorce yourselves from sin and dedicate yourselves unto Christ alone; and, if Christ is your Husband, oh, how joyful will His appearance be to you when you shall see His glorious face and sweet smiles, and are received into His embraces, and are carried by Him into His Father's house, where you shall live with, and delight in, His love forevermore.

Get Christ to be your Captain. List yourselves under His banner; wear His colors; arm yourselves with His weapons; follow His conduct; fight against His enemies; endure hardness as good soldiers, and do not shrink when you are put upon the trial; and, if you have an interest in this Captain and are victorious here over your spiritual enemies, when your Captain rides in triumph at the last day, you shall be caught up into the clouds, triumph with Him, and receive a crown of glory from Him which does not fade away.

Sinners, get an interest in Christ, in all His offices, in all His relations. It is He only who can save you from sin, wrath, and eternal death. It would be too large a subject here to treat of salvation by Christ and the way of attaining it. I may (God giving leave) hereafter treat purposely on some words whereby we may be saved from Acts 11:14: "He shall tell thee words, whereby thou and all thy house shall be saved," which I thought to have added to the end of this, with some words of advice to young men, from 1 John 2:14: "I have written unto ye young men, because ye are strong, and the word of God abideth in you, and ye have overcome the wicked one." All which I indeed, at first, intended to have joined together in one small volume with *God's Terrible Voice in the City*,* but thoughts have so multiplied in

---

* Scheduled for release by Soli Deo Gloria in 1997-98.

putting them into writing that I am even forced to separate them into three parts, which I thought at first the room of one would hold.

Chapter 13

A Word to Believers

Having spoken to sinners, I come now to speak to believers, and that in two words:
For the trial of them; and
For the comforting of them.

For the trial of believers. The doctrine of Christ's certain and sudden appearance to judgment is a most dreadful doctrine to sinners which are in sin. But it is a most comfortable doctrine to believers who are in Christ. But because many sinners who are still held fast in the bond of iniquity and are under the reigning power of some sins are apt to mistake, and without good ground persuade themselves that they are believers, who at the last day will be found to be hypocrites, and through their mistake of their state ward off those strokes of God's threatenings which are made at them and save themselves hereby from those terrible apprehensions of Christ's appearance to judge and condemn them, which if they entertained might be a means to startle and awaken them to take an effectual and speedy course for the salvation of themselves from the future vengeance; and because many true believers who are really united unto Christ by faith are apt also, through the temptation of Satan and their own ignorance and doubting, misgiving heart, to mistake themselves and look upon themselves to be hypocrites and, therefore, fear that when Christ appears that they shall be condemned by Him, being so ready to condemn themselves and, therefore, gather matter for trouble from this doctrine, which indeed is matter of the greatest comfort; therefore, it will be needful for the undeceiving of the former, that they may not falsely apply comfort, and the rectifying of the mistakes of the latter, that they may not put off comfort, to make some trials of true believers. It would be too large to present to you all the characteristics which we may find in the Word of God of true believers; therefore, I shall make mention but of one which the text holds forth, and is the second doctrine observed from the words in the beginning of our discourse.

DOCTRINE 2. There is an earnest desire in the church, or true believers, after the second appearance of the Lord Jesus Christ.

You may try yourselves whether you are true believers by your desires after Christ's appearance. This is the characteristic which the Apostle Paul gives of believers: they are such as love and, by consequence, desire the appearance of the Lord Jesus Christ. 2 Timothy 4:8: "Henceforth there is laid up for me a crown of righteousness, which the Lord the righteous Judge shall give me at that day; and not unto me only, but unto all them also that love His appearance." All such, and none but such, shall have a crown of righteousness who love Christ's appearing. Believers are said to look for Christ's coming. Hebrews 9:28: "Unto them that look for Him shall He appear the second time, without sin unto salvation." He will appear unto all, but only to them that look for Him will He appear unto salvation. Believers look for Christ's appearance with an eye of faith, hope, and desire.

Believers look for Christ's appearance with an eye of faith; they expect it as sure as death, yea, as more sure, because the death of some will be prevented by it. It is not impossible that the Lord Jesus will come in our days. They surely believe that the Lord will come.

Believers look for the appearance of Christ with an eye of hope. Titus 2:13: "Looking for that blessed hope, and the glorious appearance of the great God, and our Savior." As they have hopes of the glory of heaven, so they have hopes of the coming of Christ who will receive them into glory, who will put the crown upon their heads, and bring them with triumph into the new Jerusalem.

Believers look for the appearance of Christ with an eye of love and desire. They love and long for His appearance; they look with many a glance of love towards the place above where their Lord is, and they have many a longing wish that He would come forth, come down, and receive them unto Himself that, where He is, there they might be also. The bride said, "Come," and the desire of the spouse is, "Make haste, my beloved, and be as a roe upon the mountains of spices," Song of Solomon 8:14. Believers pray "Thy kingdom come" in the Lord's Prayer which He taught to His disciples. They desire the coming not only of the kingdom of grace, but also of the kingdom of glory. In Revelation 22:16 the church breathes forth this desire after Christ's appearance: "Amen, even so, come Lord Jesus."

Now examine yourselves, whether you are true believers, by this characteristic: do you love and desire Christ's appearance?

OBJECTION. If any object against themselves and say, "Alas! We fear then that we are not true believers because we cannot say that we love and desire Christ's appearance. We are so far from desiring it that we are afraid of it, and it is matter of the greatest trouble to think of it":

ANSWER 1. Many go under the name of believers who have only the name; take heed that none of you be found in the number of such at the last day.

ANSWER 2. Possibly, some of you may condemn yourselves without reason, as God's children are more forward to do than hypocrites who have the most reason. It may be that you do not desire that Christ should come immediately; but do you not desire that Christ should come at all? A wife may sincerely and greatly desire the coming home of her husband when he is gone on a long journey, and yet, if her house is out of order, and not fitted to her mind for the receiving of him, if she is not dressed and got into such a garb as she knows would be pleasing to him, she may be content that he would stay a little longer until she is better prepared. Yea, she may be afraid of his coming while she is unprepared. The harlot or adulteress could be content that her husband should never return, but the true wife desires the coming of her husband though, sometimes, not the immediate coming. So true believers desire Christ's coming, who is gone on a long journey to heaven, though they may not desire

His immediate coming because they are not as fitted as they desire to be for the receiving of Him. They desire His coming; they would not desire for all the world that He would stay away forever in heaven. Unbelievers could be content that Christ should stay away forever, and that they might live forever upon the earth; but believers could not be content. They may fear Christ's immediate coming because of their unpreparedness, but they desire His coming.

QUESTION. How should we know whether our desires after Christ's coming are sincere?

ANSWER 1. If you love Christ's person, it is a sign your desires after His coming are sincere. We desire the coming of friends to us whom we love. Do you love Christ in sincerity? Do you love Him for Himself, for His own excellencies, His loveliness, His love, and spiritual love tokens? Do you love Him upon a spiritual account?

ANSWER 2. If you sincerely desire the coming of Christ into your hearts, with regard to His Spirit and grace, it is a sign you have sincere desires after His coming in glory, when grace will arrive at its perfection. Can you understandingly and heartily pray, "Thy kingdom come"? I mean, that Christ's kingdom of grace should be erected in your hearts. And are you sincerely desirous to have all things within you brought into subjection and obedience thereunto? Do you sincerely and earnestly desire the presence of Christ, and the breathings of His Spirit, upon your hearts in His ordinances? It is a sign that there are at least true radical desires in you after His second appearance, though by reason of doubts and fears they may not be so express.

ANSWER 3. If you have laid up your treasure in heaven, and placed your happiness in things above; if you have cast the anchor of your hope upwards into that which is within the veil, it is a sign you have true desires after Christ's appearance, that He might give you possession of the happiness which you have made choice of.

ANSWER 4. If you are careful to please the Lord and, whether present or absent, to be accepted of Him, and are afraid of sin because it is grievous to Him, and are diligent in the use of means to fit and prepare yourselves and make all things ready for the receiving of Him, it is a sign you both look for His coming and desire it.

ANSWER 5. And lastly, if you have lively hopes of His coming, and can rejoice in these hopes; if you can with earnestness pray, "Come, Lord Jesus Christ; come quickly," this is a sign indeed of your desires, though all true believers have not attained to so great a height.

Unbelievers do not desire Christ's appearance, because they do not believe in Him, because they do not love Him, because their hearts are set upon the world, because they are under the guilt and power of sin, and because, when Christ appears, He will judge them, condemn them, and punish them; but though they do not desire Christ's coming, nor think of it, nor prepare for it, yet Christ will come, and His coming will be dreadful unto them.

Believers desire Christ's coming; they are looking for it and waiting for it; they are hoping for it and preparing for it, and He will certainly, He will quickly appear, and they shall appear with Him in glory; and His appearance will be a most comfortable and joyful appearance unto them, which leads unto the second word which I am to speak.

For the comforting of believers. Will the Lord Jesus Christ certainly and quickly appear to judgment? Then there is a full breast of the sweetest consolation at which you may stick and be satisfied and exceedingly refreshed; as every word in this doctrine speaks terror to sinners, so every word breathes forth comfort to true believers; and, therefore, I shall endeavor hence to work up your hearts unto spiritual joy.

1. Rejoice, believers, rejoice! Christ will appear to judgment. Christ will appear in His glory; the great God and our Savior will appear. He that is your Savior and Advocate will then be the Judge of the world; your Lord and King will appear attended with a glorious train of heavenly courtiers, decked with glorious beams of most excellent Majesty. Your Captain will appear, the Captain of your salvation, with the spoils of His and your enemies, and He will ride triumphantly in the clouds; your dearly beloved Friend and Husband will appear with such beauty and loveliness in His face, and with such dear love towards you in His heart, as has not entered into your hearts to conceive. The Lord Jesus Christ will be glorious in the eye of the whole world on that day, and should not this rejoice your hearts to think of the glory of your Lord, which will be then so conspicuous, and of your interest in such a person?

2. Rejoice, believers, rejoice! Christ will certainly

appear. If there were any ground to doubt the truth of this thing, you would have reason to grieve; but when the thing is so certain, when God has revealed it in His Word so clearly, when the Lord has promised it to His people so faithfully, and given His people hopes and expectations of it, He will not disappoint them. You have reason to rejoice. There is nothing more certain, as has been proved, than the second appearance of our Lord Jesus Christ at the last day.

3. Rejoice, believers, rejoice! Christ will quickly appear; the coming of the Lord draws nigh. There is a time set, though you cannot know it, because God has locked up this secret in His own bosom; yet you may know that it cannot be far off. The Lord will not tarry much longer in heaven before He comes down to judgment. Look up, then, and lift up your heads with joy, for the day of your redemption draws nigh, Luke 21:28. You will not long groan under the bondage and burden of corruption; you will not long mourn and complain under the persecutions of cruel enemies; you will not long be assaulted and buffeted with the temptations of Satan; you will not long live in the dark prison of the world. Christ will quickly be here and open the prison doors and deliver you into the glorious liberty of the children of God.

4. Rejoice, believers, rejoice! When Christ appears, you shall also appear. Possibly some of you may remain alive until His appearance; be sure, all of you shall be made alive. If you go down into the dust before, you shall not be hid there forever; you shall not be buried there in eternal oblivion; but the

Lord Jesus Christ will awaken you out of your long
sleep of death and raise you out of your beds of
darkness. He will send His angels to gather you
from the four winds. Think, oh, think, how joyful a
day this day will be unto you when the voice is pro-
claimed, "The Bridegroom is come; go ye forth to
meet Him!" When the trumpet sounds in the air,
and you are called out of your graves by the angels,
and gathered into the company of all the saints of
God which lived in all generations from the beginning of the creation; and in a moment, in the twinkling of an eye, such of you as are alive shall find
your bodies strangely transformed, and all that
come forth of the ground made incorruptible and
immortal. And when you shall see the Lord Jesus
Christ come down with such brightness, beauty,
glory, and such royal attendants, and you are caught
up to meet with Him in the air; when you shall find
yourselves in the number of those blessed and happy
ones whom the Lord will send for and receive to
Himself. When the greatest part of the world will be
left behind, crying to the rocks to cover them and
the mountains to fall upon them, to hide them from
the wrath of this furious Judge that is come to condemn them, oh, how will your hearts then be filled,
and even ravished, with transporting joy which no
heart can conceive!

5. Rejoice, believers, rejoice! When Christ appears, you shall be judged by Him; you shall not be
condemned by Him, but you shall be judged by Him.
Your Advocate will be your Judge. Who shall then lay
anything to your charge? God will then justify you;
who then shall condemn you? Christ will acquit and

absolve you; you will openly be declared righteous on that day, through the righteousness of Jesus which has been imputed to you. Christ will own you, then, for His redeemed people whom He has purchased with His own blood. Then all your works of mercy will be made mention of, all your services of Christ in the world will be had in remembrance; all your graces will be taken notice of, and the Lord will kindly accept the improvement of the smallest talent which He has entrusted you with. "Well done, thou good and faithful servant, you have been faithful over a few things, enter into the joy of your Lord," Matthew 25:21.

And if you have been persecuted for righteousness sake, if you have been imprisoned, banished, reproached, and greatly afflicted for Christ's sake; if you have left father, mother, wife, children, houses, lands, yea, and have laid down your lives for the testimony of Jesus, that you might keep a good conscience, think what entrance the Lord Jesus will give to you at that time. Oh, how will you rejoice that the Lord should confer so great honor and dignity upon you as to call you forth and enable you to suffer for His name; and think how sweetly the sentence which Christ will pronounce upon you will sound in your ears, "Come, ye blessed of My Father, inherit the Kingdom prepared for you from the foundation of the world."

6. Rejoice, believers, rejoice! When Christ appears He will reward you. He will give you a crown of glory which does not fade away; He will not only judge and sentence you to inherit the kingdom of heaven, but He will receive you into the kingdom.

He will give you possession thereof; He will carry you along with Him into glory; He will lead you and bring you into the new Jerusalem; He will show you the Father unto your satisfaction, and you shall behold His glory and share in it. He will put you into those mansions which He has prepared for you. Then, and never till then, shall you be perfectly happy.

Four Properties Of Heaven's Happiness

The forethoughts of this matter are of exceeding great comfort, especially if you consider these four properties of heaven's happiness:

1. Believers, consider the greatness of the happiness of heaven. It will be full. You will be filled therewith unto your utmost capacity; yea, beyond what here you are capable of. Consider these particulars in your happiness of heaven:

Think what bodies you will have; they will be most beautiful and glorious bodies. They will be most healthy, strong, and immortal bodies. You will then bear the image of the heavenly Adam, with regard to your bodies, as well as with regard to your souls.

Rejoice then, believers, rejoice! What if some of you have crooked and deformed bodies now? What if some of you are blind, lame, maimed, or have your bodies filled with irksome pains and weakened with long sickness? What if you live in expectation of death, and those bodies, whatever their mold and shape is, must ere long be carried to the cold stinking grave, and be turned into putrefaction? Yet re-

joice you that are believers, because your bodies will
be made so glorious in the resurrection when all
blemishes of nature will be healed, and all sickness
and pain shall be removed; because they will be
raised in incorruption and freed from any more
dominion of death forever.

Think what souls you will have. You will be glorious without; your bodies will shine, but you will be
far more glorious within. Your souls will shine
much more; then your souls shall be washed clean
from all the remainders of sin so that they shall not
have the least spot or stain. Then you shall be
cleansed from all filthiness of the flesh and spirit,
and arrive unto perfection of holiness; then the
seeds of grace will be grown up into flowers of glory,
and oh, what a fragrant garden will your souls be!
When the rough draft, as it were, of Christ here on
your hearts shall be finished and perfected by God's
pencil, and your spirits shall be made perfectly like
unto your glorious Lord, oh, how beautiful will they
be in the eyes of God!

Rejoice then, believers, rejoice! It grieves you
when you look within you and perceive so much re-
maining defilement, when you feel such strong op-
positions of the flesh against the spirit, and you find
yourselves sometimes soiled thereby. Your weakness
and infirmities trouble you, but rejoice, believers,
because in heaven you will be perfectly freed from
sin. You never will be soiled nor defiled with it any
more, but you will be made perfectly holy and perfectly happy.

Think what a habitation you shall have; you shall
have mansions in the Father's house, John 14:2; a

building of God, a house not made with hands eternal in the heavens, 2 Corinthians 5:1. Your persons and your habitation shall be glorious.

Rejoice then, believers, rejoice! What if some of you live in poor and mean cottages? Then you shall live in the glorious palace of the King of kings. What if your houses have been burned with fire, and some of you have nowhere to lay your head, and none of you have a certain dwelling place which you can secure to yourselves? Yet rejoice, because there are mansions provided for you out of which it will be impossible for you to be burned, or turned out forever. The city which is above has foundations which cannot be overturned, and the building of God, which is not made with hands, cannot be destroyed by hands, neither is exposed to flames of fire, which may demolish the fairest city in the world.

Think what company you shall have. You shall have the presence of the Father; you shall dwell with the Lord Jesus Christ, and the Spirit of God will dwell in you forever; you shall have the company of holy angels and all the glorified saints. All your companions will be most lovely and glorious.

Rejoice then, believers, rejoice! What if wicked men separate you from their company and think you unworthy of their fellowship? God will not think you unworthy of His fellowship, nor separate you from His presence. What if some of you are forced to dwell in Mesech, and are linked in near relations to some ungodly persons, and are every day vexed with their ungodly conversation? Rejoice, for in heaven you shall be freed from such company; no wicked person will be permitted to come into that place.

Think what treasures you shall have. You shall have treasures which cannot be corrupted by moth nor stolen by thieves; your riches will be durable and unsearchable.

Rejoice then, believers, rejoice! What if you are poor in the world? You are rich in faith and hope. What if you have no inheritance on earth? Yet you are heirs of the kingdom of heaven; you shall have an inheritance which is incorruptible and undefiled. What if you endure such hardship in your journey through the world? When you come home to your Father's house, you shall be freed from all want, and have such treasures to spend which can never be exhausted.

Think what honor you shall have. The meanest of you will be exalted unto higher dignity than the greatest monarch that ever lived; you will be crowned with immortal glory; you will be honored by God and the angels. You will not only have honor, but you will be made most honorable.

Rejoice then, believers, and take comfort, though you are scorned by some, and accounted as the off-scourings of the earth. You are reproached and vilified by men here, but all your reproaches, especially those which you have borne for the sake of Jesus Christ, will be wreathed into a crown and make you the more glorious in heaven. There you shall not have the least disgrace cast upon you any more, and you shall be kept from any unbecoming actions, to blot and sully you in the least; but you shall shine like so many stars or glorious suns in the kingdom of your Father.

Think what peace and rest you shall have. You

shall have a most sweet peace and tranquility of mind; no enemy without to disturb and molest you; no devil to tempt and assault you; no lusts within or distempered passions to disquiet you. Then you shall have perfect peace; then you shall rest from all wearisome employments and take up your repose forever.

Rejoice then, believers, and let this cheer your hearts in your passages through the tempestuous sea of this world; ere long you shall come to the haven where there shall be no waves or winds. Sometimes now you are troubled on every side and have no rest in your spirits; without are fightings, within are fears; but in heaven you shall be freed perfectly from all disturbance and molestation.

Think what joys and pleasures you shall have. You shall have fullness of joy, Psalm 16:11; you shall drink of the rivers of pleasures, Psalm 36:8. Oh, the delights which you shall have in the immediate view of God's face, in the sense of God's love, in the high actings of your love, in the employment which you shall have in heaven.

Rejoice then, believers, rejoice in hopes of these joys! Now you mourn and weep for your sins and, because of the eclipses of the light of God's countenance, it troubles your hearts that you can see and enjoy so little of God; that your love is so low and inconstant; that your highest services are but mean and diverted, many times, by little trifling business in the world, from conversation with God. In heaven, all tears and all sorrow will be wiped away from your eyes, and all the grounds thereof will be removed. You will come with singing into the new

Jerusalem; you will enter and live in the vision and fruition of, in the love and joy of, and spend an eternity in the presence of the Lord.

2. Believers, consider the sureness of the happiness of heaven. As surely as you are believers, so surely shall you obtain this happiness. You cannot be sure of anything in the world, but you may be sure of the glory of heaven. And, though there is not the certainty of subject, and many of you are not assured of it, but are full of doubts and fears that you fall short, yet there is the certainty of the object; the thing is sure to believers.

Rejoice then, believers, rejoice! Your names are written in the book of life, out of which they shall never be blotted. Labor to answer your doubts, and to get your hearts wrought up to a full assurance of this happiness by such arguments as these, which will evidently prove that, if you are true believers, you shall not, you cannot, miss heaven.

God has chosen you to glory. He has elected you to salvation before the world was. Acts 13:48: "As many as were ordained to eternal life believed." Hence it follows that all believers were ordained to eternal life. And 2 Thessalonians 2:13: "God hath chosen you to salvation, through sanctification of the Spirit and belief of the truth." All true believers are elected persons, and God's decree of election cannot be frustrated because God is unchangeable. Because God changes not, you are not consumed; because God changes not, you shall be saved.

God has promised this happiness to you. 1 John 2:25: "This is the promise which He hath promised, even eternal life." And Titus 1:2: "In hopes of eternal life, which God who cannot lie hath promised." If God has promised this happiness, and your faith gives you interest in the promises, and God is faithful to fulfill them (it being impossible for God to lie), then as certainly as God is true, you that are believers shall obtain them.

The Lord Jesus Christ has purchased this happiness for you. It is called the purchased possession, Ephesians 1:14. As certain as the purchase, so certain will be the possession.

The Lord Jesus has taken possession of heaven for you. The Forerunner is for us entered, Hebrews 6:20. He is preparing these mansions in the Father's house for you, John 14:2. And as certain as Christ is in heaven, so certainly shall those that are believers be received there in due time.

Christ prayed that you might have this happiness while He was on the earth. John 17:24: "Father, I will that those which Thou hast given Me be with Me where I am, that they may behold the glory which Thou hast given Me." Which prayer was made for you, if you are believers, as well as for His present disciples. Verse 20: "Neither pray I for these alone, but for them also which shall believe on Me through their word." And for this thing Christ intercedes above; and whatever He prays and intercedes for, He will prevail for you and, therefore, you shall obtain.

You are Christ's since you are believers and, therefore, all things are yours, said the Apostle, 1 Corinthians 3:22–23. Among which things to come are enumerated: you are Christ's servants and do His works, and He will give you your wages; you honor

Him in the world and, therefore, you shall be honored by Him; you follow your Master in a way of self-denial and suffering, and, if you suffer with Him, you shall reign with Him, 2 Timothy 2:12; and be glorified together, Romans 8:17; and where Christ is, there shall His servants be, John 12:26. You are Christ's members and, where the Head is, there shall the members be. You are Christ's spouse; you are joined, married to Him and, therefore, shall live with Him. All the power of earth and hell cannot separate you from His love and, therefore, cannot separate you out of heaven, Romans 8:35–39.

You are justified by faith, Romans 5:1, and, therefore, absolved from the guilt of sin; therefore freed from the condemnation of hell, Romans 8:1. Therefore, you shall not perish, seeing the cause thereof is removed; therefore you shall have eternal life, John 3:16. Whom God justifies, them He also glorifies, Romans 8:30.

You are the adopted children of God, Galatians 3:26. For you are all the children of God by faith in Christ Jesus. If children, then heirs, Romans 8:17; and if heirs, you shall be sure to have the inheritance.

You are called with a holy calling and sanctified with the Holy Spirit and, thereby, in some measure fitted and qualified for this happiness by the work of grace, conformable to the Lord in holiness. Grace is glory begun; it is called eternal life, and God has promised to perfect it, Philippians 1:6. Grace has relation to heaven as sin has relation to hell; and as sin will certainly bring men to hell if it be not pardoned and subdued, so grace will certainly bring men to heaven, because it cannot wholly be eradicated.

You have made choice of heaven for your portion. You have laid up your treasure there, and God has set your souls longing after it and given you hopes of it; and, therefore, you shall not miss it. Your desire shall be satisfied and your hopes shall not make you ashamed, Romans 5:5.

And if, besides all this, you have the witness and seal and earnest of the Spirit, giving you some first-fruits and foretastes of this happiness (though all believers do not obtain it), then you may know without question that this is a sure happiness both in itself and unto you.

Therefore, believers, exercise your faith that you may be filled with all joy and peace in believing. Believers, consider the nearness of the happiness of heaven. Christ's appearance is not far off, but your happiness may be nearer; I mean the happiness of your souls in heaven which will begin as soon as your lives come to an end. The wicked walk upon the brink of hell every day. When they die, there they are carried. You walk upon the borders of the heavenly Canaan, the paradise which is above; when you die, there shall you be conveyed. And you may die suddenly, and as suddenly you will be in glory.

Rejoice then, believers, rejoice! You may be in heaven before you are aware; it may be tomorrow. God will send for you; within a few days you may be out of the body, present with the Lord Jesus, and among the spirits of just men made perfect. When you break from the prison of the body, you will be delivered into the marvelous light of God's glory.

Rejoice to think how near your happiness is!

Believers, consider the everlastingness of the happiness of heaven. There is fullness of joy and pleasures forevermore, Psalm 16:11. When you come to heaven, there you shall abide; your happiness will be constant and eternal without diminution, inter-mixture of sin and sorrow, without interruption, or possibility that ever it should be brought to an end. It would alleviate the torments of the damned if they had any hopes of ever being let out of hell; and it would weaken the joys of the saints. You fill them with unspeakable grief if there were any danger and fear of ever being thrust out of heaven.

Rejoice then, believers! You shall rejoice forever-more in the eternal vision and fruition of God. Labor to begin your heaven's joy now; let faith realize and bring near the things which you hope for, and make evident the things which as yet you do not see but shall possess, that you may have a sweet foretaste of this happiness, and begin your heaven's work to praise the Lord for His great and unde-served love wherewith He has loved you, for these things beyond conception which, out of love, He has prepared for you.

Chapter 14

A Word to Both Sinners and Believers

Lastly, to conclude, I shall speak a word both to sinners and believers. Will the Lord Jesus Christ certainly and quickly appear to judgment? Let me then in His name persuade of three things:

1. Believe that Christ will appear; mingle the doctrine you have heard or read with faith. You have had evident proof of it; believe the thing. Sinners, believe that Christ will come to judge and condemn you if you are found in your sins. If you believed it effectually, you would quickly become saints. Believers, labor for more faith in this truth; if you believed it more strongly, you would live at a higher level.

2. Consider that Christ will appear; meditate on this thing; let it dwell on your thoughts; let it lie down with you at night and rise with you in the morning; let it sit down with you at table and walk with you abroad. Think often of the antecedents of Christ's coming, the judgment itself, and the consequences thereof, and let them make a deep impression of the last judgment on your spirits.

Sinners, consider how the wicked shall be judged; think how they shall be accused and condemned; think of the dreadful sentence and the execution thereof in hell, and then think that you are in the number of those that are in such danger unless you speedily secure yourselves by making your peace.

Believers, consider how the saints will be judged; think how Christ will acquit them and invite them to take possession, and then will give them possession of heaven; and then think that you are in the number of the blessed ones which shall be made thus happy.

3. Prepare for the appearance of Christ to judgment. And that you may be prepared as a conclusion to this doctrine, take these directions:

Be diligent that you may be found of Him in peace. That is the advice of the Apostle after his discourse on the coming of the Lord, and the glorious things of that day. "Wherefore, beloved, seeing that ye look for such things, be diligent that you may be found of Him in peace," 2 Peter 3:14.

Make your peace with God, sinners. God is your enemy; make your peace with Him. You have offended Him by your sins and His justice must be satisfied. Oh, labor to get an interest in the satisfaction of Christ. That your sins may be pardoned, and God may be reconciled, lay hold on Christ by faith, as yet you may be welcome to Him. Hereafter, it will be too late. Believers, make sure of a pardon; you cannot be too sure in a thing of such concern.

Diligently endeavor after a peace in your consciences. Sinners, get the wound which sin has made there healed with the blood of Christ. Believers, take heed of making any breaches there; maintain peace within, when you have obtained it.

Diligently follow after peace one with another. Take heed of hatred, variance, emulations, wraths, strifes, seditions, envyings, divisions, clamors, evil speakings, backbitings, whisperings, swellings, and tumults; and follow after those things which make for peace such as love, joy, humbleness of mind, meekness, long-suffering, patience, and the like, that you may be found of the Lord in peace.

Give diligence that you may be found of the Lord without spot and blameless, as the Apostle advises in 2 Peter 3: 14. Read verse 11: "Seeing all these things shall be dissolved, what manner of persons ought we to be, in all holy conversation and godliness." Get the spots of sin washed off; not only the guilt of sin removed, but also the defilement; labor to be holy in all manner of conversation; to be blameless and harmless, the children of God without rebuke in the midst of a crooked and perverse generation. Take heed of the sins of the times and places wherein you live; join not with them in their sins lest you share in their plagues at the last day. Let your conversation be as becomes the gospel; let your actions be squared by the Word, as those which must give an account and receive a reward according to their works.

Sit loose from the world. Let not your hearts be overcharged with the cares of this life, nor filled with the love of the world, and that day overtake you unaware, Luke 21:34. Remember that riches will not profit in the day of wrath, that the fashion of this world passes away, and you are passing away; and, therefore, live as strangers and sojourners.

Lay up your treasures in heaven, Matthew 6:19. And get your affections set on things above, Colossians 3:2. And then the appearance of Christ will be joyful to you because He will give you possession of heaven.

Be ready to do and suffer whatever the Lord calls you unto. Be patient in well-doing, for in due time you shall reap. Be steadfast and immovable, always abounding in the work of the Lord, because your labor shall not be in vain in the Lord, Galatians 6:9 and 1 Corinthians 15:58. And whatever afflictions you suffer for Christ, they are light and momentary; but the glory which Christ will give is weighty and eternal, 2 Corinthians 4:17.

Give Christ your hearts. Let Him have the highest place; give Him your whole heart; let Him have the choicest and chiefest of your affections; and then He will give you His kingdom, and such expressions of His love will He make unto you at His appearance as now you have not thoughts to conceive.

Maintain communion with Christ in His ordinances. Prize ordinances upon this account, because Christ walks there; and improve ordinances for this end, that you may be with Christ. Rest not in the outside and carnal part of the ordinances, but seek after Christ in them until you find Him; and labor to grow into acquaintance with Christ, and to keep fellowship with Him, and then, when He does appear, He will know you again and own you, and receive you to live with Him forever.

Stand up for the honor of Christ in the world. Confess Him before men and He will confess you before His Father in heaven, Matthew 10:32. Be not ashamed to profess yourselves His disciples, and to own His ways and truths when they are condemned and despised by the ungodly world, because if you are, He will be ashamed of you when He comes in glory, Mark 8:38.

Improve your talents for the use of the Lord, who has entrusted you with them. All of you have talents; lay them not up in a napkin, but lay them up in the service of the Lord. Whatever gifts of grace you have, put them forth in usury that you may give an account with joy unto your Lord, when He shall come to call you to an account.

Stand upon your watch. When your Savior had foretold His disciples of His coming, He exhorted them and all to watch, Mark 13:33. What I say unto you, I say unto all: "Watch, watch against sin; watch your senses, which are the inlets of sin; watch your hearts from whence are the issues of sin; watch, take heed of sleeping in sin, lest you lose your garments and be found naked."

Be frequent and fervent in prayer. Our Savior joins these duties together in His exhortations to His disciples. Luke 21:36: "Watch therefore, and pray always, that you may be counted worthy to escape all those things which shall come to pass, and to stand before the Son of man." Pray without ceasing; pray without fainting; be often upon your knees, and be earnest with the Lord that He would prepare you for this day; that He would deliver you from the dreadful wrath which shall be revealed when Christ appears, and which you have deserved for your sins. And pray that He would give you those qualifications as may embolden you at the last day to hold up your heads with confidence, that He would keep you without spot and blameless until the coming of the Lord.

Last, look for the appearance of the Lord; look with an eye of hope; labor to abound in hope by the power of the Holy Ghost; let this hope be an anchor fastened within the veil to stay your sinking hearts in the midst of these fierce storms which do or may beat upon you in the world; and look with the eye of desire. Look and long for Christ's appearance; dart up your wishes often to heaven. Oh, when shall we see the heavens opened and behold our Lord in His glory? When shall we hear the trumpet sound, and be gathered by the angels from all the quarters of the earth? When shall we put off this dust and corruption and be clothed with robes of immortality? When shall the Lord Jesus come down and show us His glory, and receive us to Himself that, where He is, there we may be also? Christ has spoken from heaven to earth, "Surely I come quickly." Let there be an echo back from earth to heaven in your desires to this voice, "Amen. Even so, come, Lord Jesus, come quickly!"

I shall conclude all with the words of the Apostle Jude, verse 24–25: "Now unto Him that is able to keep you from falling, and to present you faultless before the presence of His glory with exceeding joy, to the only wise God, our Savior, be glory and majesty, dominion and power, now and ever, Amen."